Mastering .NET Machine Learning

Master the art of machine learning with .NET and gain insight into real-world applications

Jamie Dixon

BIRMINGHAM - MUMBAI

Mastering .NET Machine Learning

First published: March 2016

Production reference: 1210316

Published by Packt Publishing Ltd.
Livery Place
35 Livery Street
Birmingham B3 2PB, UK.

ISBN 978-1-78588-840-3

www.packtpub.com

Credits

Author
Jamie Dixon

Reviewers
Reed Copsey, Jr.
César Roberto de Souza

Commissioning Editor
Vedika Naik

Acquisition Editor
Meeta Rajani

Technical Editor
Pankaj Kadam

Copy Editor
Laxmi Subramanian

Proofreader
Safis Editing

Indexer
Rekha Nair

Graphics
Jason Monteiro

Production Coordinator
Aparna Bhagat

Cover Work
Aparna Bhagat

About the Author

Jamie Dixon has been writing code for as long as he can remember and has been getting paid to do it since 1995. He was using C# and JavaScript almost exclusively until discovering F#, and now combines all three languages for the problem at hand. He has a passion for discovering overlooked gems in datasets and merging software engineering techniques to scientific computing. When he codes for fun, he spends his time using Phidgets, Netduinos, and Raspberry Pis or spending time in Kaggle competitions using F# or R.

Jamie is a bachelor of science in computer science and has been an F# MVP since 2014. He is the former chair of his town's Information Services Advisory Board and is an outspoken advocate of open data. He is also involved with his local .NET User Group (TRINUG) with an emphasis on data analytics, machine learning, and the Internet of Things (IoT).

Jamie lives in Cary, North Carolina with his wonderful wife Jill and their three awesome children: Sonoma, Sawyer, and Sloan. He blogs weekly at `jamessdixon.wordpress.com` and can be found on Twitter at `@jamie_dixon`.

Acknowledgments

I had never considered writing a book until Meeta from Packt Publishing sent me an e-mail, asking me if I was interested in writing the book that you are holding. My first reaction was excitement immediately followed by fear. I have heard that writing a book is an arduous and painful undertaking with scant reward—was I really ready to dive into that? Fortunately, writing this book was nothing of the sort—all due to the many wonderful people that helped me along the way.

First and foremost are the technical reviewers Reed Copsey, Jr. and César Roberto de Souza. Their attention to detail, their spot-on suggestions, and occasional words of encouragement made all of the difference. Next, the team at Packt of Meeta Rajani, Pankaj Kadam, and Laxmi Subramanian took my words, code samples, and screenshots and turned them into something, well, beautiful. Mathias Brandiveder, Evalina Gasborova, Melinda Thielbar, James McCaffrey, Phil Trelford, Seth Jurez, and Chris Kalle all helped me at different points with questions about what and how to present the machine learning models and ideas. Dmitry Morozov and Ross McKinlay were indispensable for explaining the finer points of type providers. Isaac Abraham helped me with the section on MBrace and Tomas Petricek helped me with the section on Deedle. Chris Matthews and Mark Hutchinson reviewed the initial outline and gave me great feedback. Ian Hoppes saved me hours (days?) by sharing his expertise on the finer points of Razor and JavaScript. Finally, Rob Seder, Mike Esposito, and Kevin Allen encouraged and supported me throughout the entire process.

To everyone I mentioned and the people I may have missed, please accept my sincerest thanks.

Finally, my deepest love for the initial proofreader, soul mate, and best wife any person could have: Jill Dixon. I am truly the luckiest man in the world to be with you.

About the Reviewers

Reed Copsey, Jr. is the executive director of the F# Software Foundation and the CTO and co-owner of C Tech Development Corporation, a software company focused on applications and tooling for the Earth Sciences. After attending the University of Chicago, he went on to consult and work in many industries, including medical imaging, geographical information systems, analysis of retail market data, and more. He has been involved with technical and business support for numerous nonprofit organizations, and most recently enjoys spending his free time involved with the software community.

He is the organizer of the Bellingham Software Developers Network, has been a Microsoft MVP in .NET since 2010, is an avid StackOverflow contributor, and regularly speaks on F# and .NET at various user groups and conferences.

César Roberto de Souza is the author of the Accord.NET Framework and an experienced software developer. During his early university years in Brazil, he decided to create the Accord.NET Framework, a framework for machine learning, image processing, and scientific computing for .NET. Targeted at both professionals and hobbyists, the project has been used by large and small companies, big corporations, start-ups, universities, and in an extensive number of scientific publications. After finishing his MSc in the Federal University of São Carlos, the success of the project eventually granted him an opportunity to work and live in Europe, from where he continues its development and interacts with the growing community of users that now helps advance the project even further.

He is a technology enthusiast, with keen interest in machine learning, computer vision, and image processing, and regularly writes articles on those topics for the CodeProject, where he has won its article writing competition multiple times.

www.PacktPub.com

eBooks, discount offers, and more

Did you know that Packt offers eBook versions of every book published, with PDF and ePub files available? You can upgrade to the eBook version at www.PacktPub.com and as a print book customer, you are entitled to a discount on the eBook copy. Get in touch with us at customercare@packtpub.com for more details.

At www.PacktPub.com, you can also read a collection of free technical articles, sign up for a range of free newsletters and receive exclusive discounts and offers on Packt books and eBooks.

https://www2.packtpub.com/books/subscription/packtlib

Do you need instant solutions to your IT questions? PacktLib is Packt's online digital book library. Here, you can search, access, and read Packt's entire library of books.

Why subscribe?

- Fully searchable across every book published by Packt
- Copy and paste, print, and bookmark content
- On demand and accessible via a web browser

To Sonoma, Sawyer, and Sloan Dixon

Table of Contents

Preface

The .NET Framework is one of the most successful application frameworks in history. Literally billions of lines of code have been written on the .NET Framework, with billions more to come. For all of its success, it can be argued that the .NET Framework is still underrepresented for data science endeavors. This book attempts to help address this issue by showing how machine learning can be rapidly injected into the common .NET line of business applications. It also shows how typical data science scenarios can be addressed using the .NET Framework. This book quickly builds upon an introduction to machine learning models and techniques in order to build real-world applications using machine learning. While by no means a comprehensive study of predictive analytics, it does address some of the more common issues that data scientists encounter when building their models.

Many books about machine learning are written with every chapter centering around a dataset and how to implement a model on that dataset. While this is a good way to build a mental blueprint (as well as some code boilerplate), this book is going to take a slightly different approach. This book centers around introducing the same application for the line of business development and one common open data dataset for the scientific programmer. We will then introduce different machine techniques, depending on the business scenario. This means you will be putting on different hats for each chapter. If you are a line of business software engineer, Chapters 2, 3, 6, and 9 will seem like old hat. If you are a research analyst, Chapters 4, 7, and 10 will be very familiar to you. I encourage you to try all chapters, regardless of your background, as you will perhaps gain a new perspective that will make you more effective as a data scientist. As a final note, one word you will not find in this book is "simply". It drives me nuts when I read a tutorial-based book and the author says "it is simply this" or "simply do that". If it was simple, I wouldn't need the book. I hope you find each of the chapters accessible and the code samples interesting, and these two factors can help you immediately in your career.

What this book covers

Chapter 1, Welcome to Machine Learning Using the .NET Framework, contextualizes machine learning in the .NET stack, introduces some of the libraries that we will use throughout the book, and provides a brief primer to F#.

Chapter 2, AdventureWorks Regression, introduces the business that we will use in this book—AdventureWorks Bicycle company. We will then look at a business problem where customers are dropping orders based on reviews of the product. It looks at creating a linear regression by hand, using Math.NET and Accord.NET to solve this business problem. It then adds this regression to the line of business application.

Chapter 3, More AdventureWorks Regression, looks at creating a multiple linear regression and a logistic regression to solve different business problems at AdventureWorks. It will look at different factors that affect bike sales and then categorize potential customers into potential sales or potential lost leads. It will then implement the models to help our website convert potential lost leads into potential sales.

Chapter 4, Traffic Stops – Barking Up the Wrong Tree?, takes a break from AdventureWorks. You will put on your data scientist hat, use an open dataset of traffic stops, and see if we can understand why some people get a verbal warning and why others get a ticket at a traffic stop. We will use basic summary statistics and decision trees to help in understanding the results.

Chapter 5, Time Out – Obtaining Data, stops with introducing datasets and machine learning models and concentrates on one of the hardest parts of machine learning— obtaining and cleaning the data. We will look at using F# type providers as a very powerful language feature that can vastly speed up this process of "data munging".

Chapter 6, AdventureWorks Redux – k-NN and Naïve Bayes Classifiers, goes back to AdventureWorks and looks at a business problem of how to improve cross sales. We will implement two popular machine learning classification models, k-NN and Naïve Bayes, to see which is better at solving this problem.

Chapter 7, Traffic Stops and Crash Locations – When Two Datasets Are Better Than One, returns back to the traffic stop data and adds in two other open datasets that can be used to improve the predictions and gain new insights. The chapter will introduce two common unsupervised machine learning techniques: k-means and PCA.

Chapter 8, Feature Selection and Optimization, takes another break from introducing new machine learning models and looks at another key part of building machine learning models—selecting the right data for the model, preparing the data for the model, and introducing some common techniques to deal with outliers and other data abnormalities.

Chapter 9, AdventureWorks Production – Neural Networks, goes back to AdventureWorks and looks at how to improve bike production by using a popular machine learning technique called neural networks.

Chapter 10, Big Data and IoT, wraps up by looking at a more recent problem—how to build machine learning models on top of data that is characterized by massive volume, variability, and velocity. We will then look at how IoT devices can generate this big data and how to deploy machine learning models onto these devices so that they become self-learning.

What you need for this book

You will need Visual Studio 2013 (any version) or beyond installed on your computer. You can also use VS Code or Mono Develop. The examples in this book use Visual Studio 2015 Update 1.

Who this book is for

The lines between business computing and scientific computing are becoming increasingly blurred. Indeed, an argument can be made that the distinction was never really as clear as it has been made out to be in the past. With that, machine learning principles and models are making their way into mainstream computing applications. Consider the Uber app that shows how far Uber drivers are from you, and product recommendations built into online retail sites such as Jet.

Also, the nature of the .NET software developer's job is changing. Earlier, when the cliché of *ours is a changing industry* was being thrown around, it was about languages (need to know JavaScript, C#, and TSql) and frameworks (Angular, MVC, WPF, and EF). Now, the cliché means that the software developer needs to know how to make sure their code is correct (test-driven development), how to get their code off of their machine onto the customer's machine (DevOps), and how to make their applications smarter (machine learning).

Also, the same forces that are pushing the business developer to retool are pushing the research analyst into unfamiliar territory. Earlier, analysts focused on data collection, exploration, and visualization in the context of an application (Excel, PowerBI, and SAS) for point-in-time analysis. The analyst would start with a question, grab some data, build some models, and then present the findings. Any kind of continuous analysis was done via report writing or just re-running the models. Today, analysts are being asked to sift through massive amounts of data (IoT telemetry, user exhaust, and NoSQL data lakes), where the questions may not be known beforehand. Also, once models are created, they are pushed into production applications where they are continually being re-trained in real time. No longer just a decision aid for humans, research is being done by computers to impact users immediately.

The newly-minted data scientist title is at the confluence of these forces. Typically, no one person can be an expert on both sides of the divide, so the data scientist is a bit of a *jack of all trades, master of none* who knows machine learning a little bit better than all of the other software engineers on the team and knows software engineering a little bit better than any researcher on the team. The goal of this book is to help move from either software engineer or business analyst to data scientist.

Conventions

In this book, you will find a number of text styles that distinguish between different kinds of information. Here are some examples of these styles and an explanation of their meaning.

Code words in text, database table names, folder names, filenames, file extensions, pathnames, dummy URLs, user input, and Twitter handles are shown as follows: "The Script1.fsx file is then added to the project."

A block of code is set as follows:

```
let multipliedAndIsEven =
    ints
    |> Array.map (fun i -> multiplyByTwo i)
    |> Array.map (fun i -> isEven i)
```

Any command-line input or output is written as follows:

```
val multipliedAndIsEven : string [] =
  [|"even"; "even"; "even"; "even"; "even"; "even"|]
```

New terms and **important words** are shown in bold. Words that you see on the screen, for example, in menus or dialog boxes, appear in the text like this: "When the **Add New Item** dialog box appears, select **Script File**."

Warnings or important notes appear in a box like this.

 Tips and tricks appear like this.

Reader feedback

Feedback from our readers is always welcome. Let us know what you think about this book—what you liked or disliked. Reader feedback is important for us as it helps us develop titles that you will really get the most out of.

To send us general feedback, simply e-mail feedback@packtpub.com, and mention the book's title in the subject of your message.

If there is a topic that you have expertise in and you are interested in either writing or contributing to a book, see our author guide at www.packtpub.com/authors.

Customer support

Now that you are the proud owner of a Packt book, we have a number of things to help you to get the most from your purchase.

Downloading the example code

You can download the example code files for this book from your account at http://www.packtpub.com. If you purchased this book elsewhere, you can visit http://www.packtpub.com/support and register to have the files e-mailed directly to you.

You can download the code files by following these steps:

1. Log in or register to our website using your e-mail address and password.
2. Hover the mouse pointer on the **SUPPORT** tab at the top.
3. Click on **Code Downloads & Errata**.
4. Enter the name of the book in the **Search** box.
5. Select the book for which you're looking to download the code files.
6. Choose from the drop-down menu where you purchased this book from.
7. Click on **Code Download**.

Once the file is downloaded, please make sure that you unzip or extract the folder using the latest version of:

- WinRAR / 7-Zip for Windows
- Zipeg / iZip / UnRarX for Mac
- 7-Zip / PeaZip for Linux

Errata

Although we have taken every care to ensure the accuracy of our content, mistakes do happen. If you find a mistake in one of our books—maybe a mistake in the text or the code—we would be grateful if you could report this to us. By doing so, you can save other readers from frustration and help us improve subsequent versions of this book. If you find any errata, please report them by visiting http://www.packtpub.com/submit-errata, selecting your book, clicking on the **Errata Submission Form** link, and entering the details of your errata. Once your errata are verified, your submission will be accepted and the errata will be uploaded to our website or added to any list of existing errata under the Errata section of that title.

To view the previously submitted errata, go to https://www.packtpub.com/books/content/support and enter the name of the book in the search field. The required information will appear under the **Errata** section.

Piracy

Piracy of copyrighted material on the Internet is an ongoing problem across all media. At Packt, we take the protection of our copyright and licenses very seriously. If you come across any illegal copies of our works in any form on the Internet, please provide us with the location address or website name immediately so that we can pursue a remedy.

Please contact us at copyright@packtpub.com with a link to the suspected pirated material.

We appreciate your help in protecting our authors and our ability to bring you valuable content.

Questions

If you have a problem with any aspect of this book, you can contact us at questions@packtpub.com, and we will do our best to address the problem.

1

Welcome to Machine Learning Using the .NET Framework

This is a book on creating and then using **Machine Learning** (**ML**) programs using the .NET Framework. Machine learning, a hot topic these days, is part of an overall trend in the software industry of analytics which attempts to make machines *smarter*. Analytics, though not really a new trend, has perhaps a higher visibility than in the past. This chapter will focus on some of the larger questions you might have about machine learning using the .NET Framework, namely: What is machine learning? Why should we consider it in the .NET Framework? How can I get started with coding?

What is machine learning?

If you check out on Wikipedia, you will find a fairly abstract definition of machine learning:

> "*Machine learning explores the study and construction of algorithms that can learn from and make predictions on data. Such algorithms operate by building a model from example inputs in order to make data-driven predictions or decisions, rather than following strictly static program instructions.*"

I like to think of machine learning as computer programs that produce different results as they are exposed to more information without changing their source code (and consequently needed to be redeployed). For example, consider a game that I play with the computer.

I show the computer this picture ● and tell it "Blue Circle". I then show it this picture ● and tell it "Red Circle". Next I show it this picture ▲ and say "Green Triangle."

Finally, I show it this picture ● and ask it "What is this?". Ideally the computer would respond, "Green Circle."

This is one example of machine learning. Although I did not change my code or recompile and redeploy, the computer program can respond accurately to data it has never seen before. Also, the computer code does not have to explicitly write each possible data permutation. Instead, we create models that the computer applies to new data. Sometimes the computer is right, sometimes it is wrong. We then feed the new data to the computer to retrain the model so the computer gets more and more accurate over time—or, at least, that is the goal.

Once you decide to implement some machine learning into your code base, another decision has to be made fairly early in the process. How often do you want the computer to learn? For example, if you create a model by hand, how often do you update it? With every new data row? Every month? Every year? Depending on what you are trying to accomplish, you might create a real-time ML model, a near-time model, or a periodic model. We will discuss the implications and implementations of each of these in several chapters in the book as different models lend themselves to different retraining strategies.

Why .NET?

If you are a Windows developer, using .NET is something you do without thinking. Indeed, a vast majority of Windows business applications written in the last 15 years use managed code—most of it written in C#. Although it is difficult to categorize millions of software developers, it is fair to say that .NET developers often come from nontraditional backgrounds. Perhaps a developer came to .NET from a BCSC degree but it is equally likely s/he started writing VBA scripts in Excel, moving up to Access applications, and then into VB.NET/C# applications. Therefore, most .NET developers are likely to be familiar with C#/VB.NET and write in an imperative and perhaps OO style.

The problem with this rather narrow exposure is that most machine learning classes, books, and code examples are in R or Python and very much use a functional style of writing code. Therefore, the .NET developer is at a disadvantage when acquiring machine learning skills because of the need to learn a new development environment, a new language, and a new style of coding before learning how to write the first line of machine learning code.

If, however, that same developer could use their familiar IDE (Visual Studio) and the same base libraries (the .NET Framework), they can concentrate on learning machine learning much sooner. Also, when creating machine learning models in .NET, they have immediate impact as you can slide the code right into an existing C#/VB.NET solution.

On the other hand, .NET is under-represented in the data science community. There are a couple of different reasons floating around for that fact. The first is that historically Microsoft was a proprietary closed system and the academic community embraced open source systems such as Linux and Java. The second reason is that much academic research uses domain-specific languages such as R, whereas Microsoft concentrated .NET on general purpose programming languages. Research that moved to industry took their language with them. However, as the researcher's role is shifted from data science to building programs that can work at real time that customers touch, the researcher is getting more and more exposure to Windows and Windows development. Whether you like it or not, all companies which create software that face customers must have a Windows strategy, an iOS strategy, and an Android strategy.

One real advantage to writing and then deploying your machine learning code in .NET is that you can get everything with one stop shopping. I know several large companies who write their models in R and then have another team rewrite them in Python or C++ to deploy them. Also, they might write their model in Python and then rewrite it in C# to deploy on Windows devices. Clearly, if you could write and deploy in one language stack, there is a tremendous opportunity for efficiency and speed to market.

What version of the .NET Framework are we using?

The .NET Framework has been around for general release since 2002. The base of the framework is the Common Language Runtime or CLR. The CLR is a virtual machine that abstracts much of the OS specific functionality like memory management and exception handling. The CLR is loosely based on the **Java Virtual Machine (JVM)**. Sitting on top of the CLR is the **Framework Class Library (FCL)** that allows different languages to interoperate with the CLR and each other: the FCL is what allows VB.Net, C#, F#, and Iron Python code to work side-by-side with each other.

Since its first release, the .NET Framework has included more and more features. The first release saw support for the major platform libraries like WinForms, ASP.NET, and ADO.NET. Subsequent releases brought in things like **Windows Communication Foundation (WCF)**, **Language Integrated Query (LINQ)**, and **Task Parallel Library (TPL)**. At the time of writing, the latest version is of the .Net Framework is 4.6.2.

In addition to the full-Monty .NET Framework, over the years Microsoft has released slimmed down versions of the .NET Framework intended to run on machines that have limited hardware and OS support. The most famous of these releases was the **Portable Class Library (PCL)** that targeted Windows RT applications running Windows 8. The most recent incantation of this is **Universal Windows Applications (UWA)**, targeting Windows 10.

At `Connect()`; in November 2015, Microsoft announced GA of the latest edition of the .NET Framework. This release introduced the .Net Core 5. In January, they decided to rename it to .Net Core 1.0. .NET Core 1.0 is intended to be a slimmed down version of the full .NET Framework that runs on multiple operating systems (specifically targeting OS X and Linux). The next release of ASP.NET (ASP.NET Core 1.0) sits on top of .NET Core 1.0. ASP.NET Core 1.0 applications that run on Windows can still run the full .NET Framework.

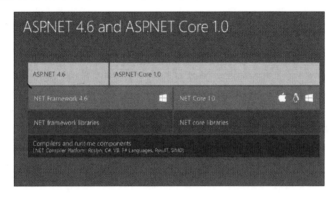

(`https://blogs.msdn.microsoft.com/webdev/2016/01/19/asp-net-5-is-dead-introducing-asp-net-core-1-0-and-net-core-1-0/`)

In this book, we will be using a mixture of ASP.NET 4.0, ASP.NET 5.0, and Universal Windows Applications. As you can guess, machine learning models (and the theory behind the models) change with a lot less frequency than framework releases so the most of the code you write on .NET 4.6 will work equally well with PCL and .NET Core 1.0. Saying that, the external libraries that we will use need some time to catch up—so they might work with PCL but not with .NET Core 1.0 yet. To make things realistic, the demonstration projects will use .NET 4.6 on ASP.NET 4.x for existing (Brownfield) applications. New (Greenfield) applications will be a mixture of a UWA using PCL and ASP.NET 5.0 applications.

Why write your own?

It seems like all of the major software companies are pitching machine learning services such as Google Analytics, Amazon Machine Learning Services, IBM Watson, Microsoft Cortana Analytics, to name a few. In addition, major software companies often try to sell products that have a machine learning component, such as Microsoft SQL Server Analysis Service, Oracle Database Add-In, IBM SPSS, or SAS JMP. I have not included some common analytical software packages such as PowerBI or Tableau because they are more data aggregation and report writing applications. Although they do analytics, they do not have a machine learning component (not yet at least).

With all these options, why would you want to learn how to implement machine learning inside your applications, or in effect, write some code that you can purchase elsewhere? It is the classic build versus buy decision that every department or company has to make. You might want to build because:

- You really understand what you are doing and you can be a much more informed consumer and critic of any given machine learning package. In effect, you are building your internal skill set that your company will most likely prize. Another way to look at it, companies are not one tool away from purchasing competitive advantage because if they were, their competitors could also buy the same tool and cancel any advantage. However, companies can be one hire away or more likely one team away to truly have the ability to differentiate themselves in their market.

- You can get better performance by executing locally, which is especially important for real-time machine learning and can be implemented in disconnected or slow connection scenarios. This becomes particularly important when we start implementing machine learning with **Internet of Things (IoT)** devices in scenarios where the device has a lot more RAM than network bandwidth. Consider the Raspberry Pi running Windows 10 on a pipeline. Network communication might be spotty, but the machine has plenty of power to implement ML models.

- You are not beholden to any one vendor or company, for example, every time you implement an application with a specific vendor and are not thinking about how to move away from the vendor, you make yourself more dependent on the vendor and their inevitable recurring licensing costs. The next time you are talking to the CTO of a shop that has a lot of Oracle, ask him/her if they regret any decision to implement any of their business logic in Oracle databases. The answer will not surprise you. A majority of this book's code is written in F# — an open source language that runs great on Windows, Linux, and OS X.

- You can be much more agile and have much more flexibility in what you implement. For example, we will often re-train our models on the fly and when you write your own code, it is fairly easy to do this. If you use a third-party service, they may not even have API hooks to do model training and evaluation, so near-time model changes are impossible.

Once you decide to go native, you have a choice of rolling your own code or using some of the open source assemblies out there. This book will introduce both the techniques to you, highlight some of the pros and cons of each technique, and let you decide how you want to implement them. For example, you can easily write your own basic classifier that is very effective in production but certain models, such as a neural network, will take a considerable amount of time and energy and probably will not give you the results that the open source libraries do. As a final note, since the libraries that we will look at are open source, you are free to customize pieces of it—the owners might even accept your changes. However, we will not be customizing these libraries in this book.

Why open data?

Many books on machine learning use datasets that come with the language install (such as R or Hadoop) or point to public repositories that have considerable visibility in the data science community. The most common ones are Kaggle (especially the Titanic competition) and the UC Irvine's datasets. While these are great datasets and give a common denominator, this book will expose you to datasets that come from government entities. The notion of getting data from government and hacking for social good is typically called **open data**. I believe that open data will transform how the government interacts with its citizens and will make government entities more efficient and transparent. Therefore, we will use open datasets in this book and hopefully you will consider helping out with the open data movement.

Why F#?

As we will be on the .NET Framework, we could use either C#, VB.NET, or F#. All three languages have strong support within Microsoft and all three will be around for many years. F# is the best choice for this book because it is unique in the .NET Framework for thinking in the scientific method and machine learning model creation. Data scientists will feel right at home with the syntax and IDE (languages such as R are also functional first languages). It is the best choice for .NET business developers because it is built right into Visual Studio and plays well with your existing C#/VB.NET code. The obvious alternative is C#. Can I do this all in C#? Yes, kind of. In fact, many of the .NET libraries we will use are written in C#.

However, using C# in our code base will make it larger and have a higher chance of introducing bugs into the code. At certain points, I will show some examples in C#, but the majority of the book is in F#.

Another alternative is to forgo .NET altogether and develop the machine learning models in R and Python. You could spin up a web service (such as AzureML), which might be good in some scenarios, but in disconnected or slow network environments, you will get stuck. Also, assuming comparable machines, executing locally will perform better than going over the wire. When we implement our models to do real-time analytics, anything we can do to minimize the performance hit is something to consider.

A third alternative that the .NET developers will consider is to write the models in T-SQL. Indeed, many of our initial models have been implemented in T-SQL and are part of the SQL Server Analysis Server. The advantage of doing it on the data server is that the computation is as close as you can get to the data, so you will not suffer the latency of moving large amount of data over the wire. The downsides of using T-SQL are that you can't implement unit tests easily, your domain logic is moving away from the application and to the data server (which is considered bad form with most modern application architecture), and you are now reliant on a specific implementation of the database. F# is open source and runs on a variety of operating systems, so you can port your code much more easily.

Getting ready for machine learning

In this section, we will install Visual Studio, take a quick lap around F#, and install the major open source libraries that we will be using.

Setting up Visual Studio

To get going, you will need to download Visual Studio on a Microsoft Windows machine. As of this writing, the latest (free) version is Visual Studio 2015 Community. If you have a higher version already installed on your machine, you can skip this step. If you need a copy, head on over to the Visual Studio home page at https://www.visualstudio.com. Download the Visual Studio Community 2015 installer and execute it.

Now, you will get the following screen:

Select **Custom** installation and you will be taken to the following screen:

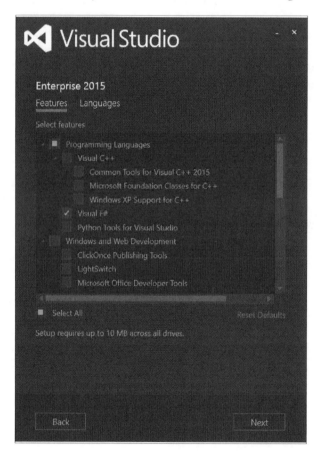

Make sure Visual F# has a check mark next to it. Once it is installed, you should see Visual Studio in your Windows Start menu.

Learning F#

One of the great features about F# is that you can accomplish a whole lot with very little code. It is a very terse language compared to C# and VB.NET, so picking up the syntax is a bit easier. Although this is not a comprehensive introduction, this is going to introduce you to the major language features that we will use in this book. I encourage you to check out `http://www.tryfsharp.org/` or the tutorials at `http://fsharpforfunandprofit.com/` if you want to get a deeper understanding of the language. With that in mind, let's create our 1st F# project:

1. Start Visual Studio.

2. Navigate to **File | New | Project** as shown in the following screenshot:

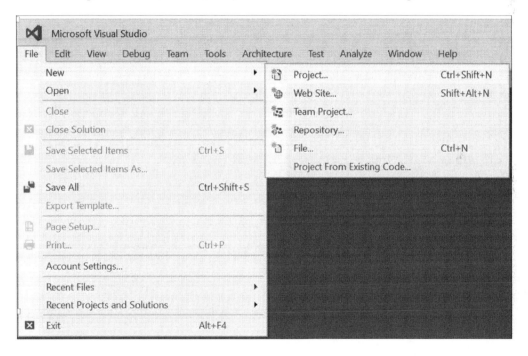

3. When the **New Project** dialog box appears, navigate the tree view to **Visual F# | Windows | Console Application**. Have a look at the following screenshot:

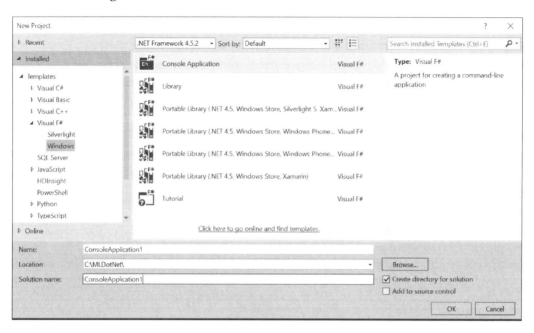

4. Give your project a name, hit **OK**, and the Visual Studio Template generator will create the following boilerplate:

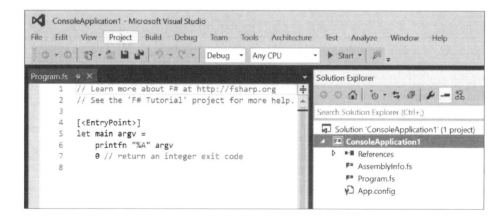

Although Visual Studio created a `Program.fs` file that creates a basic console `.exe` application for us, we will start learning about F# in a different way, so we are going to ignore it for now.

5. Right-click in the **Solution Explorer** and navigate to **Add | New Item**.

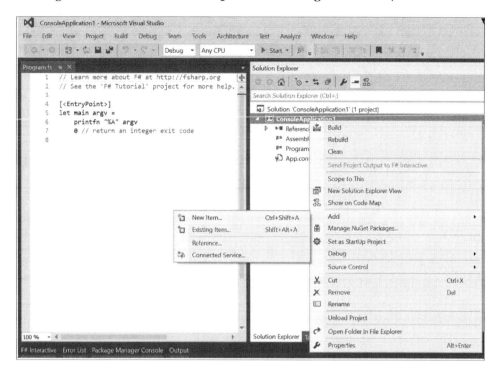

6. When the **Add New Item** dialog box appears, select **Script File**.

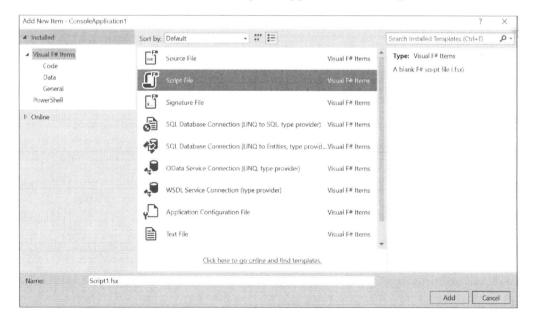

The `Script1.fsx` file is then added to the project.

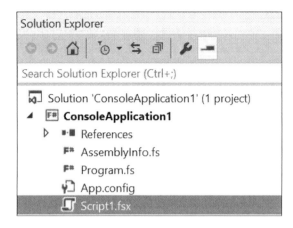

7. Once `Script1.fsx` is created, open it up, and enter the following into the file:

```
let x = "Hello World"
```

8. Highlight that entire row of code, right-click and select **Execute In Interactive** (or press *Alt + Enter*):

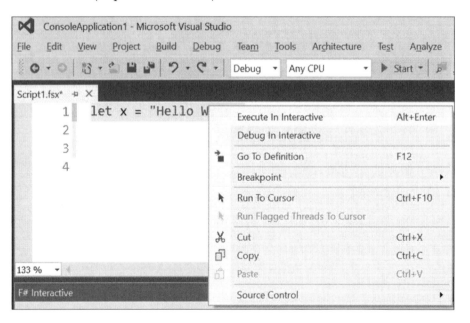

And the **F# Interactive** console will pop up and you will see this:

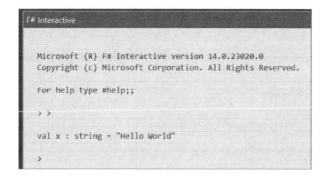

The F# Interactive is a type of REPL, which stands for Read-Evaluate-Print-Loop. If you are a .NET developer who has spent any time in SQL Server Management Studio, the F# Interactive will look very familiar to the Query Analyzer where you enter your code at the top and see how it executes at the bottom. Also, if you are a data scientist using R Studio, you are very familiar with the concept of a REPL. I have used the words REPL and FSI interchangeably in this book.

There are a couple of things to notice about this first line of F# code you wrote. First, it looks very similar to C#. In fact, consider changing the code to this:

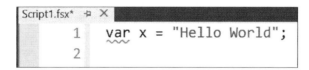

It would be perfectly valid C#. Note that the red squiggly line, showing you that the F# compiler certainly does not think this is valid.

Going back to the correct code, notice that type of x is not explicitly defined. F# uses the concept of inferred typing so that you don't have to write the type of the values that you create. I used the term *value* deliberately because unlike variables, which can be assigned in C# and VB.NET, values are immutable; once bound, they can never change. Here, we are permanently binding the name x to its value, Hello World. This notion of immutability might seem constraining at first, but it has profound and positive implications, especially when writing machine learning models.

With our basic program idea proven out, let's move it over to a compliable assembly; in this case, an .exe that targets the console. Highlight the line that you just wrote, press *Ctrl + C*, and then open up Program.fs. Go into the code that was generated and paste it in:

```
[<EntryPoint>]
let main argv =
    printfn "%A" argv
    let x = "Hello World"
    0 // return an integer exit code
```

Downloading the example code

You can download the example code files for this book from your account at http://www.packtpub.com. If you purchased this book elsewhere, you can visit http://www.packtpub.com/support and register to have the files e-mailed directly to you.

You can download the code files by following these steps:

- Log in or register to our website using your e-mail address and password.
- Hover the mouse pointer on the **SUPPORT** tab at the top.
- Click on **Code Downloads & Errata**.
- Enter the name of the book in the **Search** box.
- Select the book for which you're looking to download the code files.
- Choose from the drop-down menu where you purchased this book from.
- Click on **Code Download**.

Once the file is downloaded, please make sure that you unzip or extract the folder using the latest version of:

- WinRAR / 7-Zip for Windows
- Zipeg / iZip / UnRarX for Mac
- 7-Zip / PeaZip for Linux

Then, add the following lines of code around what you just added:

```
// Learn more about F# at http://fsharp.org
// See the 'F# Tutorial' project for more help.
open System

[<EntryPoint>]
let main argv =
    printfn "%A" argv
```

```
let x = "Hello World"
Console.WriteLine(x)
let y = Console.ReadKey()
0 // return an integer exit code
```

Press the Start button (or hit *F5*) and you should see your program run:

You will notice that I had to bind the return value from `Console.ReadKey()` to `y`. In C# or VB.NET, you can get away with not handling the return value explicitly. In F#, you are not allowed to ignore the returned values. Although some might think this is a limitation, it is actually a strength of the language. It is much harder to make a mistake in F# because the language forces you to address execution paths explicitly versus accidentally sweeping them under the rug (or into a null, but we'll get to that later).

In any event, let's go back to our script file and enter in another line of code:

```
let ints = [|1;2;3;4;5;6|]
```

If you send that line of code to the REPL, you should see this:

val ints : int [] = [|1; 2; 3; 4; 5; 6|]

This is an array, as if you did this in C#:

```
var ints = new[] {1,2,3,4,5,6};
```

Notice that the separator is a semicolon in F# and not a comma. This differs from many other languages, including C#. The comma in F# is reserved for tuples, not for separating items in an array. We'll discuss tuples later.

Now, let's sum up the values in our array:

```
let summedValue = ints |> Array.sum
```

While sending that line to the REPL, you should see this:

val summedValue : int = 21

There are two things going on. We have the |> operator, which is a pipe forward operator. If you have experience with Linux or PowerShell, this should be familiar. However, if you have a background in C#, it might look unfamiliar. The pipe forward operator takes the result of the value on the left-hand side of the operator (in this case, ints) and pushes it into the function on the right-hand side (in this case, sum).

The other new language construct is Array.sum. Array is a module in the core F# libraries, which has a series of functions that you can apply to your data. The function sum, well, sums the values in the array, as you can probably guess by inspecting the result.

So, now, let's add a different function from the Array type:

```
let multiplied = ints |> Array.map (fun i -> i * 2)
```

If you send it to the REPL, you should see this:

```
val multiplied : int [] = [|2; 4; 6; 8; 10; 12|]
```

Array.map is an example of a high ordered function that is part of the Array type. Its parameter is another function. Effectively, we are passing a function into another function. In this case, we are creating an anonymous function that takes a parameter i and returns i * 2. You know it is an anonymous function because it starts with the keyword fun and the IDE makes it easy for us to understand that by making it blue. This anonymous function is also called a lambda expression, which has been in C# and VB.NET since .Net 3.5, so you might have run across it before. If you have a data science background using R, you are already quite familiar with lambdas.

Getting back to the higher-ordered function Array.map, you can see that it applies the lambda function against each item of the array and returns a new array with the new values.

ints	Array.map(fun i -> i *2)	multiplied
1	1 *2	2
2	2*2	4
3	3*2	6
4	4*2	8
5	5*2	10
6	6*2	12

We will be using `Array.map` (and its more generic kin `Seq.map`) a lot when we start implementing machine learning models as it is the best way to transform an array of data. Also, if you have been paying attention to the buzz words of map/reduce when describing big data applications such as Hadoop, the word map means exactly the same thing in this context. One final note is that because of immutability in F#, the original array is not altered, instead, multiplied is bound to a new array.

Let's stay in the script and add in another couple more lines of code:

```
let multiplyByTwo x =
    x * 2
```

If you send it to the REPL, you should see this:

val multiplyByTwo : x:int -> int

These two lines created a named function called `multiplyByTwo`. The function that takes a single parameter `x` and then returns the value of the parameter multiplied by 2. This is exactly the same as our anonymous function we created earlier in-line that we passed into the `map` function. The syntax might seem a bit strange because of the `->` operator. You can read this as, "the function `multiplyByTwo` takes in a parameter called `x` of type `int` and returns an `int`."

Note three things here. Parameter `x` is inferred to be an `int` because it is used in the body of the function as multiplied to another `int`. If the function reads `x * 2.0`, the `x` would have been inferred as a float. This is a significant departure from C# and VB.NET but pretty familiar for people who use R. Also, there is no return statement for the function, instead, the final expression of any function is always returned as the result. The last thing to note is that whitespace is important so that the indentation is required. If the code was written like this:

```
let multiplyByTwo(x) =
x * 2
```

The compiler would complain:

Script1.fsx(8,1): warning FS0058: Possible incorrect indentation: this token is offside of context started at position (7:1).

Since F# does not use curly braces and semicolons (or the end keyword), such as C# or VB.NET, it needs to use something to separate code. That separation is whitespace. Since it is good coding practice to use whitespace judiciously, this should not be very alarming to people having a C# or VB.NET background. If you have a background in R or Python, this should seem natural to you.

Since `multiplyByTwo` is the functional equivalent of the lambda created in `Array. map (fun i -> i * 2)`, we can do this if we want:

```
let multiplied' = ints |> Array.map (fun i -> multiplyByTwo i)
```

If you send it to the REPL, you should see this:

val multiplied' : int [] = [|2; 4; 6; 8; 10; 12|]

Typically, we will use named functions when we need to use that function in several places in our code and we use a lambda expression when we only need that function for a specific line of code.

There is another minor thing to note. I used the tick notation for the value multiplied when I wanted to create another value that was representing the same idea. This kind of notation is used frequently in the scientific community, but can get unwieldy if you attempt to use it for a third or even fourth (multiplied"") representation.

Next, let's add another named function to the REPL:

```
let isEven x =
    match x % 2 = 0 with
    | true -> "even"
    | false -> "odd"
isEven 2
isEven 3
```

If you send it to the REPL, you should see this:

val isEven : x:int -> string

This is a function named `isEven` that takes a single parameter x. The body of the function uses a pattern-matching statement to determine whether the parameter is odd or even. When it is odd, then it returns the string odd. When it is even, it returns the string even.

There is one really interesting thing going on here. The match statement is a basic example of pattern matching and it is one of the coolest features of F#. For now, you can consider the match statement much like the switch statement that you may be familiar within R, Python, C#, or VB.NET, but we will see how it becomes much more powerful in the later chapters. I would have written the conditional logic like this:

```
let isEven' x =
    if x % 2 = 0 then "even" else "odd"
```

But I prefer to use pattern matching for this kind of conditional logic. In fact, I will attempt to go through this entire book without using an `if...then` statement.

With `isEven` written, I can now chain my functions together like this:

```
let multipliedAndIsEven =
    ints
    |> Array.map (fun i -> multiplyByTwo i)
    |> Array.map (fun i -> isEven i)
```

If you send it to REPL, you should see this:

```
val multipliedAndIsEven : string [] =
  [|"even"; "even"; "even"; "even"; "even"; "even"|]
```

In this case, the resulting array from the first pipe `Array.map (fun i -> multiplyByTwo i))` gets sent to the next function `Array.map (fun i -> isEven i)`. This means we might have three arrays floating around in memory: ints which is passed into the first pipe, the result from the first pipe that is passed into the second pipe, and the result from the second pipe. From your mental model point of view, you can think about each array being passed from one function into the next. In this book, I will be chaining pipe forwards frequently as it is such a powerful construct and it perfectly matches the thought process when we are creating and using machine learning models.

You now know enough F# to get you up and running with the first machine learning models in this book. I will be introducing other F# language features as the book goes along, but this is a good start. As you will see, F# is truly a powerful language where a simple syntax can lead to very complex work.

Third-party libraries

The following are a few third-party libraries that we will cover in our book later on.

Math.NET

Math.NET is an open source project that was created to augment (and sometimes replace) the functions that are available in `System.Math`. Its home page is http://www.mathdotnet.com/. We will be using Math.Net's `Numerics` and `Symbolics` namespaces in some of the machine learning algorithms that we will write by hand. A nice feature about Math.Net is that it has strong support for F#.

Accord.NET

Accord.NET is an open source project that was created to implement many common machine learning models. Its home page is `http://accord-framework.net/`. Although the focus of Accord.NET was for computer vision and signal processing, we will be using Accord.Net extensively in this book as it makes it very easy to implement algorithms in our problem domain.

Numl

Numl is an open source project that implements several common machine learning models as experiments. Its home page is `http://numl.net/`. Numl is newer than any of the other third-party libraries that we will use in the book, so it may not be as extensive as the other ones, but it can be very powerful and helpful in certain situations. We will be using Numl in several chapters of the book.

Summary

We covered a lot of ground in this chapter. We discussed what machine learning is, why you want to learn about it in the .NET stack, how to get up and running using F#, and had a brief introduction to the major open source libraries that we will be using in this book. With all this preparation out of the way, we are ready to start exploring machine learning.

In the next chapter, we will apply our newly found F# skills to create a simple linear regression to see if we can help AdventureWorks improve their sales.

2
AdventureWorks Regression

Imagine you're a business developer at AdventureWorks, a bicycle manufacturing company based in Seattle, Washington. You are responsible for three applications that run at the top of a single SQL Server instance. The applications are:

- A customer ordering website with a section for direct customer sales and another section for resellers to buy in bulk

- A desktop inventory control management application

- A reporting solution using Power BI as a frontend

All three of these applications share similar characteristics:

- They are database-first applications where their primary role is to wireframe the database

- They are all .NET applications that use standard Microsoft templating and frameworks, such as MVC for the website and Entity Frameworks for both web and desktop solutions

One day, your boss calls you into her office and says, "we are concerned about the reseller's section of the website. We've noticed through some basic charting in the Power BI that many resellers are dropping their order depending on the average customer reviews of the product.

Here is the one of the charts we are looking at:

Obviously, if we can prevent people from doing this, we will maximize sales. We want to maximize our existing code assets, so your solution needs to integrate with the existing website and we want our customers to experience the same look and feel they currently have."

This is what the current webpage looks like:

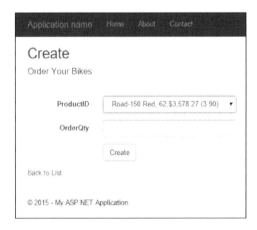

You tell your boss that you will take a look, think about it for a couple of days, and come up with some ideas. Inside, you are thrilled because this will take you out of the traditional role of web dev and into data science. After researching some different machine learning techniques, you settle on using a simple regression to help achieve this goal.

Simple linear regression

Regressions attempt to predict one number given a set of different numbers. For example, imagine we had a box where we enter in a number and another number comes out:

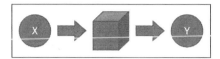

I enter the number 1 into the box, and the number 6 comes out. Then, I enter another 1 into the box and the number 7 comes out. I do this five times and I get the following results:

```
1 -> 6
1 -> 7
1 -> 6
1 -> 5
1 -> 6
```

Before entering in another one, what do you think the output will be? You probably guessed 6. However, if I asked you whether you were 100% sure that 6 would come out, you would say, "no, but it will probably be 6." In fact, you might say that 6 has a 60% chance of coming out based on prior experience (three sixes in five total attempts).

What you are doing mentally is a kind of regression. Typically, linear regressions are written using a formula like this:

```
y = x0 + x1 + x2 + E
```

Here, y is the number you want to predict and $x0$, $x1$, and $x2$ are some numbers that might affect y. Back to AdventureWorks, y is the number of bikes a retail store will order in a month, $x0$ is the month of the year, $x1$ is the order from the previous three months, and $x2$ is the number of other bikes that are being ordered by their immediate competitors. E is all of the things that our formula cannot account for that still affects the bike sales—like an individual store losing a key sales person. If we knew that $x0 + x1 + x2$ accounted for 75% of y, we would know that 25% of y cannot be explained.

Our goal, then, is to find as few x parameters as possible that have the greatest impact on y and then make a reasonable attempt to have our website reflect both the predicted value and to influence the users for our benefit.

There are many types of regressions, and we will start with the most basic, though surprisingly powerful one—the simple regression. In a simple regression, there is only one input variable and one output, so the formula is $y = x0 + E$. Because there are only two variables, we can plot them on a two-dimensional graph. For example, if we had this data:

X	Y
1	1
2	2
3	2.25
4	4.75
5	5

We can plot the data like this:

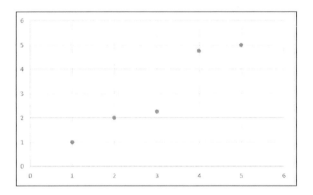

What we want to do with a simple regression is find the line that "fits" best through all of the data points:

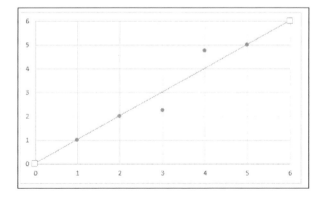

In this example, you can see that the line goes through points 1, 2, and 5. If the line does not intersect a given point, we want to know the distance from the line to the point. In this example, we want to know the distance of the dotted red line for points 3 and 4.

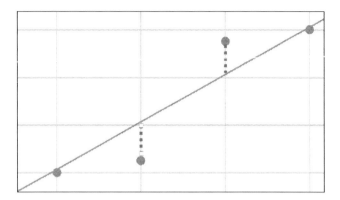

If we add up the distance of all of the dotted red lines and divide by the number of total points on our graph, we have a pretty good idea of how well this line represents the plot. If we are then given a number that is on our graph, we can make a prediction about where it will land. For example, if we are given another 2, we can predict that we will probably result in a 2. Not only that, we can make predictions about where the line is headed (slope) for inputs that we have not seen before. For example, if we input 6, we can guess that it will probably be close to 6.

In a real-word example, we typically don't have a single input for a given number. So, we might get a hundred 1s and 90% of the time the output will be 1, 5% of the time the output will be 1.25, and 5% of the time, the output will be 0.75. If we placed all the 100s on our scatter plot, we will see lots of points on 1 (or a really dark dot), some on 1.25, and some on 0.75. With this mental model in place, let's go ahead and create a simple linear regression from scratch.

Setting up the environment

Open Visual Studio 2015 and create a new F# Library:

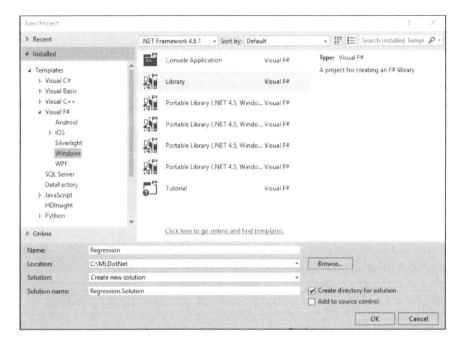

Once Visual Studio finishes creating the project and files for you, go into the solution explorer, and open `Script1.fsx` and delete all the contents in the file. You should now have an empty script file ready for your code.

Preparing the test data

The first thing we will do is create a dataset that we can use in our regression that gives us predictable results. Create an array like this:

```
let input = [|1,1.;2,2.;3,2.25;4,4.75;5,5.|]
```

Here, `input` is an array of tuples. A tuple is a data structure that contains groups of data that are unnamed—usually there are two items. The types do *not* have to be the same as a tuple's items. If you are familiar with the concept of a key/value pair, you can use that as a mental model of a tuple. The only real "gotcha" is that tuples can have many items so this it is a perfectly valid tuple: `2,true,"dog"` where the first position is an `int`, the second is a Boolean, and the third is a string.

If you highlight our single line of code and send it to the REPL using *Alt + Enter*, you will get this back:

```
val input : (int * float) [] =
  [|(1, 1.0); (2, 2.0); (3, 2.25); (4, 4.75); (5, 5.0)|]
```

The F# compiler is telling us that we have an array that contains tuples of type `int` and `float`. In this example, we will use the first value of the tuples to be the X and the second to be the Y of our simple linear regression.

With the data set up, let's think about how to calculate a regression. A more mathematical definition than what I used earlier is $y = A + Bx$, where A is the Y intercept of the line and B is the slope of the line. Therefore, we need to figure out how to calculate the intercept of the line and the slope of the line. Turns out that we need to calculate the standard deviation of the x and y values and something called the **Person's correlation**. Let's tackle each one of these separately.

Standard deviation

The best explanation of standard deviation that I have run across is at `http://www.mathsisfun.com/data/standard-deviation.html`.

Standard deviation is the square root of the variance; to calculate the variance:

1. Work out the mean (the simple average of the numbers).

2. Then, for each number, subtract the mean and square the result (the squared difference).

3. Then, work out the average of those squared differences.

So, taking MathIsFun's explanation and applying it to F#, we can write:

```
let variance (source:float seq) =
    let mean = Seq.average source
    let deltas = Seq.map (fun x -> pown (x-mean) 2) source
    Seq.average deltas
```

Sending that to the REPL gives us:

```
val variance : source:seq<float> -> float
```

Notice how there is a one-to-one correspondence between each line of the English explanation and the F# code. This is not an accident. F# is really great at matching your thought process. In fact, we even resisted to temptation to `for...each` in code when we saw those words in the English version.

There is some new F# code here that might be confusing. Notice that when I calculated the mean, I called the `Seq.average` function:

```
Seq.average source
```

And hence, the `source` argument came after the function. I could have just as well written:

```
source |> Seq.average
```

This is something you will have seen before if you worked through *Chapter 1, Welcome to Machine Learning Using the .NET Framework*. There is really no consensus in the F# community about which way is more idiomatic, though the style guidelines argue for the non-pipe forward way. Since both are supported by the languages and widely used, I use both depending on the code. Typically, when I have a string of thoughts to push together I use the pipe operator, but if there is only one calculation, I just call the function directly. Notice that I did this *after syntax* technique in all three lines: mean, deltas, and the return of the function.

With variance out of the way, we can make our standard deviation:

```
let standardDeviation values =
    sqrt (variance values)
```

Sending that to the REPL gives us:

```
val standardDeviation : values:seq<float> -> float
```

With the standard deviation ready, we can plug in our numbers. Since we will be calculating the standard deviation of *X* and *Y* independently, let's break the tuple apart into separate arrays and calculate their average and standard deviations:

```
let x = input |> Seq.map (fun (x,y) -> float x)
let y = input |> Seq.map (fun (x,y) -> y)

let mX = Seq.average x
let mY = Seq.average y

let sX = standardDeviation x
let sY = standardDeviation y
```

Sending that to the REPL gives us:

```
val x : seq<float>
val y : seq<float>
val mX : float = 3.0
val mY : float = 3.0
val sX : float = 1.414213562
val sY : float = 1.589024858
```

There is one thing new here. Notice that when calculating x, I used this syntax:

```
Seq.map(fun (x,y) -> float x)
```

With `float x` as the return. `float` is a function that casts the int into, well, a float. If you are coming from VB.NET/C#, the comparable syntax will be `(float)x`.

Pearson's correlation

Next, let's calculate the Pearson's correlation. The best explanation I have found for it is available at `http://onlinestatbook.com/2/describing_bivariate_data/calculation.html`. You can think of creating the Pearson's correlation as filling in columns in an Excel spreadsheet and then doing some calculations on the column totals. Start a grid with x and y in different rows:

	X	Y	x	y	xy	x^2	y^2
	1	1					
	2	2					
	3	2.25					
	4	4.75					
	5	5					
Total							
Mean							

Then, calculate the mean for X and Y:

	X	Y	x	y	xy	x^2	y^2
	1	1					
	2	2					
	3	2.25					
	4	4.75					
	5	5					
Total	15	15					
Mean	3	3					

Next, calculate x and y. x is calculated by subtracting the mean of X from X and y is calculated by subtracting the mean of Y from Y:

	X	Y	x	y	xy	x^2	y^2
	1	1	-2	-2			
	2	2	-1	-1			
	3	2.25	0	-0.75			
	4	4.75	1	1.75			
	5	5	2	2			
Total	15	15					
Mean	3	3					

Next, fill in xy, x^2, and y^2:

	X	Y	x	y	xy	x^2	y^2
	1	1	-2	-2	4	4	4
	2	2	-1	-1	1	1	1
	3	2.25	0	-0.75	0	0	0.563
	4	4.75	1	1.75	1.75	1	3.063
	5	5	2	2	4	4	4
Total	15	15					
Mean	3	3					

With the grid filled in, you can sum up xy, x^2, and y^2:

	X	Y	x	y	xy	x^2	y^2
	1	1	-2	-2	4	4	4
	2	2	-1	-1	1	1	1
	3	2.25	0	-0.75	0	0	0.563
	4	4.75	1	1.75	1.75	1	3.063
	5	5	2	2	4	4	4
Total	15	15			10.75	10	12.63
Mean	3	3					

The final answer is computed by dividing the sum of the xy column (Σxy) by the square root of the product of the sum of the x^2 column (Σx^2) and the sum of the y^2 column (Σy^2). So, in our example, it will be:

```
10.75/ √(10 * 12.63)
```

I now want to repeat these steps without that grid in English:

1. Calculate the mean for X.
2. Calculate the mean for Y.
3. Calculate x.
4. Calculate y.
5. Fill in xy, x^2, and y^2.
6. Sum up y^2.
7. Sum up x^2.
8. Sum up y^2.
9. Do the final formula.

And this is how I would write it in F#:

```
let pearsonsCorrelation(a:float seq, b:float seq) =
    let mX = Seq.average a
    let mY = Seq.average b
```

```
let x = a |> Seq.map (fun x -> x - mX)
let y = b |> Seq.map (fun y -> y - mY)

let xys = Seq.zip x y
let xy = xys |> Seq.map (fun (x, y) -> x*y, x*x, y*y)
let sxy = xy |> Seq.sumBy (fun (xy, x2, y2) -> xy)
let sx2 = xy |> Seq.sumBy (fun (xy, x2, y2) -> x2)
let sy2 = xy |> Seq.sumBy (fun (xy, x2, y2) -> y2)
sxy / sqrt (sx2*sy2)
```

Sending that to the REPL gives us:

```
val pearsonsCorrelation : a:seq<float> * b:seq<float> -> float
```

Again, you can see that there is almost a one-to-one correspondence between the formula and the code. There are a couple of things to note.

`Seq.zip x y` is a function that takes in two sequences of equal length and combines them together into a single tuple. So for x and y zipped:

x		y		xys
1.00		1.00		1.00,1.00
2.00	Zip	2.00	=	2.00,2.00
3.00		2.25		3.00,2.25
4.00		4.75		4.00,4.75
5.00		5.00		5.00,5.00

Another thing to notice is that there is a three-item tuple being used in the `Seq.sumBy`s. Each item of the tuple represents a different column in the grid we were filling out: xy, x^2, and y^2. Although I normally don't like to create tuples greater than two items, I can make an exception in this case because I am only using the tuple in the context of these higher-order functions. Because the data structure is contained and short-lived, a tuple is the best choice. If I needed that data structure outside of the higher-order function, a record type would have been more appropriate. We'll get more exposure to a record type later in this chapter.

A final thing to notice is the `Seq.sumBy` higher-ordered function. As you may expect, `sumBy` computes the sum of things. The key thing to realize is that the `sumBy` expects a function to be passed, not a data structure. If you just want to sum up the values in an array, you can use the `Seq.sum()` function:

```
Seq.sum ([1;2;3])
val it : int = 6

Seq.sumBy ([1;2;3])
```

```
Does not compile

Seq.sumBy (fun i -> i) [1;2;3]
val it : int = 6
```

And so to run a Pearson's correlation for *x* and *y*, type this into the script:

```
let r = pearsonsCorrelation (x,y)
```

Sending that to the REPL gives us:

val r : float = 0.9567374429

Linear regression

With standard deviation and *r* calculated, we are ready for our linear regression:

```
let b = r*(sY/sX)
let A = mY - b*mX
val b : float = 1.075
val A : float = -0.225
```

What these two values mean is that our *y* intercept is -.22, or very close to the origin, and our slope is 1.075. Laying them out on the same grid, you can see that the predicted numbers are close to the actual:

X	Y	Y'
0	0	-0.2
1	1	0.9
2	2	1.9
3	2.25	3.0
4	4.75	4.1
5	5	5.2

These are still different enough on the plot that we eye-balled earlier with the red line going directly through 1, 2, 3, 4, 5 (solid line) and the regression line taking a slightly different path (dashed line):

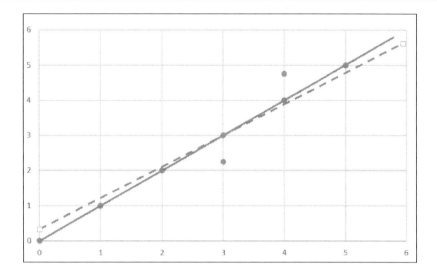

We will revisit how good this regression is at describing our data (and making predictions) in a bit. Until then, we can safely say that we have a regression, which seems to fit our data pretty well.

We now have a library we could compile for our AdventureWorks problem. However, we may not want to roll our own because this is a fairly limited implementation. For example, when we calculated variance and standard deviation, we were using the formula for the variance and standard deviation for an entire population. If we had only a small sample of the population, there is a different formula that we will implement. Also, linear regressions have several parameters that we can enter to try and *tune up* the model in our implementation. As you can guess, there is quite a bit of effort in writing your own library, and you still may not get it right. If you were wondering in the middle of the prior exercise of rolling our own, "is there an easier way?" The answer is "yes."

Math.NET

We had a brief introduction to Math.Net in *Chapter 1, Welcome to Machine Learning Using the .NET Framework*. In this section, we will add it to our project and see how it can help us do a simple linear regression. In the solution explorer of your open project, add a new script file and name it `MathDotNet.fsx`.

Next, open the NuGet Package Manager Console (**Tools | NuGet Package Manger | Package Manager Console**):

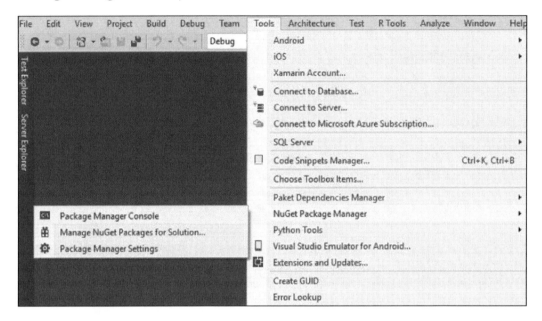

In the console, enter the following line:

```
PM> install-package MathNet.Numerics
```

You will see that the package installs successfully:

```
PM> install-package MathNet.Numerics
Attempting to gather dependencies information for package 'MathNet.Numerics.3.8.0'
'ChcikenSoftware.MathTestDrive', targeting '.NETFramework,Version=v4.5.2'
Attempting to resolve dependencies for package 'MathNet.Numerics.3.8.0' with Depen
Resolving actions to install package 'MathNet.Numerics.3.8.0'
Resolved actions to install package 'MathNet.Numerics.3.8.0'
Adding package 'MathNet.Numerics.3.8.0' to folder 'F:\Documents\Book - ML\Intro Ex
Added package 'MathNet.Numerics.3.8.0' to folder 'F:\Documents\Book - ML\Intro Exa
Added package 'MathNet.Numerics.3.8.0' to 'packages.config'
Successfully installed 'MathNet.Numerics 3.8.0' to ChcikenSoftware.MathTestDrive
```

Close the Package Manager Console and the `readme.txt` file that opens when you install Math.NET. In the future, I will assume that you know how to open and enter commands to install NuGet packages.

Regression try 1

In the script file, create the same input that we saw in the hand-rolled script and calculate the means of *x* and *y*:

```
let input = [|1,1.;2,2.;3,2.25;4,4.75;5,5.|]

let x = input |> Array.map(fun (x,y) -> float x)
let y = input |> Array.map(fun (x,y) -> y)
let mX = Array.average x
let mY = Array.average y
```

The following is the output:

```
val input : (int * float) [] =
  [|(1, 1.0); (2, 2.0); (3, 2.25); (4, 4.75); (5, 5.0)|]
val x : float [] = [|1.0; 2.0; 3.0; 4.0; 5.0|]
val y : float [] = [|1.0; 2.0; 2.25; 4.75; 5.0|]
val mX : float = 3.0
val mY : float = 3.0
```

Then, point to the Math.NET library installed with the nugget package and add a reference to it:

```
#r
"../packages/MathNet.Numerics.3.8.0/lib/net40/MathNet.Numerics.dll"
open MathNet.Numerics.Statistics
```

Next, use Math.Net to calculate the standard deviation of *x* and *y*:

```
let sX = ArrayStatistics.StandardDeviation x
let sY = ArrayStatistics.StandardDeviation y
```

The preceding code statements will give you:

```
val sX : float = 1.58113883
val sY : float = 1.7765838
```

Finally, use Math.Net to calculate the r:

```
let r = Correlation.Pearson (x,y)
```

The following will be the output:

```
val r : float = 0.9567374429
```

Now, you can calculate the regression:

```
let b = r*(sY/sX)
let A = mY - b*mX
```

And here is what you will get in the output:

```
val b : float = 1.075
```

```
val A : float = -0.225
```

There is one new thing I want to point out in the script. You had to type:

```
#r
"../packages/MathNet.Numerics.3.8.0/lib/net40/MathNet.Numerics.dll"
open MathNet.Numerics.Statistics
```

The `#r` stands for reference and points the FSI to the filesystem to locate the assembly that we want to use. The FSI loads with very few libraries installed, so you typically have to add a reference the ones you need. Notice the `".."` shorthand as the prefix for the file path. This is a relative locator that translates into the solution location.

The `open` command tells the FSI to open up the `.dll` file that we pointed to in the previous line. This is the same as `using` in C#, `Imports` in VB.NET, and `library` in R.

So, this is a much easier way to calculate the components of a simple linear regression than by hand. But wait, there is even more.

Regression try 2

Math.NET makes it even easier to calculate the regression without going into the components. In the script, enter the following code:

```
open MathNet.Numerics
let fit = Fit.Line(x,y)
let i = fst fit
let s = snd fit
```

You will get the following output:

```
val fit : float * float = (-0.225, 1.075)
```

```
val i : float = -0.225
```

```
val s : float = 1.075
```

`Math.Numerics` already has the regression available via the `Fit()` function. `Fit()` takes in two arrays (in our case, *x* and *y*) and returns a tuple. The first item of the tuple is the intercept and the second is the slope. The only new code that I introduced here are the `fst` and `snd` operators. These are shorthand notations for tuples that have a length of two. Calling `fst` on a tuple returns the first item and `snd` returns the second. If you call `fst` and `snd` on a tuple that has more than two items, you will get a type mismatch compiler error.

Accord.NET

With Math.NET doing all of our heavy lifting, we have a better way to get the results of a simple linear regression. However, there is another way I want to discuss, Accord. NET. Open the NuGet Package Manager and install the following three packages:

- Accord
- Accord.Statistics
- FSharp.Data

Note that you will get a pop-up window when you install FSharp.Data:

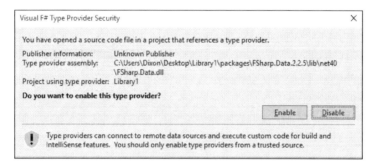

Click on **Enable**.

Regression

Back in the script file, enter the following lines of code:

```
#r "../packages/Accord.3.0.2/lib/net40/Accord.dll"
#r "../packages/Accord.Statistics.3.0.2/lib/net40/
Accord.Statistics.dll"
#r "../packages/Accord.Math.3.0.2/lib/net40/Accord.Math.dll"
```

```
open Accord
open Accord.Statistics.Models.Regression.Linear

let input = [|1,1.;2,2.;3,2.25;4,4.75;5,5.|]
let x = input |> Array.map (fun (x,y) -> float x)
let y = input |> Array.map (fun (x,y) -> y) let regression =
SimpleLinearRegression()
let sse = regression.Regress(x,y)
let intercept = regression.Intercept
let slope = regression.Slope
let mse = sse/float x.Length
let rmse = sqrt mse
let r2 = regression.CoefficientOfDetermination(x,y)
```

When you send this to the REPL, you will see the following code:

```
val input : (int * float) [] =
  [|(1, 1.0); (2, 2.0); (3, 2.25); (4, 4.75); (5, 5.0)|]
val x : float [] = [|1.0; 2.0; 3.0; 4.0; 5.0|]
val y : float [] = [|1.0; 2.0; 2.25; 4.75; 5.0|]
val regression : SimpleLinearRegression = y(x) = 1.075x +
-0.224999999999998
val sse : float = 1.06875
val intercept : float = -0.225
val slope : float = 1.075
val mse : float = 0.21375
val rmse : float = 0.4623310502
val r2 : float = 0.9153465347
```

What you see here is the exact same calculation as before with the formula kindly printed out (I have rounded it to three decimal places):

```
y(x) = 1.075x + -0.225
```

Regression evaluation using RMSE

Accord.NET goes one better than Math.NET `Fit()` as it returns the sum of the squared errors and the coefficient of determination (called r squared). In this case, the sum of squared errors is `1.06875` and the r squared is `0.915` (rounded to three decimal places). This is great because we now have two vital pieces of information:

- A model to predict
- Some way to help us evaluate how good the model is at predicting

In machine learning, it is not enough to simply implement a model and get some answers. We also have to be able to speak to know how good our answer really is. The **sum of squares error**, often called **SSE**, is a common way to evaluate a simple linear regression. To start thinking about SSE, we need to know two pieces of information for each y that we used — what we guessed and what the actual value is. Using our existing dataset:

X	Actual	Guess	Difference	Difference Squared
1	1	0.9	-0.1	0.021
2	2	1.9	-0.1	0.005
3	2.25	3.0	0.8	0.570
4	4.75	4.1	-0.7	0.449
5	5	5.2	0.2	0.024
				1.069

You can see that the model was created based on all of the y data points, and then Accord.NET went back and checked how close that model *fits* each data point. These differences are squared, then the squared values are summed. The goal is to get the sums of squares as low as possible. Once we have the SSE, we can change our model to try to get the sum of squares lower. For example, what if we changed the slope from `1.075x` to `1.000x`, which is what we were eyeballing earlier?

X	Actual	Guess	Difference	Difference Squared
1	1	0.8	-0.2	0.048
2	2	1.8	-0.2	0.048
3	2.25	2.8	0.5	0.281
4	4.75	3.8	-1.0	0.941
5	5	4.8	-0.2	0.048
				1.367

Since we have all five data points that are available for the initial model calculation, you are not going to improve on the model by making manual changes like this. The original regression is the best way of describing the relationship among these five data points. It is important to note that the SSE is a context-free measure. This means 1.069 does not have any value in and of itself. We only know that 1.069 is better than 1.367. Basically, we want the SSE to be as low as possible.

A slightly better variation of the SSE is the **Mean Square Error (MSE)**. The MSE is the SSE divided by the number of observations of the regression:

X	Actual	Guess	Difference	Difference Squared
1	1	0.9	-0.1	0.021
2	2	1.9	-0.1	0.005
3	2.25	3.0	0.8	0.570
4	4.75	4.1	-0.7	0.449
5	5	5.2	0.2	0.024
			SSE	1.069
			MSE	0.213775

In this case, the MSE is `0.2138`. Like the MSE, the number itself is not particularly useful. However, if we take the square root of the MSE, often called the **Root Of Mean Square Error**, or **RMSE**, the result is an error measure in the same units as our original numbers.

```
RMSE = Square Root of MSE = sqrt(.2137) = .462
```

In our case, the RMSE is `0.462` means that any given guess is likely off by 0.46. When you talk to other data scientists at your next cocktail party (you do go to cocktail parties with data scientists, don't you?), you will typically use the RMSE when evaluating the predictive capabilities of a simple linear model.

Using the RMSE, we now have a measure of how accurate our model is when predicting values. We also have a second measure, called the r2, that calculates how much correlation our model has. The r2 takes the r (in this case, Pearson's correlation) and squares it. The r2 is always between zero and one, with zero meaning that there is no correlation between x and y and one meaning that the regression line perfectly fits the data. In practical terms, we want a low as possible RMSE with a high as possible r2.

Regression and the real world

So far, we really haven't done any machine learning, in that we can't make our model any better. The initial regression is the best and explains 91.5% of the data. However, the world does not work in such a straightforward manner.

The challenge is that we will start applying a simple linear regression on a dataset that represents human activity (in our case, AdventureWorks sales), and human activity is fraught with uncertainty. Consider a more realistic data frame with a product, its list price, and its customer reviews:

ProductId	Name	ListPrice	ReviewerName	Rating
759	Road-650 Red, 58	782.99	sean andrews	5
759	Road-650 Red, 58	782.99	dikra langerak	3
759	Road-650 Red, 58	782.99	kasper latt	4
759	Road-650 Red, 58	782.99	oskari maki	5
759	Road-650 Red, 58	782.99	clarence fletcher	2
759	Road-650 Red, 58	782.99	chloe lee	5
759	Road-650 Red, 58	782.99	leana nguyen	1
759	Road-650 Red, 58	782.99	jack reid	3
759	Road-650 Red, 58	782.99	mark castro	4
759	Road-650 Red, 58	782.99	leta adams	4
759	Road-650 Red, 58	782.99	izzie bates	5

Notice that the rating seems to have some wide variance. Some customers gave the bike a 5 while others gave it a 1 or 2. You would think for the same product, the average reviews would be fairly similar. Perhaps we have a problem with manufacturing quality or perhaps the price is such that low-end customers expect more from what they perceive to be a very expensive bike and high-end customers are thrilled with the value they got from what they perceive to be a low-cost bike. Now can we start with our model? Yes! Let's take the data from AdventureWorks and see how it stacks up with an initial model using Accord.NET.

Regression against actual data

As this is the first time we are using AdventureWorks, there are a couple of housekeeping items we need to take care of. We will be using the AdventureWorks 2014 full database found at `https://msftdbprodsamples.codeplex.com/releases/view/125550`. If you want to bring the data locally, you can do that by restoring the `.bak` file from their website. If you go this route, note that I added some additional data to the `Production.ProductReview` table for this chapter. You will need to run the `populateProductReview.sql` script found in this chapter's GitHub repository after your database is installed to match the examples found in the book. In addition, you will have to generate your own connection string. If you just want to use the data on our server, you can use the connection string that is in the upcoming code sample.

You might be thinking that I am nuts to put a connection string out in the public domain like this. First, don't tell anyone you have it. Second, if by some stroke of fortune millions of people buy this book and they all pound on this server to do the examples, I will be happy to pay Microsoft more $$ for the compute time.

In Visual Studio, add a new script to your project and call it `AccordDotNet2.fsx`. Then, add the following references and open the script file:

```
#r "System.Transactions.dll"
#r "../packages/Accord.3.0.2/lib/net40/Accord.dll"
#r "../packages/Accord.Statistics.3.0.2/lib/net40/Accord.Statistics.
dll"
#r "../packages/Accord.Math.3.0.2/lib/net40/Accord.Math.dll"
#r "../packages/FSharp.Data.2.2.5/lib/net40/FSharp.Data.dll"


open Accord
open Accord.Statistics
open Accord.Statistics.Models.Regression.Linear


open System
open System.Data.SqlClient
```

Next, add a record type, a list of that record type, a connection string, and a query:

```
type ProductReview = {ProductID:int; TotalOrders:float;
AvgReviews:float}

let reviews = ResizeArray<ProductReview>()

[<Literal>]
let connectionString =
"data source=nc54a9m5kk.database.windows.net;initial catalog=Adventure
Works2014;user
id=chickenskills@nc54a9m5kk;password=sk1lzm@tter;"

[<Literal>]
let query = "Select
            A.ProductID, TotalOrders, AvgReviews
            From
            (Select
            ProductID,
            Sum(OrderQty) as TotalOrders
            from [Sales].[SalesOrderDetail] as SOD
            inner join [Sales].[SalesOrderHeader] as SOH
            on SOD.SalesOrderID = SOH.SalesOrderID
            inner join [Sales].[Customer] as C
```

```
                        on SOH.CustomerID = C.CustomerID
                        Where C.StoreID is not null
                        Group By ProductID) as A
                        Inner Join
                        (Select
                        ProductID,
                        (Sum(Rating) + 0.0) / (Count(ProductID) + 0.0) as
        AvgReviews
                        from [Production].[ProductReview] as PR
                        Group By ProductID) as B
                        on A.ProductID = B.ProductID"
```

There are three new language features here. The first is a record type called
`ProductReview`. Record types are immutable named data structures and stand
in contrast to tuples, which are unnamed. You can think of a record type as an
immutable DTO/POCO that you might encounter in the VB.NET/C# world.
`ProductReview` has three members: `ProductId`, `TotalOrders`, and `AvgReviews`.
You can think of these members as properties of a POCO in the C#/VB.NET world.

The second new language feature is the attribute added to the `connectionString`
and query values. Most .NET developers are familiar with attributes, so you should
be comfortable using them. By making `connectionString` and query literal, I can
pass them into type providers in the script file.

Finally, we will use a `ResizeArray` datatype to keep our `seq` of product reviews.
Because arrays are immutable in F# and we don't know how many reviews we will
be getting back from the database, we need to use a special array that does allow
resizing. This is equivalent to `System.Collections.Generic.List<>` that you
might be familiar with in your C#/VB.NET code.

Next, add some ADO.Net code to extract the data from the database and put it into
the list:

```
let connection = new SqlConnection(connectionString)
let command = new SqlCommand(query,connection)
connection.Open()
let reader = command.ExecuteReader()
while reader.Read() do
    reviews.Add({ProductID=reader.GetInt32(0);
    TotalOrders=(float)(reader.GetInt32(1));
    AvgReviews=(float)(reader.GetDecimal(2))})
```

This code should be familiar to most .Net developers. Sending it to the REPL, we can see:

```
type ProductReview =
  {ProductID: int;
   TotalOrders: float;
   AvgReviews: float;}
val reviews : System.Collections.Generic.List<ProductReview>
val connectionString : string =
  "data source=nc54a9m5kk.database.windows.net;initial catalog=A"+[72
chars]
val query : string =
  "Select
                A.ProductID, AvgOrders, AvgReviews
  "+[814 chars]
val connection : System.Data.SqlClient.SqlConnection =
  System.Data.SqlClient.SqlConnection
val command : System.Data.SqlClient.SqlCommand =
  System.Data.SqlClient.SqlCommand
val reader : System.Data.SqlClient.SqlDataReader
val it : unit = ()
```

With the data coming down, let's see if our models reflect what our manager noticed in the power bi' charting:

```
let x = reviews |> Seq.map (fun pr -> pr.AvgReviews) |> Seq.toArray
let y = reviews |> Seq.map (fun pr -> pr.TotalOrders) |> Seq.toArray
let regression = SimpleLinearRegression()
let sse = regression.Regress(x,y)
let mse = sse/float x.Length
let rmse = sqrt mse
let r2 = regression.CoefficientOfDetermination(x,y)
```

You will see the following:

```
val regression : SimpleLinearRegression =
  y(x) = 1277.89025884053x + -4092.62506538369
val sse : float = 39480886.74
val mse : float = 203509.7254
val rmse : float = 451.1205221
val r2 : float = 0.2923784167
```

We now see a `0.29 r2` and a `451 rmse`, which shows a weak relationship between customer reviews and order quantity and that there is a 450 order margin of error.

Another point is that simple linear regressions tend to have a problem with outliers. We'll have a lot to say about this topic in the next chapter. Also, by doing a one-shot analysis, we have a large problem with over-fitting. We'll be talking about over-fitting extensively in *Chapter 8, Feature Selection and Optimization*. For now, I just wanted to acknowledge that although we have a pretty good model, it is far from perfect. However, it is still better than eyeballing a chart and it does have some statistical validity. We now have a model and we can predict some sales. How do we put this in production?

AdventureWorks app

We will start by thinking about how we want to prevent users from abandoning orders based on low product reviews. One option would be to drop the review entirely. While this will prevent that undesirable effect of people dropping orders because of a low rating, it also prevents the desirable effect of people purchasing items based on a high rating. We could also hide the ratings for low-score items, but that would be seen through very easily. Another possibility is to lower the price of low-rated products, but lowering prices is anathema to most companies. Perhaps a better way is to have our site have knowledge of low-rated products and give people an incentive to order them by prefilling the amount that most people order for that given review. Consumer behaviorists have demonstrated that if you prefill a quantity, the consumer is less likely to abandon their purchase.

Setting up the environment

Go get a copy of AdventureWorks UI from GitHub at this uri. Next, open the copy using Visual Studio 2015.

Now, follow these steps, which will guide you to set up the environment:

1. Let's go into our **Solution Explorer** and add an F# project (**File | New Project**).

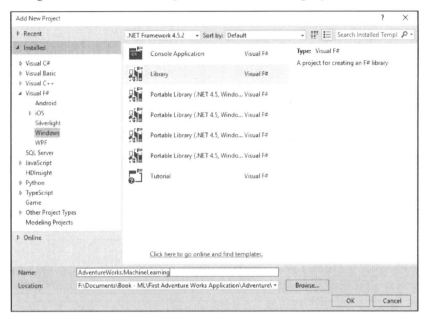

2. Delete the script file and rename `Library1.fs` to `OrderPrediction.fs`.

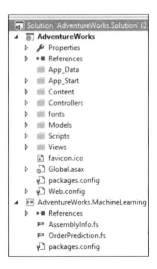

3. Open NuGet Package Manager and install Accord.NET to the F# project:

```
PM> install-package Accord
PM> install-package Accord.Statistics
```

4. Make sure that the default project is `AdventureWorks.MachineLearning`:

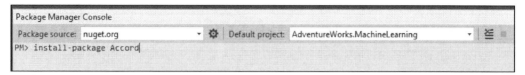

5. Open up `OrderPrediction.fs` and rename `Class1` to `OrderPrediction`.

```
namespace AdventureWorks.MachineLearning

type OrderPrediction() =
    member this.X = "F#"
```

6. Then, rename `X` to `PredictQuantity` with a single integer parameter of `ProductId` and a return value of a float. For now, make it `0.0`. Make the type public.

```
namespace AdventureWorks.MachineLearning

type public OrderPrediction() =
    member this.PredictQuantity(productId:int) = 0.0
```

7. Compile the F# project.

Updating the existing web project

Next, go to the C# project in the **Solution Explorer** and add a reference to the F# project:

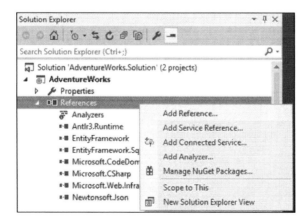

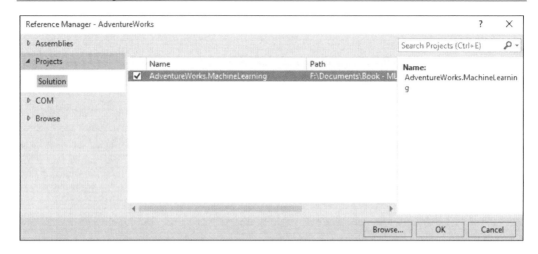

Go into `PurchaseOrderDetailsController.cs` and add a `using` statement to `AdventureWorks.MachineLearning`:

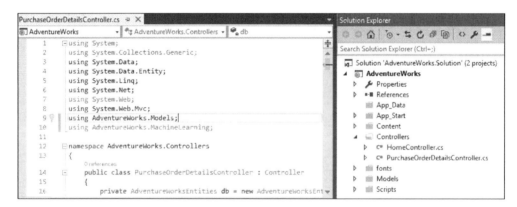

Next, create an endpoint that can take in a `productId` and predict the quantity of the order:

```
// GET: PurchaseOrderDetails/PredictQuantity/1
public Int32 PredictQuantity(int id)
{
    var orderPrediction = new OrderPrediction();
    return (Int32)orderPrediction.PredictQuantity(id);
}
```

Forgive me that this is RPC and not very RESTful. The intention of this exercise is about machine learning and not web development. If you want to rewrite, this is a more MVC idiomatic form, feel free.

With the controller set up, hop over to the Create view:

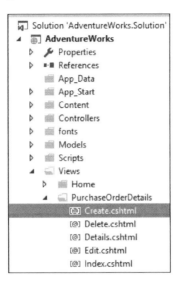

Add the following JavaScript at the bottom of the page in the `@section Scripts` block:

```
@section Scripts {
    @Scripts.Render("~/bundles/jqueryval")
<script type="text/javascript">
        $(document).ready(function(){
            $("#ProductID").change(function(){
                var productID = $(this).val();
                $.get("/PurchaseOrderDetails/PredictQuantity/" +
                  productID, function(result){
                    $("#OrderQty").val(result);
                });
            });
        });
</script>
}
```

With that in place, you should be able to run the project and after selecting a new product from the dropdown, the order quantity should populate with a `0.0`.

Implementing the regression

With the app wired up, let's hop back to the F# project and implement the prediction for real. First, make sure that you have a reference to `System.Data`.

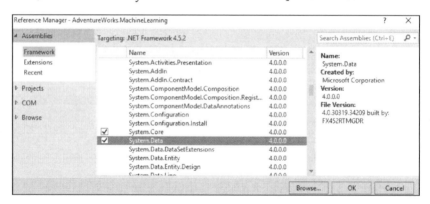

Next, open up `OrderPrediction.fs` and enter this in the following code:

> Since this is (almost) verbatim from the REPL project, you can go ahead with copying and pasting if you want to avoid some typing.

```
namespace AdventureWorks.MachineLearning

open Accord
open Accord.Statistics
```

```
open Accord.Statistics.Models.Regression.Linear

open System
open System.Data.SqlClient
open System.Collections.Generic

type internal ProductReview = {ProductID:int; TotalOrders:float;
AvgReviews: float}

type public OrderPrediction () =
    let reviews = List<ProductReview>()

    [<Literal>]
    let connectionString = "data
source=nc54a9m5kk.database.windows.net;initial
catalog=AdventureWorks2014;user
id=chickenskills@nc54a9m5kk;password=sk1lzm@tter;"

    [<Literal>]
    let query = "Select
                A.ProductID, TotalOrders, AvgReviews
                From
                (Select
                ProductID,
                Sum(OrderQty) as TotalOrders
                from [Sales].[SalesOrderDetail] as SOD
                inner join [Sales].[SalesOrderHeader] as SOH
                on SOD.SalesOrderID = SOH.SalesOrderID
                inner join [Sales].[Customer] as C
                on SOH.CustomerID = C.CustomerID
                Where C.StoreID is not null
                Group By ProductID) as A
                Inner Join
                (Select
                ProductID,
                (Sum(Rating) + 0.0) / (Count(ProductID) + 0.0) as
                  AvgReviews
                from [Production].[ProductReview] as PR
                Group By ProductID) as B
                on A.ProductID = B.ProductID"

    member this.PredictQuantity(productId:int) =
        use connection = new SqlConnection(connectionString)
        use command = new SqlCommand(query,connection)
        connection.Open()
```

```
use reader = command.ExecuteReader()
while reader.Read() do
    reviews.Add({ProductID=reader.
GetInt32(0);TotalOrders=(float)(reader.GetInt32(1));AvgReviews=(float)
(reader.GetDecimal(2))})

let x = reviews |> Seq.map (fun pr -> pr.AvgReviews) |>
    Seq.toArray
let y = reviews |> Seq.map (fun pr -> pr.TotalOrders) |>
    Seq.toArray
let regression = SimpleLinearRegression()
let sse = regression.Regress(x,y)
let mse = sse/float x.Length
let rmse = sqrt mse
let r2 = regression.CoefficientOfDetermination(x,y)

let review = reviews |> Seq.find (fun r -> r.ProductID =
    productId)
regression.Compute(review.AvgReviews)
```

The only change from the REPL code is that `connection`, `command`, and `reader` are now assigned with the `use` keyword and not `let`. This is equivalent to the `using` statement in C# so that all resources are cleaned up in the most efficient manner.

With that in place, you can run the UI and see the actual value being predicted from the regression that uses all of our data:

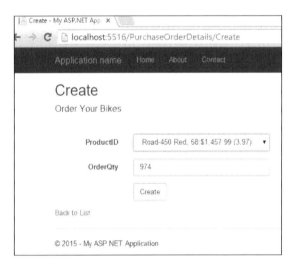

Congratulations! You have successfully wired up a website with a simple linear regression. This prediction is dynamic because the regression is calculated on every page refresh. This means as more data goes into our database, the websites reflect changes in the product reviews at real time. The software architect in you should be pulling the alarm because this will have a severe impact on performance; we pull the aggregate data and then do the regression calculation on each call. We will discuss better strategies later in the book that allow our site to have real-time or near-time performance to go with a machine learning algorithm.

Summary

This chapter dipped our toes into the water of creating a machine learning model and implementing those models in a line of business application. There are many things that we glossed over that will get all of your data science friends mad, such as my dumbed-down formula for a regression, overfitting, and using a regression without dealing with outliers. Also, the web developers in the room have plenty to be mad about, including my rudimentary website design and injecting a data-intensive operation in a page load. Fear not. We will address these issues (and many more) in the coming chapters.

3

More AdventureWorks Regression

In the last chapter, you had your software developer hat on and you stuck your toe into machine learning waters. You created a simple linear regression and implemented it in your website. The regression attempted to explain how customer reviews affected bike sales quantity to retail shops. In this chapter, we are going to pick up where we left off and use a multiple linear regression to explain bike sales with more precision. Then we will switch over to a logistic regression to see if we can predict whether an individual customer will or will not purchase a bike based on the same factors. We will then consider how to implement the regression in an experiment that will help with the model's accuracy and repeatability. Finally, we will wrap up by considering some of the strengths and weaknesses of regressions.

Introduction to multiple linear regression

A multiple linear regression has the same concept as a simple linear regression, in that we are trying to find the best fit. The major difference is that we have more than one independent variable that is trying to explain the dependent variable. If you remember from the last chapter, we made a regression like this: $Y = x0 + E$, where Y was bike sales and $x0$ was average ratings.

If we want to see whether there is a relationship between average rating and price of the bike on bike sales, we can use the formula $Y = x0 + x1 + E$, where Y is bike sales, $x0$ is the average ratings, and $x1$ is the price of the bike.

Intro example

Before diving into actual data, let's dissect a multiple linear regression. Open up Visual Studio and create a new F# library project. Add a script file called `AccordDotNet.fsx`. Next, add a NuGet reference to `Accord.Statistics`. If you are unfamiliar with how to do any of those tasks, review *Chapter 1, Welcome to Machine Learning Using the .NET Framework*, and *Chapter 2, AdventureWorks Regression*, where each step is detailed using screenshots.

At the top of your script, add in the following references:

```
#r "../packages/Accord.3.0.2/lib/net40/Accord.dll"
#r "../packages/Accord.Statistics.3.0.2/lib/net40/Accord.Statistics.
dll"
#r "../packages/Accord.Math.3.0.2/lib/net40/Accord.Math.dll"

open Accord
open Accord.Statistics.Models.Regression.Linear
```

Next, let's create a dummy dataset. In this case, let's see if there is a relationship between a student's age, their IQ, and their GPA. Since there are two independent variables (x0 and x1), we will create an input value called, well, xs and see it with five observations. Since there are two values for each observation, xs is a jagged array.

```
let xs = [| [|15.0;130.0|];
 [|18.0;127.0|];[|15.0;128.0|];[|17.0;120.0|];[|16.0;115.0|] |]
```

Sending it to the REPL, we get:

```
val xs : float [] [] =
  [|[|15.0; 130.0|]; [|18.0; 127.0|]; [|15.0; 128.0|];
[|17.0; 120.0|]; [|16.0; 115.0|]|]
```

In this dataset, the first observation is a 15 year old with a 130 IQ, the second is an 18 year old with a 127 IQ, and so on. With the inputs taken care of, let's create the y, which is the student's GPA:

```
let y = [|3.6;3.5;3.8;3.4;2.6|]
```

Sending to the REPL, we get:

```
val y : float [] = [|3.6; 3.5; 3.8; 3.4; 2.6|]
```

The first student has a 3.6 GPA, the second has a 3.5, and so on. Notice that since our output is a single number, we only need a simple array to hold the values. With our inputs taken care of, let's create a multiple linear regression with our xs and y:

```
let regression = MultipleLinearRegression(2, true)
let error = regression.Regress(xs, y)

let a = regression.Coefficients.[0]
let b = regression.Coefficients.[1]
let c = regression.Coefficients.[2]
```

Sending this to the REPL, we get:

```
val regression : MultipleLinearRegression =

  y(x0, x1) = 0.0221298495645295*x0 + 0.0663103721298495*x1 +
-5.20098970704672
val error : float = 0.1734125099

val a : float = 0.02212984956

val b : float = 0.06631037213

val c : float = -5.200989707
```

There are a couple of things to notice. First, Accord printed the formula of our multiple linear regression for us as y(x0, x1) = 0.0221298495645295*x0 + 0.0663103721298495*x1 + -5.20098970704672. The key thing to notice is that you cannot interpret the results of multiple regressions the same as the simple regression, for example, summing x1 and x2 together to be the slope of a line would be incorrect. Rather, each x is the slope of the line if the other x is held constant. So, in this case, if x1 is held constant, each change of one unit of x0 changes y .022. Back to our example, we can say that if we increase a person's age by one year, a person's GPA increases by .022, holding the IQ constant. Similarly, we can say that for every one point drop in a person's IQ, the person's GPA drops 0.066, holding the person's age constant. We can't use a scatterplot to show all of the results of a multiple regression the way we can with a simple regression because you would need an axis for each x value and that quickly will get unwieldy, if not impossible.

Next, let's see how good our regression is using our old friends r2 and rmse:

```
let sse = regression.Regress(xs, y)
let mse = sse/float xs.Length
let rmse = sqrt(mse)
let r2 = regression.CoefficientOfDetermination(xs,y)
```

Sending this to the REPL, we get:

```
val sse : float = 0.1734125099
val mse : float = 0.03468250198
val rmse : float = 0.186232387
val r2 : float = 0.7955041157
```

Notice that `sse` is the same as the error from above. Accord.NET returns `sse` as an error, so I will just use that in the future. Also, looking at our result, we can see that we have an `r2` of `.79`, which is pretty good and that our `rmse` is `.18`, which is also low enough that the regression is a viable one.

Keep adding x variables?

If two x variables are good, are three better? Let's take a look. Let's add another variable, in this case, the student's prior year GPA as a third x value. Go back to the REPL and add this:

```
let xs' = [| [|15.0;130.0;3.6|];[|18.0;127.0;3.5|];
            [|15.0;128.0;3.7|];[|17.0;120.0;3.5|];
            [|17.0;120.0;2.5|]  |]

let regression' = MultipleLinearRegression(3,true)
let error' = regression'.Regress(xs',y)

let a' = regression'.Coefficients.[0]
let b' = regression'.Coefficients.[1]
let c' = regression'.Coefficients.[2]
let d' = regression'.Coefficients.[3]

let mse' = error'/float xs'.Length
let rmse' = sqrt(mse')
let r2' = regression'.CoefficientOfDetermination(xs',y)
```

Sending this to the REPL, we get:

```
val xs' : float [] [] =
  [| [|15.0; 130.0; 3.6|]; [|18.0; 127.0; 3.5|]; [|15.0; 128.0; 3.7|];
     [|17.0; 120.0; 3.5|]; [|17.0; 120.0; 2.5|]|]
val regression' : MultipleLinearRegression =
  y(x0, x1, x2) = -0.0202088664499619*x0 + 0.0116951379763468*x1 +
  0.834082578324918*x2 + -0.552984300435694
val error' : float = 0.01071166747
```

```
val a' : float = -0.02020886645

val b' : float = 0.01169513798

val c' : float = 0.8340825783

val d' : float = -0.5529843004

val mse' : float = 0.002142333495

val rmse' : float = 0.0462853486

val r2' : float = 0.9873683167
```

So the r2 is now up to 99%, which means we can explain 99% of the change in a person's GPA using their age, IQ, and prior year GPA. Also, note that the rmse is .04, which is nice and low. We have a pretty good model.

AdventureWorks data

With the demo out of the way, let's implement a multiple linear regression back at the bike company. Since we are using more realistic data, I don't think we will get a 99% r2, but we can hope. In your **Solution Explorer**, add another F# script called AccordDotNet2.fsx. Then, add a reference to System.Transactions so that we can use ADO.NET to access our data. Go back to AccordDotNet2.fsx and add the following code:

```
#r "System.Transactions.dll"
#r "../packages/Accord.3.0.2/lib/net40/Accord.dll"
#r "../packages/Accord.Statistics.3.0.2/lib/net40/
Accord.Statistics.dll"
#r "../packages/Accord.Math.3.0.2/lib/net40/Accord.Math.dll"

open Accord
open Accord.Statistics
open Accord.Statistics.Models.Regression.Linear

open System
open System.Data.SqlClient

type ProductInfo = {ProductID:int; AvgOrders:float;
AvgReviews: float; ListPrice: float}

let productInfos =  ResizeArray<ProductInfo>()

[<Literal>]
let connectionString = "data
source=nc54a9m5kk.database.windows.net;initial
catalog=AdventureWorks2014;user id=chickenskills@
nc54a9m5kk;password=sk1lzm@tter;"
```

```fsharp
[<Literal>]
let query = "Select
            A.ProductID, AvgOrders, AvgReviews, ListPrice
            From
            (Select
            ProductID,
            (Sum(OrderQty) + 0.0)/(Count(Distinct SOH.CustomerID)
              + 0.0) as AvgOrders
            from [Sales].[SalesOrderDetail] as SOD
            inner join [Sales].[SalesOrderHeader] as SOH
            on SOD.SalesOrderID = SOH.SalesOrderID
            inner join [Sales].[Customer] as C
            on SOH.CustomerID = C.CustomerID
            Where C.StoreID is not null
            Group By ProductID) as A
            Inner Join
            (Select
            ProductID,
            (Sum(Rating) + 0.0) / (Count(ProductID) + 0.0) as
              AvgReviews
            from [Production].[ProductReview] as PR
            Group By ProductID) as B
            on A.ProductID = B.ProductID
            Inner Join
            (Select
            ProductID,
            ListPrice
            from [Production].[Product]
            ) as C
            On A.ProductID = C.ProductID"

let connection = new SqlConnection(connectionString)
let command = new SqlCommand(query,connection)
connection.Open()
let reader = command.ExecuteReader()
while reader.Read() do
    productInfos.Add({ProductID=reader.GetInt32(0);
                      AvgOrders=(float)(reader.GetDecimal(1));
                      AvgReviews=(float)(reader.GetDecimal(2));
                      ListPrice=(float)(reader.GetDecimal(3));})
```

Notice that this is very similar to the code that you wrote in the prior chapter. In fact, you might want to copy and paste that code and make the following changes:

1. Add a `ListPrice` field to the `ProductInfo` record type.
2. Update the query to add a clause to pull down the list price of the bike.
3. Update `productInfos`. Add a method to include the third value we are bringing down.

The code itself shapes a data frame of a number of orders, average reviews, and average price by `productId` in SQL and brings it local. Sending this code to the REPL, we get the following:

```
type ProductInfo =
  {ProductID: int;
   AvgOrders: float;
   AvgReviews: float;
   ListPrice: float;}
val productInfos : Collections.Generic.List<ProductInfo>
val connectionString : string =
  "data source=nc54a9m5kk.database.windows.net;initial catalog=A"+[72
chars]
val query : string =
  "Select
           A.ProductID, AvgOrders, AvgReviews, ListP"+[937 chars]
val connection : SqlConnection = System.Data.SqlClient.SqlConnection
val command : SqlCommand = System.Data.SqlClient.SqlCommand
val reader : SqlDataReader
val it : unit = ()
```

With the data down, let's create a multiple linear regression. Add the following code to the script file:

```
    let xs =
        productInfos
        |> Seq.map (fun pi -> [|pi.AvgReviews; pi.ListPrice|])
        |> Seq.toArray
    let y =
        productInfos
        |> Seq.map (fun pi -> pi.AvgOrders)
        |> Seq.toArray
```

```
let regression = MultipleLinearRegression(2, true)
let error = regression.Regress(xs, y)

let a = regression.Coefficients.[0]
let b = regression.Coefficients.[1]
let c = regression.Coefficients.[2]

let mse = error/float xs.Length
let rmse = sqrt mse
let r2 = regression.CoefficientOfDetermination(xs, y)
```

Sending this code to the REPL, we get:

```
val regression : MultipleLinearRegression =
  y(x0, x1) = 9.68314848116308*x0 + -0.000913619922709572*x1 +
-26.1836956342657
val error : float = 682.6439378
val a : float = 9.683148481
val b : float = -0.0009136199227
val c : float = -26.18369563
val mse : float = 7.037566369
val rmse : float = 2.652841188
val r2 : float = 0.3532529168
```

By adding the price of the bike, our r2 moves from .29 to .35. Also, our rmse moves from 2.77 to 2.65. This change means we have a more accurate model with a smaller amount of error. Because this is better, let's add this to our production application.

Adding multiple regression to our production application

Open up the AdventureWorks solution that you started working on in the last chapter. In the **Solution Explorer**, navigate to the AdventureWorks.MachineLearning project and open OrderPrediction.fs.

Locate the ProductReview type and replace it with this:

```
type ProductInfo = {ProductID:int; AvgOrders:float;
AvgReviews: float; ListPrice: float}
```

Next, go into the `OrderPrediction` type and find the line where the reviews value is assigned and replace it with this:

```
let productInfos = ResizeArray<ProductInfo>()
```

Next, locate the query value and replace its contents with this:

```
[<Literal>]
let query = "Select
            A.ProductID, AvgOrders, AvgReviews, ListPrice
            From
            (Select
            ProductID,
            (Sum(OrderQty) + 0.0)/(Count(Distinct SOH.CustomerID) +
0.0) as AvgOrders,
            Sum(OrderQty) as TotalOrders
            from [Sales].[SalesOrderDetail] as SOD
            inner join [Sales].[SalesOrderHeader] as SOH
            on SOD.SalesOrderID = SOH.SalesOrderID
            inner join [Sales].[Customer] as C
            on SOH.CustomerID = C.CustomerID
            Where C.StoreID is not null
            Group By ProductID) as A
            Inner Join
            (Select
            ProductID,
            (Sum(Rating) + 0.0) / (Count(ProductID) + 0.0) as
              AvgReviews
            from [Production].[ProductReview] as PR
            Group By ProductID) as B
            on A.ProductID = B.ProductID
            Inner Join
            (Select
            ProductID,
            ListPrice
            from [Production].[Product]
            ) as C
            On A.ProductID = C.ProductID"
```

Next, scroll down to the `PredictQuantity` function and locate the `reader.Read()` line of codes. Replace it with this:

```
            while reader.Read() do
                productInfos.Add({ProductID=reader.GetInt32(0);
                            AvgOrders=
                                (float)(reader.GetDecimal(1));
```

```
                    AvgReviews=
                      (float)(reader.GetDecimal(2));
                    ListPrice=
                      (float)(reader.GetDecimal(3));})
```

Finally, remove all of the remaining code in the `PredictQuantity` function starting with:

```
let x = reviews |> Seq.map(fun pr -> pr.AvgReviews) |> Seq.toArray
```

Replace it with this:

```
let xs =
    productInfos
    |> Seq.map (fun pi -> [|pi.AvgReviews; pi.ListPrice|])
    |> Seq.toArray
let y =
    productInfos
    |> Seq.map (fun pi -> pi.AvgOrders)
    |> Seq.toArray
let regression = MultipleLinearRegression(2, true)
let error = regression.Regress(xs, y)

let a = regression.Coefficients.[0]
let b = regression.Coefficients.[1]
let c = regression.Coefficients.[2]

let mse = error/float xs.Length
let rmse = sqrt mse
let r2 = regression.CoefficientOfDetermination(xs, y)

let productInfo =
    productInfos
    |> Seq.find (fun r -> r.ProductID = productId)
let xs' = [|[|productInfo.AvgReviews;
  productInfo.ListPrice|]|]
regression.Compute(xs') |> Seq.head
```

Notice we have to create a jagged array even though we are only entering in one `productInfo` for the final `regression.Compute()`. Also, notice that the `Compute` function returns an array, but since we are only entering in one value, the resulting array will always have a length of one. We used the `Seq.head` to pull the first value of the array. The head function comes in quite handy at certain times and we will be seeing it again in this book.

Build the project and open up the UI; you can see that our prediction has been adjusted:

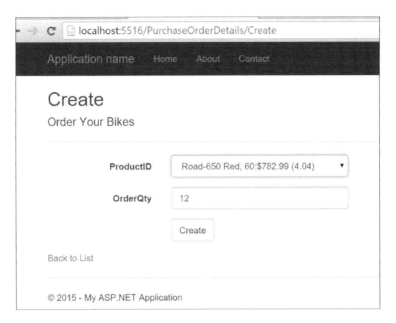

Considerations when using multiple x variables

At this point, you might be thinking, "This is great! I can keep adding more and more variables to my multiple linear regression and I will get a better and better r2 and a lower `rmse`." As Lee Corso might say, "Not so fast!" Without getting too far into the details, every time you add a new feature of a linear multiple regression, you will always get a better result, or, at least, not a worse result. This means, if you add in the average temperature from different cities on June 29, 1999, the model might improve. Also, as you increase the number of features, the chance of introducing unwanted side effects into your model increases; we will talk about that in a little bit. In fact, I have seen some models where the number of features outnumber the number of observations. As a rule, this is a not a good idea.

To combat feature growth, you can take two approaches. First, you can combine common sense with Occam's Razor. Occam's Razor is the notion that given a choice of possible solutions, the simplest one should always be chosen. This combination of sense and simplicity is more common and powerful than most people realize. The gray matter between the ears is a pretty powerful computer in its own right and can do a good job of seeing patterns and making relationships.

Indeed, the business analyst who has spent time in the domain might know of relationships that are not apparent to an external data scientist looking at a laundry list of features or a basic machine learning model that is thrown at the data. Granted, humans do have biases and sometimes miss relationships, but on the whole, they are still good at matching patterns. Applying Occam's Razor to feature selection means that you are trying to find the fewest number of features that has the greatest impact on the model's predictability.

Let's head over to our friendly business analyst at AdventureWorks and ask him what he thinks influences the quantity of bicycles purchased by our resellers. He says, "Well, I think that price and customer reviews are certainly very important, but I think that the weight of the bike influences our resellers. The heavier the bike, the less likely they are to order some."

Adding a third x variable to our model

With the business analyst's idea in mind, let's add a third independent variable to our model, bike weight. Go back to the **Solution Explorer** and add another script file. Add the following code to the script:

```
#r "System.Transactions.dll"
#r "../packages/Accord.3.0.2/lib/net40/Accord.dll"
#r "../packages/Accord.Statistics.3.0.2/lib/net40/
   Accord.Statistics.dll"
#r "../packages/Accord.Math.3.0.2/lib/net40/Accord.Math.dll"

open Accord
open Accord.Statistics
open Accord.Statistics.Models.Regression.Linear

open System
open System.Data.SqlClient

type ProductInfo = {ProductID:int; AvgOrders:float;
   AvgReviews: float; ListPrice: float; Weight: float}

let productInfos = ResizeArray<ProductInfo>()

[<Literal>]
let connectionString = "data source=nc54a9m5kk.database.windows.
net;initial
catalog=AdventureWorks2014;user
id=chickenskills@nc54a9m5kk;password=sk1lzm@tter;"
```

```
[<Literal>]
let query = "Select
            A.ProductID, AvgOrders, AvgReviews, ListPrice, Weight
            From
            (Select
            ProductID,
            (Sum(OrderQty) + 0.0)/(Count(Distinct SOH.CustomerID)
              + 0.0) as AvgOrders
            from [Sales].[SalesOrderDetail] as SOD
            inner join [Sales].[SalesOrderHeader] as SOH
            on SOD.SalesOrderID = SOH.SalesOrderID
            inner join [Sales].[Customer] as C
            on SOH.CustomerID = C.CustomerID
            Where C.StoreID is not null
            Group By ProductID) as A
            Inner Join
            (Select
            ProductID,
            (Sum(Rating) + 0.0) / (Count(ProductID) + 0.0) as
              AvgReviews
            from [Production].[ProductReview] as PR
            Group By ProductID) as B
            on A.ProductID = B.ProductID
            Inner Join
            (Select
            ProductID,
            ListPrice,
            Weight
            from [Production].[Product]
            ) as C
            On A.ProductID = C.ProductID"

let connection = new SqlConnection(connectionString)
let command = new SqlCommand(query, connection)
connection.Open()
let reader = command.ExecuteReader()
while reader.Read() do
    productInfos.Add({ProductID=reader.GetInt32(0);
                      AvgOrders=(float)(reader.GetDecimal(1));
                      AvgReviews=(float)(reader.GetDecimal(2));
                      ListPrice=(float)(reader.GetDecimal(3));
                      Weight=(float)(reader.GetDecimal(4));})
```

```
let xs =
    productInfos
    |> Seq.map (fun pi -> [|pi.AvgReviews; pi.ListPrice;
      pi.Weight|])
    |> Seq.toArray
let y =
    productInfos
    |> Seq.map (fun pi -> pi.AvgOrders)
    |> Seq.toArray
let regression = MultipleLinearRegression(3, true)
let error = regression.Regress(xs, y)

let a = regression.Coefficients.[0]
let b = regression.Coefficients.[1]
let c = regression.Coefficients.[2]
let d = regression.Coefficients.[3]

let mse = error/float xs.Length
let rmse = sqrt mse
let r2 = regression.CoefficientOfDetermination(xs, y)
```

Sending this to the REPL, notice that our `r2` goes to `.36` and our `rmse` drops to `2.63`:

val regression : MultipleLinearRegression =

  y(x0, x1, x2) = 8.94836007927991*x0 + -0.00103754084861455*x1 +
-0.0848953592695415*x2 + -21.2973971475571

val error : float = 671.2299241

val a : float = 8.948360079

val b : float = -0.001037540849

val c : float = -0.08489535927

val d : float = -21.29739715

val mse : float = 6.919896125

val rmse : float = 2.630569544

val r2 : float = 0.3640667242

Our analyst's intuition about price and customer reviews was spot on, the weight... not so much. Using Occam's Razor, we can use price and customer reviews for our model and ignore the weight variable.

Logistic regression

Now that we are becoming more comfortable with regressions, let's introduce another type of regression—the logistic regression. Up to this point, the regressions have had a numeric output value—like predicting a person's GPA or predicting the number of bikes sold. Logistic regressions use the same technique of fitting a group of independent features to a line, but they do not attempt to predict a number. Rather, a logistic regression attempts to predict a binary value (yes/no, true/false, tastes great/less filling) and then assigns a probability to that value.

Intro to logistic regression

Since you have already had an introduction to regressions, we can skip straight to the code and see one in action. Open up the regression project and add a script called `AccordDotNet7.fsx`. Copy in the following lines of code:

```
#r "../packages/Accord.3.0.2/lib/net40/Accord.dll"
#r "../packages/Accord.Statistics.3.0.2/lib/net40/Accord.Statistics.
dll"
#r "../packages/Accord.Math.3.0.2/lib/net40/Accord.Math.dll"

open Accord
open Accord.Statistics.Analysis
open Accord.Statistics.Models.Regression
open Accord.Statistics.Models.Regression.Fitting

let xs = [| [|0.5|];[|0.75|];
            [|1.0|];[|1.25|];[|1.5|];[|1.75|];[|1.75|];
            [|2.0|];[|2.25|];[|2.5|];[|2.75|];
            [|3.0|];[|3.25|];[|3.5|];
            [|4.0|];[|4.25|];[|4.5|];[|4.75|];
            [|5.0|];[|5.5|];|]

let y = [|0.0;0.0;0.0;0.0;0.0;0.0;1.0;0.0;1.0;0.0;
          1.0;0.0;1.0;0.0;1.0;1.0;1.0;1.0;1.0;1.0|]
```

Sending this to the REPL gives us:

```
val xs : float [] [] =
  [|[|0.5|]; [|0.75|]; [|1.0|]; [|1.25|]; [|1.5|]; [|1.75|];
[|1.75|]; [|2.0|];
    [|2.25|]; [|2.5|]; [|2.75|]; [|3.0|]; [|3.25|]; [|3.5|]; [|4.0|];
[|4.25|];
    [|4.5|]; [|4.75|]; [|5.0|]; [|5.5|]|]
val y : float [] =
```

```
   [|0.0; 0.0; 0.0; 0.0; 0.0; 0.0; 1.0; 0.0; 1.0; 0.0; 1.0; 0.0; 1.0;
0.0; 1.0;
    1.0; 1.0; 1.0; 1.0; 1.0|]
```

I pulled this dataset from Wikipedia and it represents 20 students, how many hours of studying they did the day before an exam, and whether they passed the exam represented as `0.0` for failure and `1.0` for pass. Looking at the `xs`, student 0 studied 0.5 hours and looking at the `y`, we can see that s/he did not pass the exam.

Next, let's create our regression analysis and look at some results:

```
let analysis = new LogisticRegressionAnalysis(xs, y)
analysis.Compute() |> ignore
let pValue = analysis.ChiSquare.PValue
let coefficientOdds = analysis.Regression.GetOddsRatio(0)
let hoursOfStudyingOdds = analysis.Regression.GetOddsRatio(1)
let coefficients = analysis.CoefficientValues
```

Sending this to the REPL gives this:

```
val analysis : LogisticRegressionAnalysis
val pValue : float = 0.0006364826185
val coefficientOdds : float = 0.01694617045
val hoursOfStudyingOdds : float = 4.502556825
val coefficients : float [] = [|-4.077713403; 1.504645419|]
```

There are plenty of new things going on here, so let's take a look at them in turn. After we create an analysis, we compute the regression. The next item is `pValue`. `pValue` is a common measure of accuracy for logistic regressions. As we saw earlier, linear regressions typically use `rmse` and `r2` as a way to measure model accuracy. Logistic regressions can use those measures, but usually don't. Unlike the linear regression where the model spits out an exact number using something called *least-squares*, the logistic regression uses something called *maximum-likelihood* where the regression iterates and tries different combinations of the input values to maximize the likelihood of the result. Therefore, the logistic regression needs to be run many times over the dataset and we can configure how precise we want the model to be. Graphically, it looks like this:

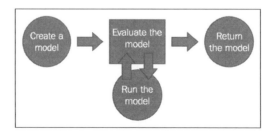

Coming back to `pValue`, it is a measure of how well our model compares to the `null` hypothesis, or basically, how well our model compares to a completely random model. If the `pValue` is less than 0.05, our model is valid. If the number is above 0.05, the model is no better than a random one. You might be asking yourself, "What is so special about 0.05?" The exact answer resides in some low-level mathematical functions that are beyond the scope of this book. The rough answer is, well, that is what everyone uses so that is what Accord baked in. If you don't find that explanation satisfactory, take a look at this post on Wikipedia (`https://en.wikipedia.org/wiki/P-value`). In any event, the 0.0006 is very good.

Moving on to the next values, we see `GetOddsRatio` results:

```
val coefficientOdds : float = 0.01694617045
val hoursOfStudyingOdds : float = 4.502556825
```

What this means is that if we didn't study at all, we would have 1.6% chance of passing the exam. If we want to pass the exam, we need to study 4.5 hours. Next, take a look at the coefficients:

```
val coefficients : float [] = [|-4.077713403; 1.504645419|]
```

Accord.NET passes back an array for the coefficients, with the first value being the intercept. With these, you can create a formula to predict if a student can pass the exam given any input of hours of studying. For example, here are the predictions from our base dataset:

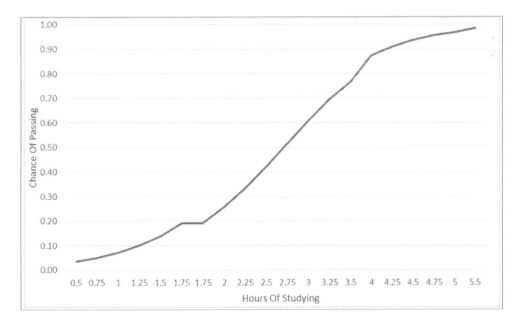

If we want to start playing with beer and hours of studying combinations (for example, "Will I pass if I study for 4.5 hours?"), we can do that using the `Compute` function. At the bottom of the script file, enter in:

```
let result = analysis.Regression.Compute([|3.75|])
```

Send it to the REPL for this:

```
val result : float = 0.8270277278
```

So you have an 82% chance of passing if you study for 3.75 hours.

Adding another x variable

Next, let's add in another variable to our model—the number of beers you drank the night before the exam. Go back to your script file and add this to the bottom:

```
let xs' = [| [|0.5;2.5|];
    [|0.75;1.5|];
            [|1.0;4.0|];
    [|1.25;1.0|];
    [|1.5;0.0|];
    [|1.75;3.0|];
    [|1.75;0.0|];
            [|2.0;3.0|];
            [|2.25;1.0|];
            [|2.5;4.5|];
            [|2.75;1.5|];
            [|3.0;1.0|];
            [|3.25;2.5|];
            [|3.5;0.0|];
            [|4.0;2.0|];
            [|4.25;1.5|];
            [|4.5;4.5|];
            [|4.75;0.0|];
            [|5.0;1.0|];
            [|5.5;0.0|];|]
```

```
let analysis' = new LogisticRegressionAnalysis(xs', y)
analysis'.Compute() |> ignore
let pValue' = analysis'.ChiSquare.PValue
let coefficientOdds' = analysis'.Regression.GetOddsRatio(0)
let hoursOfStudyingOdds' = analysis'.Regression.GetOddsRatio(1)
let numberOfBeersDrankOdds' = analysis'.Regression.GetOddsRatio(2)
let coefficients' = analysis'.CoefficientValues
```

Sending this to the REPL, we see:

```
val analysis' : LogisticRegressionAnalysis
val pValue' : float = 0.002336631577
val coefficientOdds' : float = 0.02748131566
val hoursOfStudyingOdds' : float = 4.595591714
val numberOfBeersDrankOdds' : float = 0.7409200941
val coefficients' : float [] = [|-3.594248936;
1.525097521; -0.2998624947|]
```

Evaluating the results, we still need to study 4.59 hours to pass, holding the number of beers constant. Also, we will need to drink less than .74 of a beer to pass. Notice that the odds ratio is positive, even though consuming more beer actually decreases our chance to pass. We know that there is an inverse relationship between the number of beers and the odds of passing because the coefficient for beer (-.029986) is negative.

Now, we can start trading off studying hours and drinking beer on the chance of us passing the exam. Go to the script file and add in studying 4.5 hours and drinking one beer:

```
let result' = analysis'.Regression.Compute([|4.50; 1.00|])
```

Sending it to the REPL:

```
val result' : float = 0.9511458187
```

So you have a 95% chance of passing if you drink a beer and study 4.5 hours. To further cement your odds, try filling out "B" on question 4 to push you over the top—that always worked for me in middle school.

Applying a logistic regression to AdventureWorks data

So going back to a more realistic dataset, let's take a look at AdventureWorks. Go ahead and add a new script file to the project. Call it `AccordDotNet8.fsx`. Copy and paste the following code into the script file:

```
#r "System.Transactions.dll"
#r "../packages/Accord.3.0.2/lib/net40/Accord.dll"
#r "../packages/Accord.Statistics.3.0.2/lib/net40/
Accord.Statistics.dll"
#r "../packages/Accord.Math.3.0.2/lib/net40/Accord.Math.dll"
```

```
open Accord
open Accord.Statistics.Filters
open Accord.Statistics.Analysis
open Accord.Statistics.Models.Regression
open Accord.Statistics.Models.Regression.Fitting

open System
open System.Data.SqlClient

type ProductInfo = {ProductID:int; Color:string;
AvgReviews: float; Markup: float}
let productInfos = ResizeArray<ProductInfo>()

[<Literal>]
let connectionString = "data source=nc54a9m5kk.database.windows.
net;initial
catalog=AdventureWorks2014;user
id=chickenskills@nc54a9m5kk;password=sk1lzm@tter;"

[<Literal>]
let query = "Select
    A.ProductID,
    A.Color,
    B.AvgReviews,
    A.MarkUp
    From
    (Select P.ProductID,
      Color,
      ListPrice - StandardCost as Markup
      from [Sales].[SalesOrderDetail] as SOD
        inner join [Sales].[SalesOrderHeader] as SOH
        on SOD.SalesOrderID = SOH.SalesOrderID
        inner join [Sales].[Customer] as C
        on SOH.CustomerID = C.CustomerID
      inner join [Production].[Product] as P
      on SOD.ProductID = P.ProductID
      inner join [Production].[ProductSubcategory] as PS
      on P.ProductSubcategoryID = PS.ProductSubcategoryID
      Where C.StoreID is null
      and PS.ProductCategoryID = 1) as A
    Inner Join
    (Select PR.ProductID,
      (Sum(Rating) + 0.0) / (Count(ProductID) + 0.0) as AvgReviews
        from [Production].[ProductReview] as PR
        Group By ProductID) as B
```

```
        on A.ProductID = B.ProductID"

    let connection = new SqlConnection(connectionString)
    let command = new SqlCommand(query, connection)
    connection.Open()
    let reader = command.ExecuteReader()
    while reader.Read() do
        productInfos.Add({ProductID=reader.GetInt32(0);
                          Color=(string)(reader.GetString(1));
                          AvgReviews=(float)(reader.GetDecimal(2));
                          Markup=(float)(reader.GetDecimal(3));})
```

Sending this to the REPL, you should see:

```
type ProductInfo =
  {ProductID: int;
   Color: string;
   AvgReviews: float;
   Markup: float;}
val productInfos : List<ProductInfo>
val connectionString : string =
  "data source=nc54a9m5kk.database.windows.net;initial
catalog=A"+[72 chars]
val query : string =
  "Select
    A.ProductID,
    A.Color,
    B.AvgReviews,
    A."+[803 chars]
val connection : SqlConnection = System.Data.SqlClient.SqlConnection
val command : SqlCommand = System.Data.SqlClient.SqlCommand
val reader : SqlDataReader
val it : unit = ()
```

There's no new code here, so we can safely press on. However, I would like to note that this query might take a bit longer than any other query we have run against the database so far. This has an implication for how we architect our code when we integrate it to our application. We will discuss this in length in *Chapter 5, Time Out – Obtaining Data*, but for now, we just want to note it.

Going back to the script file, go ahead and add this code to the bottom:

```
type ProductInfo' = {ProductID:int; BlackInd:float; BlueInd:float;
RedInd:float; SilverInd:float; OtherInd: float; AvgReviews: float;
HighMargin:float}

let getProductInfo'(productInfo:ProductInfo) =
        {ProductInfo'.ProductID=productInfo.ProductID;
        BlackInd = (match productInfo.Color with | "Black" -> 1.0
          | _ -> 0.0);
        BlueInd = (match productInfo.Color with | "Blue" -> 1.0
          | _ -> 0.0);
        RedInd = (match productInfo.Color with | "Red" -> 1.0
          | _ -> 0.0);
        SilverInd = (match productInfo.Color with
          | "Silver" -> 1.0 | _ -> 0.0);
        OtherInd = (match productInfo.Color with | "Silver"
          | "Blue" | "Red"  -> 0.0 | _ -> 1.0);
        AvgReviews = productInfo.AvgReviews;
        HighMargin = (match productInfo.Markup > 800.0 with
          | true -> 1.0 | false -> 0.0);}

let productInfos' =
    productInfos
    |> Seq.map (fun pi -> getProductInfo'(pi))
let xs =
    productInfos'
    |> Seq.map (fun pi -> [|pi.BlackInd; pi.BlueInd; pi.RedInd;
      pi.SilverInd; pi.OtherInd; pi.AvgReviews|])
    |> Seq.toArray
let y =
    productInfos'
    |> Seq.map (fun pi -> pi.HighMargin)
    |> Seq.toArray

let analysis = new LogisticRegressionAnalysis(xs, y)
analysis.Compute() |> ignore
let pValue = analysis.ChiSquare.PValue
let coefficientOdds = analysis.Regression.GetOddsRatio(0)
let blackIndOdds = analysis.Regression.GetOddsRatio(1)
let blueIndOdds = analysis.Regression.GetOddsRatio(2)
let redIndOdds = analysis.Regression.GetOddsRatio(3)
let silverIndOdds = analysis.Regression.GetOddsRatio(4)
let otherIndOdds = analysis.Regression.GetOddsRatio(5)
let ratingsOdds = analysis.Regression.GetOddsRatio(6)
let coefficients = analysis.CoefficientValues
```

Sending this to the REPL, you should get:

```
val analysis : LogisticRegressionAnalysis
val pValue : float = 0.0
val coefficientOdds : float = 4.316250806e-07
val blackIndOdds : float = 6.708924364
val blueIndOdds : float = 0.03366007966
val redIndOdds : float = 0.0897074697
val silverIndOdds : float = 0.04618907808
val otherIndOdds : float = 0.003094736179
val ratingsOdds : float = 127.5863311
val coefficients : float [] =
  [|-14.65570849; 1.903438635; -3.391442724; -2.411201239;
-3.075011914;
    -5.778052618; 4.848793242|]
```

There are some new pieces of code to look at and two new concepts. First, notice that a new record type was created for `ProductInfo` and the colors are broken out from a single column (`ProductType.Color`) to a series of 0.0/1.0 columns (`ProductType'.BlackInd`, `ProductType'BlueInd`, and so on). The reason I did not make the columns bool is that Accord.NET expects inputs to be a float and 0.0/1.0 serves the purpose just as well. These columns are called "dummy" variables and they are used by logistic regressions to accommodate categorical data. At this point, you are probably asking, "What the heck is categorical data?" Fair question.

Categorical data

You might not have noticed, but all of the x variables that we have used until this last query have been numeric—number of bikes sold, average reviews, number of beers drank, and the like. These values are considered continuous because they can be of infinite value. I can have one, two, or three beers. Similarly, the average reviews of a bike can be 3.45, 3.46, and so on. Because these values are treated as numbers, they can be added, averaged, and manipulated in all of the ways that you've learned since first grade. Note that continuous values can be range-bound: the average review can only be between 0.0 and 5.0 because that is what we limited users to enter.

Categorical values are different. Typically, they are integers that stand in for a non-numeric concept. For example, 0 might be male and 1 might be female. Similarly, the status of the sales order might be 1 for open, 2 for pending, 3 for closed, and 4 for returned. Although these values are stored in the database as integers, they cannot be added, averaged, or otherwise manipulated. Categorical values may also be stored as strings, like we have seen for a bike color: "black", "blue", and the like. In this case, the range of strings is limited to a set from which numbers can be chosen.

Going back to our analysis, we have the bike color, which is a categorical value and is being stored as a string. We can't send this string to Accord.NET as a single x variable because the `LogisticRegressionAnalysis` only takes in floats in the array. Note that in other statistical packages like R or SAS, you can pass in a string because there is behind-the-scenes code that translates those string values to numeric. So, back to color. We want to use it, but it has to become a float. We could create a new field called `ColorId` and hook up a translation function that turns each of the colors to a numeric representation like this:

```
let getColorId (color:string) =
    match color.ToLower() with
    | "black" -> 1.0
    | "blue" -> 2.0
    | "red" -> 3.0
    | "silver" -> 4.0
    | _ -> 5.0
```

And we will do that in other places in the book. However, using those numeric values makes no sense in our logistic regression because there is no real meaning in comparing values: an `oddsRatio` of 2.3 means what? In fact, no type of regression can make sense of categorical data coded in this way. Instead of building nonsensical values, we create dummy variables that can be interpreted with meaning in a regression. For each of the possible values of our categorical variable, we create a bool column that indicates whether that particular record has that value. Technically, we can create one less than the total possible values, but I find it easier to reason and display a column for each value. We can then pass these dummy variables into a regression and get a meaningful response.

Also notice that I did the pattern matching for the colors assignment on one line like this:

```
BlackInd = (match productInfo.Color with | "Black" -> 1.0
| _ -> 0.0);
```

There is some heated controversy in the F# community about whether this is considered bad form: some people want to see each possible outcome of the pattern matching statement to be on one line, and others do not. I find it much more readable to keep everything on one line in cases like this, but I acknowledge it is a bit harder for someone new to F# from a curly-braced language like C#. If, however, you use ternary operators you should be comfortable with the syntax.

Also, notice that we changed our continuous variable of `Markup` to `High Margin` using this line of code:

```
HighMargin = (match productInfo.Markup > 800.0 with | true -> 1.0
| false -> 0.0);}
```

Attachment point

Since logistic regressions need to have a 0.0 or 1.0 as a y variable, we need a way of splitting the data into something that has both business meaning and can be evaluated into 0.0 or 1.0. How did I pick $800? I eyeballed it after doing this in the database:

```
Select
ProductID,
P.Name,
ProductNumber,
Color,
StandardCost,
ListPrice,
ListPrice - StandardCost as Markup
from [Production].[Product] as P
Inner Join [Production].[ProductSubcategory] as PS
on P.ProductSubcategoryID = PS.ProductSubcategoryID
Where PS.ProductCategoryID = 1
Order by ListPrice - StandardCost
```

That $800 number is often called the "attachment point" and is often the most discussed part of any logistic regression model. In the real world, that number is often set by the President of a small company on the back of a napkin, or, in a large company, a multi-disciplinary team that takes six weeks. The key thing to remember is that you want that number in your `config` file (if you are running your regression at real-time) or a separate variable at the top of your script (if doing it ad hoc). Note that to make our script even smarter, it is possible to inject in another model that determines the attachment point dynamically, so it will not require a human to update it, but that will be an exercise for another day.

Analyzing results of the logistic regression

Let's look at the odds ratios and coefficients, and we'll see two things stand out. First, notice that black odds (6.7) is much higher than all of the other numbers and that it has a positive coefficient while all of the other colors have a negative one. Since all of the bikes are available in all the colors, in this context, we can reasonably conclude that black is the new black. People are buying our higher margin bikes and preferring the color black when they do so.

The other striking number is the average review's `OddsRatio`, which is 127. How can a number that usually falls between 3 and 5 have an odds ratio of 127? Should we interpret it to mean that increasing the average review 1,270 times will move a customer from a low-margin to a high-margin bike? Well, no. When we get an abnormally high `OddsRatio`, it means that our predictors are highly correlated with each other (you might hear data scientists talk about sparse matrices, and the like here). As we learned from Occam's Razor, we want to remove variables whenever we can. Since ratings and colors are correlated (which is in itself an interesting discovery), let's drop the average rating and only focus on color.

Since black seems to be associated with higher margin products, what should we do? Should we suggest to the management that we should be like Harry Ford and offer our bikes, "In any color they like, as long as it is black?" No, we want to offer other colors, because some people don't want black and we want their business. However, what we can do is use black to drive higher-margin sales. Here is a small snippet from the order form for individuals on our website:

Notice that the colors are ordered in a random manner and are placed after the customer selects the model. What if we moved the colors to the first selection to get the user in the "black frame of mind" and then offer models? Also, perhaps we should move the color selection so that black is on top?

While this is pretty good, this is a book about machine learning and there is little machine learning here to this point (unless you count the logistic regression's methodology in determining the answer, which I don't). How can we update our site automatically as customers' preferences change? What if all the cool kids started riding silver bikes? How can we quickly take advantage of this? How can the machine learn faster than the research analysts running the model periodically?

We could do what we did in the last chapter and run the model on each page creation, create an evaluator of the model, and then populate the select list. However, if you remember about how long it took to run, it is a suboptimal solution because by the time it takes to run the model, most of our customers would abandon the site (though if they were using a mobile device, we can always blame the network connection; developers have never done this before). As an alternative, what if we created a process when the website started that constantly runs the model and caches the result? This way, each time the page is created, the data behind the select list is as fresh as it can be. Let's drop into Visual Studio and make it happen.

Adding logistic regression to the application

Open up the `AdventureWorks` solution and go to the `AdventureWorks.MachineLearning` project:

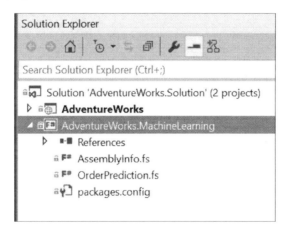

Add a new F# source file and name it `ColorPrediction.fs`. You will notice that it is placed at the bottom of the project. The order of the files is important in an F# project because of the type inference system. What you can do is right-click on the file and move it up above the `.config` file:

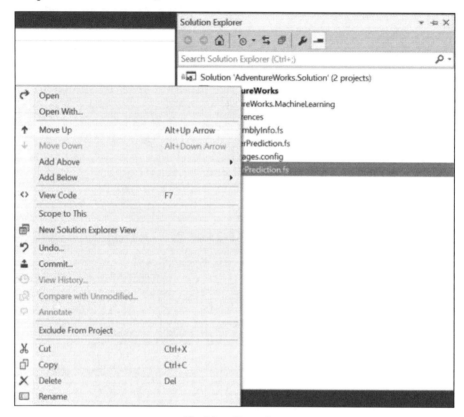

The Move Up option

Go into the `ColorPrediction.fs` file and replace all the existing code with the following code:

```
namespace AdventureWorks.MachineLearning

open Accord
open Accord.Statistics.Filters
open Accord.Statistics.Analysis
open Accord.Statistics.Models.Regression
open Accord.Statistics.Models.Regression.Fitting

open System
open System.Data.SqlClient
```

Next, let's add in the types that we created in the regression project and the one type we need for this compiled assembly. While we're at it, add in the list of `ProductInfos` and the connection string and query values from the regression project:

```
type ProductInfo = {ProductID:int; Color:string;
AvgReviews: float; Markup: float}
type ProductInfo' = {ProductID:int; BlackInd:float; BlueInd:float;
RedInd:float; SilverInd:float; OtherInd: float; AvgReviews: float;
HighMargin:float}

type public ColorPrediction () =
    let productInfos = ResizeArray<ProductInfo>()

    [<Literal>]
    let connectionString = "data source=nc54a9m5kk.database.windows.
net;
initial catalog=AdventureWorks2014;user
id=chickenskills@nc54a9m5kk;password=sk1lzm@tter;"

    [<Literal>]
    let query = "Select
        A.ProductID,
        A.Color,
        B.AvgReviews,
        A.MarkUp
        From
        (Select P.ProductID,
          Color,
          ListPrice - StandardCost as Markup
          from [Sales].[SalesOrderDetail] as SOD
            inner join [Sales].[SalesOrderHeader] as SOH
            on SOD.SalesOrderID = SOH.SalesOrderID
            inner join [Sales].[Customer] as C
            on SOH.CustomerID = C.CustomerID
            inner join [Production].[Product] as P
            on SOD.ProductID = P.ProductID
            inner join [Production].[ProductSubcategory] as PS
            on P.ProductSubcategoryID = PS.ProductSubcategoryID
            Where C.StoreID is null
            and PS.ProductCategoryID = 1) as A
        Inner Join
        (Select PR.ProductID,
            (Sum(Rating) + 0.0) / (Count(ProductID) + 0.0) as
            AvgReviews
```

```
        from [Production].[ProductReview] as PR
        Group By ProductID) as B
    on A.ProductID = B.ProductID"
```

Next, let's add a method that will return an ordered list of colors with the most important one on top:

```
member this.GetColors(attachmentPoint) =
    let connection = new SqlConnection(connectionString)
    let command = new SqlCommand(query, connection)
    connection.Open()
    let reader = command.ExecuteReader()
    while reader.Read() do
        productInfos.Add({ProductID=reader.GetInt32(0);
          Color=(string)(reader.GetString(1));
          AvgReviews=(float)(reader.GetDecimal(2));
          Markup=(float)(reader.GetDecimal(3));})

    let getProductInfo'(productInfo:ProductInfo) =
            {ProductInfo'.ProductID=productInfo.ProductID;
            BlackInd = (match productInfo.Color with |
              "Black" -> 1.0 | _ -> 0.0);
            BlueInd = (match productInfo.Color with |
              "Blue" -> 1.0 | _ -> 0.0);
            RedInd = (match productInfo.Color with |
              "Red" -> 1.0 | _ -> 0.0);
            SilverInd = (match productInfo.Color with |
              "Silver" -> 1.0 | _ -> 0.0);
            OtherInd = (match productInfo.Color with |
              "Silver" | "Blue" | "Red" | "Silver" -> 0.0 |
              _ -> 1.0);
            AvgReviews = productInfo.AvgReviews;
            HighMargin = (match productInfo.Markup >
              attachmentPoint with | true -> 1.0 |
              false -> 0.0);}

    let productInfos' =
        productInfos
        |> Seq.map (fun pi -> getProductInfo'(pi))
    let xs =
        productInfos'
        |> Seq.map (fun pi -> [|pi.BlackInd; pi.BlueInd;
        pi.RedInd; pi.SilverInd; pi.OtherInd; pi.AvgReviews|])
        |> Seq.toArray
    let
```

```
        y = productInfos'
        |> Seq.map (fun pi -> pi.HighMargin)
        |> Seq.toArray

    let colors = [|"Black";"Blue";"Red";"Silver";"Other"|]

    let analysis = new LogisticRegressionAnalysis(xs, y)
    match analysis.Compute() with
        | true ->
            let coefficientValues = analysis.CoefficientValues
            |> Seq.skip 1
            let colors' = Seq.zip colors coefficientValues
            colors' |> Seq.mapi (fun i (c,cv) -> c,
            (abs(cv)/cv), analysis.Regression.GetOddsRatio(i))
                        |> Seq.map (fun (c, s, odr) -> c, s * odr)
                        |> Seq.sortBy (fun (c, odr) -> odr)
                        |> Seq.map (fun (c, odr) -> c)
                        |> Seq.toArray
        | false -> colors
```

Most of the code is the same as the work we did in the regression project, but there is some new code that needs some explanation. There is now a string array called `colors` that lists all of the colors that we sent to our regression. After the `analysis.Compute()` is called, we remove the first value from the `analysis.CoefficientValues` via this line:

```
analysis.CoefficientValues |> Seq.skip 1
```

Skip is a handy function that allows us to, well, skip the first rows of `Seq`. We are calling it here because the `analysis.CoefficientValues` returns the coefficient in the first value of the array.

Next, we call the following:

```
let colors' = Seq.zip colors coefficientValues
```

We have seen `Seq.zip` before. We are gluing together the colors array with the coefficient values array so each row is a tuple of the color name and its coefficient. With that array set up, we then implement the final transformation pipeline:

```
                colors' |> Seq.mapi (fun i (c,cv) -> c,
                    (abs(cv)/cv),
                    analysis.Regression.GetOddsRatio(i+1))
                            |> Seq.map (fun (c, s, odr) -> c, s * odr)
                |> Seq.sortByDescending (fun (c,odr)-> odr)
                            |> Seq.map (fun (c, odr) -> c)
                            |> Seq.toArray
```

The first step is as follows:

```
|> Seq.mapi(fun i (c,cv) -> c, (abs(cv)/cv),
analysis.Regression.GetOddsRatio(i+1))
```

This applies a `mapi` function to `colors`. `Seq.mapi` is a high order function that is just like the `Seq.map` function with one extra parameter, the index of each row. So the index `i` is passed in and then the tuple `(c,cv)`, which is the color and the `coefficientValue`. We return a tuple with the color, a -1 or +1 depending on the sign of the `coefficientValue`, and the odds ratio ->, which we look up based on the index.

The next step is as follows:

```
|> Seq.map(fun (c, s, odr) -> c, s * odr)
```

This applies another function that returns the color and a signed odds ratio. If you remember from before, `Regression.GetOddsRatio` is always positive. We are applying the sign so we can order the ratios from most probable to the least probable.

The next step is as follows:

```
|> Seq.sortByDescending(fun (c,odr)-> odr)
```

This applies a function that sorts the array based on the odds ratio so that the tuple with the highest `oddsRatio` is on top.

The next two steps turn the tuple into a simple string. The color name then transforms our `Seq` to an array:

```
|> Seq.map(fun (c, odr) -> c)
|> Seq.toArray
```

With the code in place, let's hop over to our MVC project and implement it. Find the `Global.asax` file and open it up. Replace the code with the following:

```
using System;
using System.Collections.Generic;
using System.Configuration;
using System.Linq;
using System.Threading;
using System.Web;
using System.Web.Mvc;
using System.Web.Optimization;
using System.Web.Routing;
using AdventureWorks.MachineLearning;
```

```
namespace AdventureWorks
{
    public class MvcApplication : System.Web.HttpApplication
    {
        static Object _lock = new Object();
        Timer _timer = null;
        static String[] _bikeColors = null;

        protected void Application_Start()
        {
            AreaRegistration.RegisterAllAreas();
            FilterConfig.RegisterGlobalFilters(GlobalFilters.Filters);
            RouteConfig.RegisterRoutes(RouteTable.Routes);
            BundleConfig.RegisterBundles(BundleTable.Bundles);
            _bikeColors = new string[5] { "Red", "White", "Blue",
                "Black", "Silver" };
            _timer = new Timer(UpdateBikeColors,null,0,
              TimeSpan.FromMinutes(1).Milliseconds);
        }

        private void UpdateBikeColors(object state)
        {
            var attachmentPoint = Double.Parse
              (ConfigurationManager.AppSettings
                ["attachmentPoint"]);
            var colorPrediction = new ColorPrediction();
            BikeColors =
              colorPrediction.GetColors(attachmentPoint);
        }

        public static String[] BikeColors
        {
            get
            {
                lock(_lock)
                {
                    return _bikeColors;
                }
            }
            set
            {
                lock(_lock)
                {
                    _bikeColors = value;
```

```
                }
            }
        }
    }
}
```

Some of this code might be new, so let's take a closer look. First, we created two class-level variables: `_lock` and `_timer`. We use `_lock` to prevent our color array to be read while our regression could be updating it. You can see `_lock` in action in the public property that exposes the color array:

```
public static String[] BikeColors
{
    get
    {
        lock(_lock)
        {
            return _bikeColors;
        }
    }
    set
    {
        lock(_lock)
        {
            _bikeColors = value;
        }
    }
}
```

Next, we create a method that will be called when our timer fires:

```
private void UpdateBikeColors(object state)
{
    var attachmentPoint = Double.Parse
      (ConfigurationManager.AppSettings
        ["attachmentPoint"]);
    var colorPrediction = new ColorPrediction();
    BikeColors =
      colorPrediction.GetColors(attachmentPoint);
}
```

Notice that we are creating an instance of our `ColorPrediction` class, which then invokes the `GetColors` method. We assign the `BikeColors` property with the return of our recently-calculated solution.

Finally, we instantiate the `_timer` variable in the `Application.Start` method, passing in the method that gets invoked when the timer counts down:

```
_timer = new Timer
    (UpdateBikeColors,null,0,TimeSpan.FromMinutes(1).Milliseconds);
```

This means, every minute we call the color prediction to run the logistic regression based on the most recent data. Meanwhile, clients will be calling our website continuously and they will be getting an array of colors based on the most recent calculation.

Next, go to the `.config` file and add the attachment point to the `appSettings` section:

```
<add key="attachmentPoint" value="800" />
```

Finally, open the `individualOrder` controller and replace the hardcoded values of colors with our generated one in the `Create` method:

```
var colors = MvcApplication.BikeColors;
```

Run the site and you will see that our color list has changed:

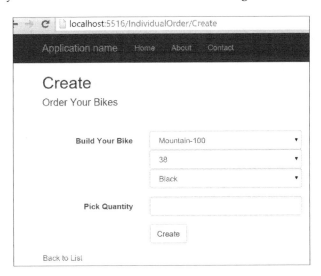

We now have a pretty good model that seems to be working in production, without a major performance hit. However, our solution so far has a fatal flaw. We are guilty of overfitting. As mentioned in *Chapter 2, AdventureWorks Regression*, overfitting, is the notion that the model we create only works against the data we have on hand and fails miserably when we introduce it to new data. Every machine learning technique has a problem with overfitting, and there are some common ways to mitigate its impact. We will look at that in the coming chapters.

Summary

We covered a lot of ground in this chapter. We looked at multiple linear regressions, logistic regressions, and then considered a couple of techniques to normalize our dataset. Along the way, we learned some new F# code and learned a way to update a machine learning model without impact on our end user experience.

In the next chapter, we take a break from AdventureWorks and line of business development and start working with some open data as a data scientist using a decision tree. As Dick Clark used to say, "The hits just keep coming."

4
Traffic Stops – Barking Up the Wrong Tree?

In the prior two chapters, you were a software developer who was injecting machine learning into their existing line of business application. In this chapter, we are going to put on our research analyst hat and see if we can discover some hidden insights from an existing dataset.

The scientific process

The research analyst historically followed this pattern of discovery and analysis:

With the rise of the data scientist, that workflow has changed to something like this:

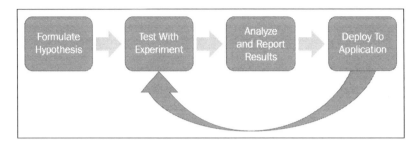

Notice how the work does not end after reporting the results of a model. Rather, the data scientist is often responsible for moving the working models from their desktop and into a production application. With this new responsibility, comes new power, to reverse-paraphrase Spider-Man. The data scientist's skillset becomes broader because they have to understand software engineering techniques to go along with their traditional skill set.

One thing that the data scientist knows by heart is this following workflow. Inside the Test With Experiment block, there is this:

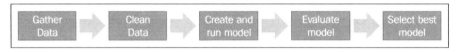

In terms of time spent, the **clean data** block is very large compared to the other blocks. This is because most of the work effort is spent with data acquisition and preparation. Historically, much of this **data munging** was dealing with missing, malformed, and illogical data. The traditional way to try to minimize the work effort on this step was to create data warehouses and clean the data as it transferred from the source system into the warehouse (sometimes called the Extract, Transform, Load, or ETL process). While this had some limited success, it was a fairly expensive endeavor and a fixed schema meant that changes became particularly difficult. More recent efforts in this space have surrounded gathering data in its native format, dumping it into **data lakes** and then building jobs on top of the lake that are specific to the data's native format and structure. Sometimes, this is called *putting the data in a rectangle* because you may be taking unstructured data, cleaning and aggregating it, and then outputting it in a two-dimensional data frame. The power of this data frame is that you can then combine it with other data frames to do some more interesting analysis.

Open data

One of the most exciting civic movements that align with Big Data and Machine Learning is **Open Data**. Although there is not as much buzz around it, it's a very exciting and important transformation in data science. The premise of open data is that local, state, and national governments will become much more accountable and efficient if they expose the public data that they currently maintain in a RESTful format. Currently, most government agencies might have paper records, charge a significant sum to output an ad-hoc query, or occasionally have an FTP site with some `.xls` or `.pdf` files that get refreshed from time to time. Open Data is a movement that takes the same, if not more, data and places it on a web service that can be consumed by applications and/or research analysts. The key thing is security and privacy of the data. Historically, some government agencies have practised security by obscurity (we have the records online but the only way to get to it is by our custom web frontend) and open data makes that kind of defense obsolete. Truth be told, security by obscurity has never really worked (how hard is it to write a screen scraper?) and all it has really done is made it harder for well-intentioned people to accomplish their goals.

The rise of open data also coincides with the formulation of groups of people who are hacking for civic good. Sometimes these are ad hoc meetup groups that center on a single technology stack and other groups are much more formal. For example, Code for America has *brigades* in many cities across the world. If you are interested in helping a local chapter, you can find information on their website `http://www.codeforamerica.org/`.

Hack-4-Good

Let's pretend we are a member of a local chapter of a fictional organization civic hacking called "Hack-4-Good". At the latest meeting, the leader announces, "Through a public record request, we have obtained all of the traffic stop information in our town. Does anyone know what to do with this dataset?" You immediately throw your hand in the air and say, "Heck yeah, Baby!" Okay, maybe you don't use those exact words but your enthusiasm is undeniable.

Since you are a research analyst by training, the first thing you want to do is load the data into your IDE and start exploring the data.

Open up Visual Studio and create a new Solution called `Hack4Good.TrafficStop.Solution`:

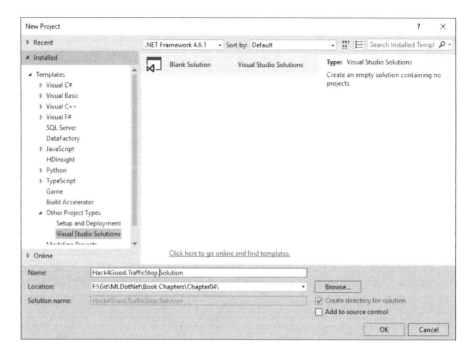

Add a new F# Library project to the solution:

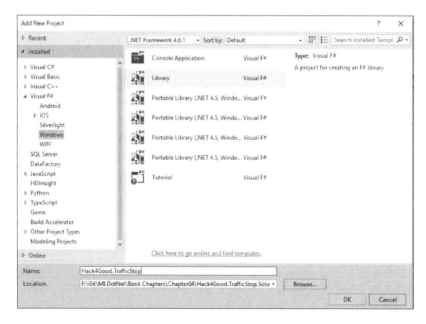

FsLab and type providers

Now that the project skeleton has been set up, open up the `Script.fsx` file and remove all of its contents. Next, let's take a look at a really neat library called FsLab (`http://fslab.org/`). Go to the NuGet package manager console and enter this:

```
PM> Install-Package fslab
```

Next, we will install SqlClient, so we can access our data. Go to the NuGet package manager and enter:

```
PM> Install-Package FSharp.Data.SqlClient
```

With the ceremony out of the way, let's get to coding. Let's first bring the traffic ticket dataset into our script. Go into `Script.fsx` and enter this at the top:

```
#load "../packages/FsLab.0.3.11/FsLab.fsx"
```

You should get a series of dialog boxes from Visual Studio that looks like this:

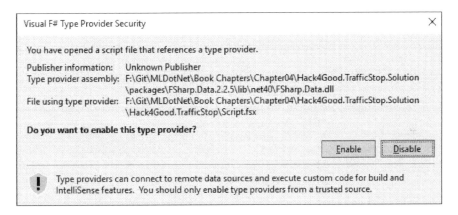

Click on **Enable**. As a general point, whenever you get a dialog box from Visual Studio like this, click on **Enable**. For example, depending on our machine's configuration, you might get these dialog boxes when you run the following `open` statements.

Back in our script, enter this:

```
#r "System.Data.Entity.dll"
#r "FSharp.Data.TypeProviders.dll"
#r "System.Data.Linq.dll"

open System
open Foogle
```

```
open Deedle
open FSharp.Data
open FSharp.Charting
open System.Data.Linq
open System.Data.Entity
open Microsoft.FSharp.Data.TypeProviders
```

Next, enter this into the script:

```
[<Literal>]
let connectionString =
"data source=nc54a9m5kk.database.windows.net;
initial catalog=Traffic;
user id=chickenskills@nc54a9m5kk;password=sk1lzm@tter;"

type EntityConnection =
SqlEntityConnection<connectionString,Pluralize = true>
let context = EntityConnection.GetDataContext()
context.dbo_TrafficStops |> Seq.iter(fun ts -> printfn "%s"
ts.StreetAddress)
```

The first line should look familiar; it's a connection string just like we used in the last chapter. The only difference is the database. But what's with the next line of code?

```
type EntityConnection =
SqlEntityConnection<connectionString,Pluralize = true>
```

This is an example of a type provider. Type providers are one of the best features of F# and it is unique to the language. I like to think of type providers as **object relational mapping (ORM)** on steroids. This type provider is inspecting the database and generating F# types for me to use in the REPL—which we will see in action in a second. In fact, the type provider is sitting on top of **Entity Framework (EF)**, which is sitting on top of ADO.NET. If you got excited about how much more productive you were when you went from hand-rolling ADO.NET code to EF, you should be equally excited about how much more productive you can be working with type providers; it is really the next generation of data access. Another cool thing is that type providers are not just for relational database management systems—there is a JSON type provider, a .csv type provider, and others. You can read more about type providers at https://msdn.microsoft.com/en-us/library/hh156509.aspx and once you see them in action, you will find them indispensable in your coding tasks.

Back to the code. The next line is:

```
let context = EntityConnection.GetDataContext()
```

It creates the actual instance of the type to be used. The next line is where the rubber meets the road:

```
context.dbo_TrafficStops |> Seq.iter(fun ts -> printfn "%s"
ts.StreetAddress)
```

In this line, we are traversing the `TrafficStop` table and printing out the street address. If you highlight all of the code in the script so far and send it to the REPL, you will see the last part of 30,000 addresses:

```
128 SW MAYNARD RD/KILMAYNE DR

1 WALNUT ST TO US 1 RAMP NB/US 1 EXIT 101 RAMP NB

2333 WALNUT ST

1199 NW MAYNARD RD/HIGH HOUSE RD

3430 TEN TEN RD


val connectionString : string =
  "data source=nc54a9m5kk.database.windows.net;initial catalog=T"+[61
chars]
type EntityConnection =
  class
    static member GetDataContext : unit -> EntityConnection.ServiceTypes.
SimpleDataContextTypes.EntityContainer
      + 1 overload
    nested type ServiceTypes
  end
val context :
  EntityConnection.ServiceTypes.SimpleDataContextTypes.EntityContainer
val it : unit = ()
```

Before we press on, I want to mention how cool type providers are. With three lines of code, I defined a database schema, connected to it, and then pulled down records. Not only that, but the result set from the database is `IEnumerable`. So everything I have done with `Seq` in prior chapters to transform and shape the data, I can do here.

Data exploration

With this new found power, let's start exploring. Enter this into the script:

```
context.dbo_TrafficStops |> Seq.head
```

Sending to the REPL, we will see the following:

```
val it : EntityConnection.ServiceTypes.dbo_TrafficStops =
  SqlEntityConnection1.dbo_TrafficStops
    {CadCallId = 120630019.0;
    DispositionDesc = "VERBAL WARNING";
    DispositionId = 7;
    EntityKey = System.Data.EntityKey;
    EntityState = Unchanged;
    Id = 13890;
    Latitude = 35.7891;
    Longitude = -78.8289;
    StopDateTime = 6/30/2012 12:36:38 AM;
    StreetAddress = "4348 NW CARY PKWY/HIGH HOUSE RD";}
>
```

We see our data frame has some interesting elements we can analyze: the date and time of the traffic stop, the geocoordinate of the traffic stop, and the final disposition of the stop. We also have some data that does not seem useful for analysis: the `CadCallId` which is probably the primary key of the source system. This might be useful for later auditing. We also have `StreetAddress`, which is the same as the geocoordinate, but in a less analyzable form. Finally, we have some fields thrown in by Entity Framework (`EntityKey`, `EntityState`, and `Id`).

Let's make a data frame with only the fields we care about. Enter this into the script:

```
let trafficStops =
    context.dbo_TrafficStops
    |> Seq.map(fun ts -> ts.StopDateTime, ts.Latitude,
    ts.Longitude, ts.DispositionId)
```

And sending it to the REPL, we get this:

```
val trafficStops :
  seq<System.Nullable<System.DateTime> * System.Nullable<float> *
    System.Nullable<float> * System.Nullable<int>>

>
```

It is interesting that although F# really, really tries to prevent you from using null, it does support it. In fact, all four of our fields are nullable. I'll show you how to deal with nulls a bit further on in the chapter as they are often a major headache when coding.

There is one more data frame we should create before getting too far down the analysis. As a general rule, the machine learning models that we use, prefer primitive types such as ints, floats, and bools. They have a much harder time with strings, especially strings that represent categorical data. You probably noticed that I brought in `DispositionId` into the `trafficStops` data frame and not `DispositionDesc`. However, we still don't want to lose that description because we might want to refer to it later. Let's create a separate data frame for this lookup data. In the script, enter this:

```
let dispoistions =
    context.dbo_TrafficStops
    |> Seq.distinctBy(fun ts -> ts.DispositionId,
    ts.DispositionDesc)
    |> Seq.map (fun d -> d.DispositionId, d.DispositionDesc)
    |> Seq.toArray
```

And then send it to the REPL to get this:

```
val dispoistions : (System.Nullable<int> * string) [] =
  [|(7, "VERBAL WARNING"); (15, "CITATION"); (12, "COMPLETED AS
REQUESTED");
    (4, "WRITTEN WARNING"); (13, "INCIDENT REPORT"); (9, "ARREST");
    (14, "UNFOUNDED"); (19, "None Provided");
    (10, "NO FURTHER ACTION NECESSARY"); (5, "OTHER    SEE NOTES");
    (2, "UNABLE TO LOCATE"); (16, "FIELD CONTACT");
    (6, "REFERRED TO PROPER AGENCY"); (17, "BACK UP UNIT");
    (11, "CIVIL PROBLEM"); (1, "FURTHER ACTION NECESSARY"); (3, "FALSE
ALARM");
    (18, "CITY ORDINANCE VIOLATION")|]


>
```

Looking at the code, we have a couple of new things. First, we are using the high order function `Seq.distinctBy`, which you can probably guess return records with the distinct values specified in the argument. Interestingly, the entire traffic stop record is being returned, not just the values in the lambda. If you are wondering which record gets picked by F# to represent the distinct disposition, you have to chalk it up to magic. Okay, maybe not. As it was traversing the data frame, F# picked the first record where there was a new unique value for `DispositionID` and `DispositionDesc`. In any event, since we only care about the `DispositionId` and `DispositionDesc`, we then mapped the traffic stop record into a tuple on this line of code: `Seq.map (fun d -> d.DispositionId, d.DispositionDesc`. That should look familiar to you by now.

With our data frames set up, let's start digging into the data. One of the nice things about having a `DateTime` value is that it represents many different factors that might be worth exploring. For example, how many traffic stops are performed by month? What about the day of the week? Is there a time factor in the stops? Does more happen at night or in the day? Let's start writing some code. Go to the script and enter this code block:

```
let months =
    context.dbo_TrafficStops
    |> Seq.groupBy (fun ts -> ts.StopDateTime.Value.Month)
    |> Seq.map (fun (m, ts) -> m, Seq.length ts)
    |> Seq.sortBy (fun (m, ts) -> m)
    |> Seq.toArray
```

And sending it to the REPL, you should see this:

```
val months : (int * int) [] =
  [|(1, 2236); (2, 2087); (3, 2630); (4, 2053); (5, 2439); (6, 2499);
    (7, 2265); (8, 2416); (9, 3365); (10, 1983); (11, 2067); (12, 1738)|]


>
```

Just a quick glance tells you that there are a whole lot of traffic stops being performed in September, and December looks like a light month. Digging into the code, there is a new high-order function that I used:

```
    |> Seq.groupBy (fun ts -> ts.StopDateTime.Value.Month)
```

groupBy is a very powerful function, but it can be a bit confusing the first time you use it (it was for me, at least). I came to a better understanding of groupBy by working backwards and looking at the output of a simple array. Go into the script file and enter this:

```
let testArray = [|1;1;2;3;4;5;3;4;5;5;2;1;5|]
testArray |> Array.groupBy (id)
```

Sending that to the REPL gives this:

```
val testArray : int [] = [|1; 1; 2; 3; 4; 5; 3; 4; 5; 5; 2; 1; 5|]
val it : (int * int []) [] =
  [|(1, [|1; 1; 1|]); (2, [|2; 2|]); (3, [|3; 3|]); (4, [|4; 4|]);
    (5, [|5; 5; 5; 5|])|]
```

You will notice that the output is a tuple. The first item of the tuple is the value on which the groupBy grouped the data. The next item is a subarray with only the values from the original array that match the tuple's first item. Diving into the ones, (1, [|1; 1; 1|]), we can see that the number 1 was the groupBy value and that there were three 1s in the original array. groupBy can be applied to record types too. Consider this data frame. From left to right, the columns are USState, Gender, YearOfBirth, NameGiven, and NumberOfInstances:

USState	Gender	YearOfBirth	NameGiven	NumberOfInstances
AK	F	1910	Annie	12
AK	F	1910	Anna	10
AK	F	1910	Margaret	8
AL	F	1910	Annie	90
AL	F	1910	Anna	88
AL	F	1910	Margaret	86
AZ	F	1910	Annie	46
AZ	F	1910	Anna	34
AZ	F	1910	Margaret	12

Applying a `groupBy` on `NameGiven` to this data frame gives the following output:

fst	snd					
Annie	AK	F	1910	Annie	12
	AL	F	1910	Annie	90
	AZ	F	1910	Annie	46
Anna	AK	F	1910	Anna	10
	AL	F	1910	Anna	88
	AZ	F	1910	Anna	34
Margaret	AK	F	1910	Margaret	8
	AL	F	1910	Margaret	86
	AZ	F	1910	Margaret	12

With the `fst` of the tuple the `NameGiven`, and the `snd` being a data frame with only the records that match the `fst`.

Let's continue with the next line of code `|> Seq.map (fun (m, ts) -> m, ts |> Seq.length)`.

We can see that we are mapping the original tuple of month and `trafficStops` to a new tuple of month and the length of the array that was `snd` of the original tuple. This effectively reduces our data into a sequence of length 12 (one for each month). The `fst` is the month and the `snd` is the number of stops that occurred. Next we sort it by month and then push it to an array.

With this pattern set, let's do a couple of more `groupBy`. Let's do `Day` and `DayOfWeek`. Go into the script and enter this:

```
let dayOfMonth =
    context.dbo_TrafficStops
    |> Seq.groupBy (fun ts -> ts.StopDateTime.Value.Day)
    |> Seq.map (fun (d, ts) -> d, Seq.length ts)
    |> Seq.sortBy (fun (d, ts) -> d)
    |> Seq.toArray

let weekDay =
    context.dbo_TrafficStops
    |> Seq.groupBy (fun ts -> ts.StopDateTime.Value.DayOfWeek)
    |> Seq.map (fun (dow, ts) -> dow, Seq.length ts)
    |> Seq.sortBy (fun (dow, ts) -> dow)
    |> Seq.toArray
```

You will notice one subtle change from the month analysis that we just did — `| >
Seq.map (fun (dow, ts) -> dow, Seq.length ts)` has a different syntax for
getting the length of the `snd`. Instead of writing `ts |> Seq.length`, I wrote `Seq.
length ts`. Both styles are perfectly valid F#, but the latter is considered more
idiomatic. I will begin using this style more frequently in the book.

So once we send this to the REPL, we can see:

```
val dayOfMonth : (int * int) [] =
  [|(1, 918); (2, 911); (3, 910); (4, 941); (5, 927); (6, 840);
(7, 940);
    (8, 785); (9, 757); (10, 805); (11, 766); (12, 851); (13, 825); (14,
911);
    (15, 977); (16, 824); (17, 941); (18, 956); (19, 916); (20, 977);
    (21, 988); (22, 906); (23, 1003); (24, 829); (25, 1036);
(26, 1031);
    (27, 890); (28, 983); (29, 897); (30, 878); (31, 659)|]


val weekDay : (System.DayOfWeek * int) [] =
  [|(Sunday, 3162); (Monday, 3277); (Tuesday, 3678);
(Wednesday, 4901);
    (Thursday, 5097); (Friday, 4185); (Saturday, 3478)|]
```

Looking at the results, it should be pretty obvious what we are doing. The 25th of
every month looks like the day where most of the traffic stops occur and Thursday
sure has a lot of stops. I wonder what would happen if the 25th fell on a Thursday
for a given month?

Before we dive deeper into the data, I want to point out that the last three blocks of
code are very similar. They all follow this pattern:

```
let weekDay =
    context.dbo_TrafficStops
      |> Seq.groupBy (fun ts -> ts.StopDateTime.Value.XXXXX)
      |> Seq.map (fun (fst, snd) -> fst, Seq.length snd)
      |> Seq.sortBy (fun (fst, snd) -> fst)
      |> Seq.toArray
```

Instead of having three chunks of code that are almost identical, is there a way we
can consolidate them into a single function? Yes there is. What if we wrote a function
like this:

```
let transform grouper mapper =
    context.dbo_TrafficStops
      |> Seq.groupBy grouper
```

```
                  |> Seq.map mapper
                               |> Seq.sortBy fst
                               |> Seq.toArray
```

And then we called it like this:

```
    transform (fun ts -> ts.StopDateTime.Value.Month)
    (fun (m, ts) -> m, Seq.length ts)
    transform (fun ts -> ts.StopDateTime.Value.Day)
    (fun (d, ts) -> d, Seq.length ts)
    transform (fun ts -> ts.StopDateTime.Value.DayOfWeek)
    (fun (dow, ts) -> dow, Seq.length ts)
```

Would that work? You bet your bippy. Sending it to the REPL, we can see we are getting the same results:

```
val transform :
  grouper:(EntityConnection.ServiceTypes.dbo_TrafficStops -> 'a) ->
    mapper:('a * seq<EntityConnection.ServiceTypes.dbo_TrafficStops> ->
              'b * 'c) -> ('b * 'c) [] when 'a : equality and 'b :
comparison
val it : (System.DayOfWeek * int) [] =
  [|(Sunday, 3162); (Monday, 3277); (Tuesday, 3678); (Wednesday, 4901);
    (Thursday, 5097); (Friday, 4185); (Saturday, 3478)|]
```

Those of you coming from C# and VB.NET might have gotten very uncomfortable with the transform's interface. You probably would have been much more comfortable with this syntax:

```
    let transform (grouper, mapper) =
```

The () and the commas make it look much more like C# and VB.NET. Although both are perfectly valid F#, this is another place where it is considered more idiomatic to remove the parenthesis and the commas. I will begin using this style more frequently in this book.

Also, notice that I am passing two functions into the transform function. This is very different from imperative C#/VB.NET where we usually pass data into a method. I have noticed that functional programming is more about bringing the operations to the data than bringing the data to the operations, which has profound implications once we start applying machine learning to big data.

Going back to our transform function, we can see that the mapper function is pretty the same in the three times we invoked it: (fun (dow, ts) -> dow, Seq.length ts). The only difference is the name we gave the first part of the tuple. This seems like another great place where we can consolidate some code. Let's rewrite transform like this:

```
let transform grouper  =
    context.dbo_TrafficStops
    |> Seq.groupBy grouper
    |> Seq.map (fun (fst, snd) -> fst, Seq.length snd)
    |> Seq.sortBy fst
    |> Seq.toArray

transform (fun ts -> ts.StopDateTime.Value.Month)
transform (fun ts -> ts.StopDateTime.Value.Day)
transform (fun ts -> ts.StopDateTime.Value.DayOfWeek)
```

And sending that to the REPL, we get this:

```
val transform :
  grouper:(EntityConnection.ServiceTypes.dbo_TrafficStops -> 'a) ->
    ('a * int) [] when 'a : comparison

>

val it : (System.DayOfWeek * int) [] =
  [|(Sunday, 3162); (Monday, 3277); (Tuesday, 3678); (Wednesday, 4901);
    (Thursday, 5097); (Friday, 4185); (Saturday, 3478)|]
```

Pretty cool, huh? We will be doing this kind of programming more and more in this book. Once you get the hang of it, you will start seeing patterns in your code that you never had seen before, and you have yet another powerful arrow in your toolbox (as I mix metaphors).

Since you are now up to speed on groupBy, I want to rewrite our transform function to ditch it. Instead of using the groupBy and map functions, let's rewrite it using the countBy high order function. While we are at it, let's rename our function to something that is a bit more intention revealing. Type this into the script:

```
let getCounts counter =
    context.dbo_TrafficStops
    |> Seq.countBy counter
    |> Seq.sortBy fst
    |> Seq.toArray

getCounts (fun ts -> ts.StopDateTime.Value.DayOfWeek)
```

Sending this to the REPL, we get the same values:

```
val getCounts :
  counter:(EntityConnection.ServiceTypes.dbo_TrafficStops -> 'a) ->
    ('a * int) [] when 'a : comparison
val it : (System.DayOfWeek * int) [] =
  [|(Sunday, 3162); (Monday, 3277); (Tuesday, 3678);
  (Wednesday, 4901);
    (Thursday, 5097); (Friday, 4185); (Saturday, 3478)|]
```

Visualization

Looking at the data in the REPL is a good start, but pictures are a much more powerful and effective way to communicate information. For example, is there some kind of monthly seasonality for traffic stops? Let's put the data into a chart to find out. In your script, enter this:

```
let months' = Seq.map (fun (m,c) -> string m,c) months
Chart.LineChart months'
```

Your REPL should look like this:

```
val months' : seq<string * int>
val it : FoogleChart = (Foogle Chart)

>
```

Your default browser should be trying to open and should show you this:

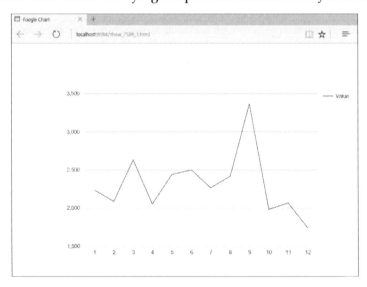

So we see the spike in September and the drop off in December that had already caught our eye. If the date/time has some curious patterns, what about the geolocation? Enter this into the script file:

```
let locations =
    context.dbo_TrafficStops
    |> Seq.filter (fun ts -> ts.Latitude.HasValue &&
    ts.Longitude.HasValue )
    |> Seq.map (fun ts -> ts.StreetAddress, ts.Latitude.Value,
    ts.Longitude.Value)
    |> Seq.map (fun (sa,lat,lon) -> sa, lat.ToString(),
    lon.ToString())
    |> Seq.map (fun (sa,lat,lon) -> sa, lat + "," + lon)
    |> Seq.take 2
    |> Seq.toArray
```

```
Chart.GeoChart(locations,DisplayMode=GeoChart.DisplayMode.Markers,
    Region="US")
```

Not very helpful. The problem is that the FsLab geomap covers Google's `geoMap` API, and that API only goes to the country level. Instead of using Fslab then, we can roll our own. This is a fairly complex process using Bing maps, WPF dependency properties, and the like, so I will not explain it in this book. The code is available for you to review on the download section of our site. So, close your eyes and pretend the last 3 hours I spent working on this went by in 2 seconds and we have this map:

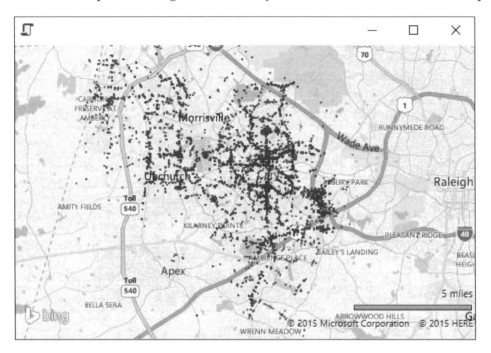

So what can we tell off the bat? There are traffic stops everywhere, though they seem to concentrate on main streets. Based on the initial analysis, the term "speed trap" might be less about location and more about month, day, and time. Also, we can't draw too much from this map because we don't know the traffic patterns—more stops might be on more traveled streets or might be an indicator of key areas where there are traffic stops. To help us dig into the data more, let's move away from simple descriptive statistics and apply a common machine learning technique called a decision tree.

Decision trees

The principle of decision tree is this: you can use a tree-like structure to make predictions. Here is a cantonal example of whether we will play tennis today:

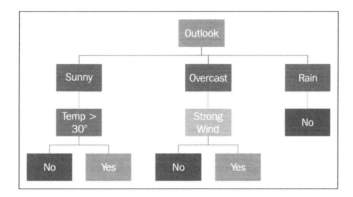

Each decision is called a node and the final result (in our case, the **Yes/No** boxes) is called the leaf. The analogy to a tree is somewhat appropriate. In fact, I would call it a decision branch with each decision called a crook and the final results being called leaves. However, J.R. Quinlan didn't ask me in 1986 when he invented this methodology. In any event, the number of levels of the tree is called the height of the tree. In our prior example, the tree has a maximum height of two. The nodes that are possible for a given point is called the features. In our prior example, Outlook has three features (sunny, overcast, and rain) and Strong Wind has two features (yes and no).

One of the real benefits of the decision tree is its simplicity of conveying information. Humans often do mental decision trees as long as the number of nodes are small and the calculation to move to the next node is simple. (Should I order decaf or regular? Do I need to study tonight?) Computers come in handy when there are many nodes and the calculations are complex. For example, we can hand the computer a whole bunch of historical data from people who decide to play tennis and it can determine that, for sunny days, the actual decision point is not 30°, but 31.2°. Something to keep in mind though is that decision trees often become less meaningful as the number of features increase and the depth gets too large. We'll look at ways to handle this a little bit later.

Accord

Let's make a decision tree with our traffic stop data. Go back to Visual Studio, open up **Solution Explorer**, and add a new script called `Accord.fsx`. Enter this into the script:

```
#r "System.Data.Entity.dll"
#r "FSharp.Data.TypeProviders.dll"
#r "System.Data.Linq.dll"

open System
open System.Data.Linq
open System.Data.Entity
open Microsoft.FSharp.Data.TypeProviders

[<Literal>]
let connectionString = "data
source=nc54a9m5kk.database.windows.net;initial
catalog=Traffic;user
id=chickenskills@nc54a9m5kk;password=sk1lzm@tter;"

type EntityConnection =
SqlEntityConnection<connectionString,Pluralize = true>
let context = EntityConnection.GetDataContext()
```

This code is the same that you used in `Script.fsx`. Send it to the REPL to make sure you copy-pasted it correctly:

```
val connectionString : string =
  "data source=nc54a9m5kk.database.windows.net;initial catalog=T"+[61
chars]
type EntityConnection =
  class
    static member GetDataContext : unit -> EntityConnection.ServiceTypes.
SimpleDataContextTypes.EntityContainer
    + 1 overload
    nested type ServiceTypes
  end
val context :
  EntityConnection.ServiceTypes.SimpleDataContextTypes.EntityContainer

>
```

Next, open up the NuGet package manager and enter in the following command:

```
PM> Install-Package Accord.MachineLearning
```

Go back to the script and enter in this:

```
#r "../packages/Accord.3.0.2/lib/net40/Accord.dll"
#r "../packages/Accord.MachineLearning.3.0.2/lib/net40/
Accord.MachineLearning.dll"
#r "../packages/Accord.Statistics.3.0.2/lib/net40/
Accord.Statistics.dll"
open Accord
open Accord.MachineLearning
open Accord.MachineLearning.DecisionTrees
open Accord.MachineLearning.DecisionTrees.Learning
```

With that out of the way, let's create a data structure that we can pass to Accord. As I mentioned earlier, decision trees often have a problem with a large number of features. A common technique to mitigate this is to bin the data. When you bin the data, you take your original data and put them into large groups. For example, we can take all of the times for the traffic stops and bin them into AM or PM, depending on whether they occurred before or after noon. Binning is a commonly used technique in data science—sometimes justifiably and sometimes just as a way to make the model conform to a desired output.

Going back to our script, create the following record type for our decision tree:

```
type TrafficStop = {Month:int; DayOfWeek:DayOfWeek; AMPM: string;
ReceivedTicket: bool option }
```

You will see that I created two bins of data. The first is called AMPM and it is for the time of the stop. The second is called ReceviedTicket as a Boolean. If you remember, there are 18 different values for the disposition. We only care whether the person received a ticket (called citation), so we are binning citations to true and noncitations to false. There is one more thing that you probably noticed— ReceivedTicket isn't simply a bool, it is a bool option. As you might remember, F# really doesn't like nulls. Although it can support null, F# instead encourages you to use something called an option type in its place.

An option type can have two values: Some<T> or None. If you are not familiar with the syntax of Some<T>, it means that Some is limited to only one type. Therefore, you can write Some<bool>, Some<int>, or Some<string>. With an option type, you can verify if a field has a value that you care about: Some or None. Not only that, the compiler forces you to be explicit with the choice. This compiler checking forces you to be explicit with the value and is an extremely powerful construct. Indeed, it is one of the reasons that F# code often has fewer bugs than other languages because it forces the developer to confront problems sooner and prevents them from sweeping them under the rug into a null where they can be accidentally ignored.

Going back to our code, let's write two functions that will bin our original data:

```
let getAMPM (stopDateTime:System.DateTime) =
    match stopDateTime.Hour < 12 with
    | true -> "AM"
    | false -> "PM"

let receviedTicket (disposition:string) =
    match disposition.ToUpper() with
    | "CITATION" -> Some true
    | "VERBAL WARNING" | "WRITTEN WARNING" -> Some false
    | _ -> None
```

Sending that to the REPL, we see:

```
val getAMPM : stopDateTime:DateTime -> string

val receviedTicket : disposition:string -> bool option
```

Notice that ReceivedTicket returns three possibilities with the option type: Some true, Some false, and None. The reason I did not include the other disposition values into Some false versus None was because we are only concentrating on traffic violations, not all of the reasons why an officer might stop a car. This kind of filtering is often used in data science to help make the dataset align with what we are trying to prove. We are not getting into more detail here about filtering as there are entire books written about the best way to deal with outliers and non-conforming data.

Back to our code. Let's take the data out of the database and put it into our TrafficStop record type. Go into the script and enter this:

```
let dataFrame = context.dbo_TrafficStops
                |> Seq.map (fun ts -> {Month=ts.StopDateTime.Value.
Month;DayOfWeek=ts.StopDateTime.Value
.DayOfWeek;
```

```
                                        AMPM=getAMPM(ts.StopDateTime.
    Value);
    ReceviedTicket= receviedTicket(ts.DispositionDesc) })
                    |> Seq.filter (fun ts -> ts.ReceviedTicket.IsSome)
                    |> Seq.toArray
```

Sending this to the REPL, we see the last bit of all of our records in the data frame:

```
{Month = 7;
 DayOfWeek = Sunday;
 AMPM = "PM";
 ReceviedTicket = Some false;}; {Month = 7;
                                 DayOfWeek = Sunday;
                                 AMPM = "PM";
                                 ReceviedTicket = Some false;}; ...|]


>
```

With the data shaped somewhat, let's get it ready for Accord. As I mentioned earlier, Accord wants the input data for the decision tree to be in a int [] [] and the output to be in a int []. However, it also needs the inputs to be tagged to make the model work. We achieve that by passing in an array of attributes. Back in the script file, add this code block:

```
let month = DecisionVariable("Month",13)
let dayOfWeek = DecisionVariable("DayOfWeek",7)
let ampm = DecisionVariable("AMPM",2)

let attributes =[|month;dayOfWeek;ampm|]
let classCount = 2
```

Sending this to the REPL, we see:

```
val month : Accord.MachineLearning.DecisionTrees.DecisionVariable

val dayOfWeek : Accord.MachineLearning.DecisionTrees.DecisionVariable

val ampm : Accord.MachineLearning.DecisionTrees.DecisionVariable

val attributes : Accord.MachineLearning.DecisionTrees.DecisionVariable []
=
   [|Accord.MachineLearning.DecisionTrees.DecisionVariable;
     Accord.MachineLearning.DecisionTrees.DecisionVariable;
     Accord.MachineLearning.DecisionTrees.DecisionVariable|]
val classCount : int = 2
```

Some of the sharp-eyed people reading this book might have noticed that the month decision variable has a range of 13 and not 12. This is because the values for month are 1-12 and Accord needs 13 to account for the possibility of any feature value up to 13 (like 12.99—we know that won't exist but Accord does not). Day of week is 0 to 6, so it gets a 7.

So going back to our script, add in the following blocks:

```
let getAMPM' (ampm: string) =
    match ampm with
    | "AM" -> 0
    | _ -> 1

let receivedTicket' value =
    match value with
    | true -> 1
    | false -> 0

let inputs =
    dataFrame
    |> Seq.map (fun ts -> [|(ts.Month); int ts.DayOfWeek;
    getAMPM'(ts.AMPM)|])
    |> Seq.toArray

let outputs =
    dataFrame
    |> Seq.map (fun ts ->
    receivedTicket'(ts.ReceviedTicket.Value))
    |> Seq.toArray
```

Sending this to the REPL, we get the end of our data frame being converted into int arrays:

```
[|7; 0; 0|]; [|7; 0; 0|]; [|7; 0; 0|]; [|7; 0; 0|]; [|7; 0; 0|];
[|7; 0; 0|]; [|7; 0; 0|]; [|7; 0; 0|]; [|7; 0; 0|]; [|7; 0; 0|];
[|7; 0; 1|]; [|7; 0; 1|]; [|7; 0; 1|]; [|7; 0; 1|]; [|7; 0; 1|];
[|7; 0; 1|]; [|7; 0; 1|]; [|7; 0; 1|]; [|7; 0; 1|]; [|7; 0; 1|];
[|7; 0; 1|]; [|7; 0; 1|]; [|7; 0; 1|]; [|7; 0; 1|]; [|7; 0; 1|];
[|7; 0; 1|]; [|7; 0; 1|]; [|7; 0; 1|]; [|7; 0; 1|]; [|7; 0; 1|];
...|]

val outputs : int [] =
  [|0; 1; 0; 1; 0; 0; 1; 0; 0; 0; 0; 0; 0; 1; 0; 0; 0; 0; 0; 0; 1; 1; 1;
0; 1;
```

```
   0; 0; 0; 0; 0; 1; 0; 0; 0; 0; 0; 1; 1; 1; 0; 1; 1; 0; 1; 0; 0; 1; 0;
0; 0;
   0; 0; 0; 1; 0; 1; 0; 0; 0; 0; 1; 0; 0; 0; 0; 0; 0; 0; 0; 0; 1; 1; 0;
0; 0;
   1; 0; 0; 0; 0; 0; 0; 0; 0; 0; 0; 0; 0; 1; 0; 0; 0; 0; 0; 0; 0; 0; 0;
0; 0;
   ...|]
```

```
>
```

With everything setup, let's go ahead and run our tree. Enter this to the script:

```
let tree = DecisionTree(attributes, classCount)
let id3learning = ID3Learning(tree)
let error = id3learning.Run(inputs, outputs)
```

Sending this to the REPL gives us:

val error : float = 0.2843236362

Just like all the other models we have seen so far, we need both an output from the model and some information about how good our model is at predicting based on the data that we provided. In this case, the model is off by 28%, which is pretty high for a decision tree. With the model created, we can now ask the tree to predict if we will get a ticket or a warning on a Saturday in October in the evening.

Enter this script:

```
let query = ([|10;6;1|])
let output = tree.Compute(query)
```

Sending it to the REPL, we see:

val query : int [] = [|10; 6; 1|]

val output : int = 0

It looks like we will get a warning and not a ticket.

As I mentioned, 28% is high for a decision tree. Is there a way to get that number down? Perhaps binning will help. Go back to the REPL and type in this:

```
dataFrame
    |> Seq.countBy (fun ts -> ts.Month)
    |> Seq.sort
    |> Seq.iter (fun t -> printfn "%A" t)
```

```
dataFrame
    |> Seq.countBy (fun ts -> ts.DayOfWeek)
    |> Seq.sort
    |> Seq.iter (fun t ->  printfn "%A" t)


dataFrame
    |> Seq.countBy (fun ts -> ts.AMPM)
    |> Seq.sort
    |> Seq.iter (fun t ->  printfn "%A" t)


dataFrame
    |> Seq.countBy (fun ts -> ts.ReceviedTicket)
    |> Seq.sort
    |> Seq.iter (fun t ->  printfn "%A" t)
```

Sending this to the REPL, we see:

```
(1, 2125)
(2, 1992)
(3, 2529)
(4, 1972)
(5, 2342)
(6, 2407)
(7, 2198)
(8, 2336)
(9, 3245)
(10, 1910)
(11, 1989)
(12, 1664)
(Sunday, 3019)
(Monday, 3169)
(Tuesday, 3549)
(Wednesday, 4732)
(Thursday, 4911)
(Friday, 4012)
(Saturday, 3317)
("AM", 9282)
("PM", 17427)
(Some false, 19081)
(Some true, 7628)

val it : unit = ()
```

Perhaps we can bin the months of the year in quarters? Let's create a function that does that. Go into the script file and enter this:

```
let getQuarter(month:int) =
    match month with
    | 1 | 2 | 3 -> 1
    | 4 | 5 | 6 -> 2
    | 7 | 8 | 9 -> 3
    | _ -> 4

let inputs' =
    dataFrame
    |> Seq.map (fun ts -> [|getQuarter((ts.Month));
    int ts.DayOfWeek; getAMPM'(ts.AMPM)|])
    |> Seq.toArray

let outputs' =
    dataFrame
    |> Seq.map (fun ts ->
    receivedTicket'(ts.ReceviedTicket.Value))
    |> Seq.toArray

let error' = id3learning.Run(inputs', outputs')
```

Sending this to the REPL, we see this:

```
val error' : float = 0.2851473286
```

This did not improve our model. Perhaps we can keep working with the data, or perhaps there is not a correlation between a ticket/warning based on the data that we have. Walking away from a model is often one of the hardest things you have to do in data science, especially if you have spent a considerable amount of time on it, but it is often the right thing to do.

numl

Before we leave decision trees, I want to look at another way of calculating them. Instead of using Accord.Net, I want to introduce another .Net machine learning library called **numl**. numl is a new kid on the block and can offer a lower barrier entry to machine learning. Although not as expansive as Accord, it does offer many common models, including a decision tree.

Go to **Solution Explorer** and add another script called `numl.fsx`. Then go into the NuGet package manager and pull down numl:

```
PM> Install-Package numl
```

Go back to the numl script and enter in the following code:

```
#r "System.Data.Entity.dll"
#r "FSharp.Data.TypeProviders.dll"
#r "System.Data.Linq.dll"

open System
open System.Data.Linq
open System.Data.Entity
open Microsoft.FSharp.Data.TypeProviders

[<Literal>]
let connectionString = "data
source=nc54a9m5kk.database.windows.net;initial
catalog=Traffic;user
id=chickenskills@nc54a9m5kk;password=sk1lzm@tter;"

type EntityConnection =
SqlEntityConnection<connectionString,Pluralize = true>
let context = EntityConnection.GetDataContext()

type TrafficStop = {Month:int; DayOfWeek:DayOfWeek; AMPM: string;
ReceivedTicket: option<bool>}

let getAMPM (stopDateTime:System.DateTime) =
    match stopDateTime.Hour < 12 with
    | true -> "AM"
    | false -> "PM"

let receviedTicket (disposition:string) =
    match disposition.ToUpper() with
    | "CITATION" -> Some true
    | "VERBAL WARNING" | "WRITTEN WARNING" -> Some false
    | _ -> None


let dataFrame =
    context.dbo_TrafficStops
    |> Seq.map (fun ts ->
     {Month=ts.StopDateTime.Value.Month;DayOfWeek=
     ts.StopDateTime.Value.DayOfWeek;
       AMPM=getAMPM(ts.StopDateTime.Value); ReceivedTicket=
         receviedTicket(ts.DispositionDesc) })
    |> Seq.filter (fun ts -> ts.ReceivedTicket.IsSome)
    |> Seq.toArray
```

This is the same code as the `Accord.fsx` script, so you can copy and paste it from there. Send it to the REPL to make sure you copy-pasted it correctly. Next, add in this block to reference numl.

```
#r "../packages/numl.0.8.26.0/lib/net40/numl.dll"
open numl
open numl.Model
open numl.Supervised.DecisionTree
```

Next, enter this block of code:

```
type TrafficStop' = {[<Feature>] Month:int; [<Feature>]
DayOfWeek:int;
    [<Feature>] AMPM: string; [<Label>] ReceivedTicket: bool}

let dataFrame' =
    dataFrame
    |> Seq.map (fun ts -> {TrafficStop'.Month = ts.Month;
    DayOfWeek = int ts.DayOfWeek; AMPM=ts.AMPM;
    ReceivedTicket=ts.ReceivedTicket.Value})
    |> Seq.map box

let descriptor = Descriptor.Create<TrafficStop'>()
```

Sending that to the REPL, returns this:

```
type TrafficStop' =
  {Month: int;
   DayOfWeek: int;
   AMPM: string;
   ReceivedTicket: bool;}
val dataFrame' : seq<obj>
val descriptor : Descriptor =
  Descriptor (TrafficStop') {
    [Month, -1, 1]
    [DayOfWeek, -1, 1]
    [AMPM, -1, 0]
  * [ReceivedTicket, -1, 1]
}
```

There are two things to notice here. First, just like Accord, numl wants the input to its modeling engine to be in a certain format. In this case, it is not arrays of ints. Rather, it wants object types (as of the time of writing). In order to know what to make of each object, it needs to have attributes associated with each element, hence the `TrafficStop'` type that has either `[Feature]` or `[Label]` added. As you can guess, features are for input and labels are for outputs. The second thing to notice is that we call `|> Seq.map box`. This converts our types such as int, string, and bool to object, which is what numl wants.

With that out of the way, we can see what numl comes up with. Enter this into the script window:

```
let generator = DecisionTreeGenerator(descriptor)
generator.SetHint(false)
let model = Learner.Learn(dataFrame', 0.80, 25, generator)
```

Sending that to the REPL, we get:

```
val generator : DecisionTreeGenerator
val model : LearningModel =
  Learning Model:
  Generator numl.Supervised.DecisionTree.DecisionTreeGenerator
  Model:
  [AM, 0.0021]
   |- 0
   |   [Month, 0.0021]
   |    |- 1 ≤ x < 6.5
   |    |   [DayOfWeek, 0.0001]
   |    |    |- 0 ≤ x < 3
   |    |    |   +(False, -1)
   |    |    |- 3 ≤ x < 6.01
   |    |    |   +(False, -1)
   |    |- 6.5 ≤ x < 12.01
   |    |   +(False, -1)
   |- 1
   |   +(False, -1)


  Accuracy: 71.98 %


>
```

One of the nice things about numl is that the `ToString()` overload prints out a graphical representation of our tree. This is a great way to quickly visually inspect to see what we have. You can also see that the accuracy of the model is pretty much the same as Accord. If you run this script several times, you will get slightly different answers because of the way numl splits the data. Taking another look at the tree, let's see if we can interpret it in more detail.

The modeling engine found that the best feature to start splitting on was AM/PM. If the traffic stop was in the afternoon, you will get a warning and not a ticket. If it was in the morning, we moved down to the next decision point on the tree. What we can see is that, if the traffic stop occurred in the AM between July and December, we would not get a ticket. If the AM traffic stop was between Jan and June, we would have to go to the next level, which is the day of the week. In this case, the model split between Sunday-Tuesday and Wednesday-Saturday. You will notice that both terminal nodes are false too. Where is the true? Can the model predict that I will get a ticket? No, this model cannot reasonably predict when you will get a ticket. As before, we will have to leave this model behind. However, this exercise was not a waste because we will use this data with some more data and a different model to create something that has some practical value.

One last question before we leave this chapter, "What machine learning is going on here?" We can say that numl is using machine learning because it is doing several iterations with the data. But what does that mean? If you look at the last line of code we wrote, `let model = Learner.Learn(dataFrame', 0.80, 25, generator)`, you can see that the third argument is 25. This is the number of times the model is run and then numl picks the best model. In effect, then, the machine is "learning" but evaluating several possible models and selecting one for us. I don't really consider this machine learning because we are not introducing new data to the learning to make it smarter.

In the next chapter, we will look at using testing and training sets to accomplish some of that, but we still have the problem that this is a point-in-time analysis. How would you make this model self-teaching? Point of fact, I would not bother with the model in its current state because the model has been demonstrated to be useless. However, if the model was useful, I can imagine a scenario where we constantly update the dataset and run the model based on more datasets that our open data friends can get their hands on. With that, we can have an application running that might remind drivers before they leave the house in the morning that based on the date/time/weather/other factors, they should be taking it easier than normal. Perhaps a simple text or tweet to the driver? In any event, once we have a real model, we can see an application like this in action.

Summary

In this chapter, we put on our data scientist hat and took a look at using F# to do data exploration and analysis. We were exposed to open data and the awesomeness of type providers. We then implemented a decision tree, though ultimately we concluded that the data did not show a significant relationship.

In the next chapter, we will address some of the issues that we have been glossing over so far and take a deep dive into obtaining, cleaning, and organizing our data.

5

Time Out – Obtaining Data

In this chapter, we are going to break from looking at various machine learning models. Instead, we are going to revisit some of the issues that I glossed over in *Chapter 2*, *AdventureWorks Regression*, *Chapter 3*, *More AdventureWorks Regression*, and *Chapter 4*, *Traffic Stops – Barking Up the Wrong Tree?*. We are going to look at different ways in which we can obtain data using Visual Studio and type providers. We will then look at how type providers help us solve problems of missing data, how we can use parallelism to speed up our data extraction, and how we can use type providers on secured web services.

Overview

One of the underappreciated skills that a data scientist must possess is the ability to gather and assimilate heterogeneous data. Heterogeneous data is data from different sources, structures, and formats. Heterogeneous stands in contrast to homogenous data which assumes that all of the data that is imported is the same as all of the other data that may already exist. When the data scientist gets heterogeneous data, one of the first things they will do is transform the data to a point that it can be combined with the other data. The most common shape of that transformation is the **data frame**—sometimes called the *rectangle* because the columns are attributes and the rows are the data. For example, here is a data frame that we have seen earlier:

ProductID	Sales	Cust Review	LogReiews	Cust Review
757	156	3.94	2.193124598	3.94
993	272	3.48	2.434568904	3.48
960	281	3.57	2.44870632	3.57
989	282	3.39	2.450249108	3.39
978	292	3.31	2.465382851	3.31

Ideally, each frame has a unique key that allows it to be combined with other data frames. In this case, **ProductID** is the primary key. If you are thinking that this is a lot like RDBMS theory—you are right.

One of the bigger differences between a research analysts and a line of business developer is how they approach using data in their project. For the software engineer, data elements must be meticulously defined, created, and tracked. For the research analyst, all of that mental effort is noise that is tangential to solving the problem.

This is where the power of type providers comes in. Instead of spending any effort on extracting data, we spend our time transforming, shaping, and analyzing it.

SQL Server providers

Even though there is lots of buzz surrounding `no-sql` databases like MongoDb and unstructured data stores like *data lakes* (or *data swamps*, depending on your point of view), a significant percentage of data that our industry works with is still stored in relational databases. As we have seen in prior chapters, the data scientist must be able to effectively communicate with relational databases using SQL. However, we also saw that F# offers the ability to use something called a type provider to access SQL Server.

Non-type provider

Let's go back to the SQL that was used in *Chapter 3, More AdventureWorks Regression,* to bring down the Average Orders, Average Reviews, and List Price for individual customers and see how to do it differently. Go into Visual Studio and create an F# Windows Library called `TypeProviders`.

Notice that I am using .NET Framework 4.5.2. The framework's minor version does not matter, as long as it is 4.x. It is important to note that you cannot use type providers with **Portable Class Libraries (PCLs)**.

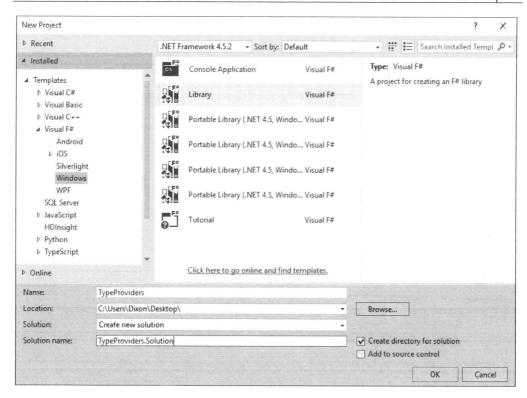

Once Visual Studio generates the files for you, go ahead and delete `Library1.fs` and remove all the contents of `Script1.fsx`. Rename `Scipt1.fsx` to `SqlServerProviders.fsx`. Next, add a reference to `System.Transactions`:

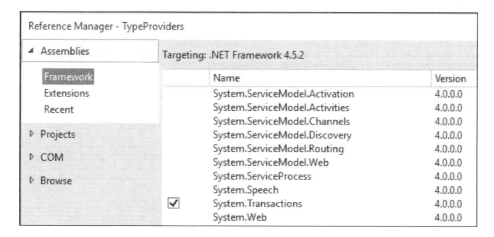

Go into SqlServerProviders.fsx and add this code (you can copy it from *Chapter 3, More AdventureWorks Regression,* it is identical):

```
#r "System.Transactions.dll"

open System
open System.Text
open System.Data.SqlClient

type ProductInfo = {ProductID:int; AvgOrders:float; AvgReviews: float;
ListPrice: float}

let productInfos = ResizeArray<ProductInfo>()

[<Literal>]
let connectionString = "data source=nc54a9m5kk.database.windows.
net;initial catalog=AdventureWorks2014;user id= PacktReader;password=
P@cktM@chine1e@rning;"

[<Literal>]
let query =
    "Select
    A.ProductID, AvgOrders, AvgReviews, ListPrice
    From
    (Select
    ProductID,
    (Sum(OrderQty) + 0.0)/(Count(Distinct SOH.CustomerID) + 0.0)
      as AvgOrders
    from [Sales].[SalesOrderDetail] as SOD
    inner join [Sales].[SalesOrderHeader] as SOH
    on SOD.SalesOrderID = SOH.SalesOrderID
    inner join [Sales].[Customer] as C
    on SOH.CustomerID = C.CustomerID
    Where C.StoreID is not null
    Group By ProductID) as A
    Inner Join
    (Select
    ProductID,
    (Sum(Rating) + 0.0) / (Count(ProductID) + 0.0) as AvgReviews
    from [Production].[ProductReview] as PR
    Group By ProductID) as B
    on A.ProductID = B.ProductID
    Inner Join
    (Select
```

```
            ProductID,
            ListPrice
            from [Production].[Product]
            ) as C
            On A.ProductID = C.ProductID"

    let connection = new SqlConnection(connectionString)
    let command = new SqlCommand(query,connection)
    connection.Open()
    let reader = command.ExecuteReader()
    while reader.Read() do
        productInfos.Add({ProductID=reader.GetInt32(0);
                            AvgOrders=(float)(reader.GetDecimal(1));
                            AvgReviews=(float)(reader.GetDecimal(2));
                            ListPrice=(float)(reader.GetDecimal(3));})

    productInfos
```

There are 52 lines of total code here, 26 of which are SQL inside the string called query. This seems like a lot of work for something that appears to be pretty basic. Also, if we want to change our output rectangle, we would have to rewrite this SQL and hope we got it right. Also, we now need to know some fairly advanced SQL even though we don't care one whit that the data is stored in a SQL Server database. How can type providers help us here?

SqlProvider

Go back into Visual Studio, open up the nugget package manager, and enter this:

```
PM> Install-Package SQLProvider -prerelease
```

Next, go into the script file and add this:

```
#r "../packages/SQLProvider.0.0.11-alpha/lib/ FSharp.Data.SQLProvider.
dll"
```

Warning

Type Providers are constantly changing their version number. Therefore, SQLProvider.0.0.11 will fail unless you edit it. To determine the correct version, go into the packages folder in your solution and look at the path.

Once you put in the correct version of the provider, you might get a dialog box that looks like this (this is from the last chapter):

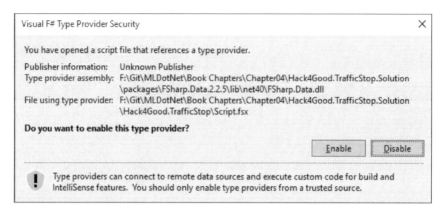

Click on **Enable**. Heading back to the script, go ahead and enter the following code:

```
open System
open System.Linq
open FSharp.Data.Sql

[<Literal>]
let connectionString = "data source=nc54a9m5kk.database.windows.
net;initial catalog=AdventureWorks2014;user id= PacktReader;password=
P@cktM@chine1e@rning;"

type AdventureWorks = SqlDataProvider<Common.DatabaseProviderTypes.
MSSQLSERVER,
  connectionString>
let context = AdventureWorks.GetDataContext()

Sending that to the FSI gives us this:
val connectionString : string =
  "data source=nc54a9m5kk.database.windows.net;initial
    catalog=A"+[72 chars]
type AdventureWorks = SqlDataProvider<...>
val context : SqlDataProvider<...>.dataContext
```

Enter the following code in the script file:

```
let customers =
    query {for c in context.Sales.Customer do
            where (c.StoreId > 0)
            select c.CustomerId}
            |> Seq.toArray
```

Sending that to the FSI gives us the following:

```
val customers : int [] =
  [|1; 2; 3; 4; 5; 6; 7; 8; 9; 10; 11; 12; 13; 14; 15; 16; 17; 18; 19;
20; 21;
    22; 23; 24; 25; 26; 27; 28; 29; 30; 31; 32; 33; 34; 35; 36; 37; 38;
39; 40;
    41; 42; 43; 44; 45; 46; 47; 48; 49; 50; 51; 52; 53; 54; 55; 56; 57;
58; 59;
    60; 61; 62; 63; 64; 65; 66; 67; 68; 69; 70; 71; 72; 73; 74; 75; 76;
77; 78;
    79; 80; 81; 82; 83; 84; 85; 86; 87; 88; 89; 90; 91; 92; 93; 94; 95;
96; 97;
    98; 99; 100; ...|]
```

There are a couple of things to notice here. First, we are sending a query (sometimes referred to as a *computational expression*) to the type provider. In this case, we are selecting all customers where the `storeId` is greater than `0` — the individual customers. The expression is everything between the {} symbols. Notice that it is LINQ-syntax, because it is LINQ. If you are not familiar, LINQ stands for **language Integrated Query** and is a language within a language — it allows for querying capabilities to be placed inside your .NET language of choice. The other thing to notice is that the results of the expression are piped to our familiar F# `seq` type. This means we can get any result from the expression and use `seq` to further shape or refine the data. To see this in action, enter this into the script file:

```
let products =
    query {for soh in context.Sales.SalesOrderHeader do
            join sod in context.Sales.SalesOrderDetail on
              (soh.SalesOrderId = sod.SalesOrderId)
            join c in context.Sales.Customer on
              (soh.CustomerId = c.CustomerId)
            join p in context.Production.Product on
              (sod.ProductId = p.ProductId)
            where (c.CustomerId |=| customers)
            select (p.ProductId)}
            |> Seq.distinct
            |> Seq.toArray
```

When you send it to the FSI, you should see an array of product IDs:

```
val products : int [] =
  [|776; 777; 778; 771; 772; 773; 774; 714; 716; 709; 712; 711; 762; 758;
745;
    743; 747; 715; 742; 775; 741; 708; 764; 770; 730; 754; 725; 765; 768;
753;
```

```
    756; 763; 732; 729; 722; 749; 760; 726; 733; 738; 766; 755; 707; 710;
761;
    748; 739; 744; 736; 767; 717; 769; 727; 718; 759; 751; 752; 750; 757;
723;
    786; 787; 788; 782; 783; 779; 780; 781; 815; 816; 808; 809; 810; 823;
824;
```

Going back to the code, we are joining three tables from the **AdventureWorks** database together via their foreign keys:

```
join sod in context.Sales.SalesOrderDetail on (soh.SalesOrderId = sod.
SalesOrderId)
join c in context.Sales.Customer on (soh.CustomerId = c.CustomerId)
join p in context.Production.Product on (sod.ProductId = p.ProductId)
```

In the next line, we are selecting only those customers that are in the customers' table that we created previously. Notice that we are using the F# in operator of |=|:

```
where (c.CustomerId |=| customers)
```

Finally, we are selecting only the product IDs and then pulling down all of the values and then selecting the unique values:

```
select (p.ProductId)}
|> Seq.distinct
|> Seq.toArray
```

Let's keep going and see what else we can do. Enter the following into the script:

```
let averageReviews =
    query {for pr in context.Production.ProductReview do
            where (pr.ProductId |=| products)
            select pr}
            |> Seq.groupBy(fun pr -> pr.ProductId)
            |> Seq.map(fun (id,a) -> id, a |> Seq.sumBy(fun pr ->
              pr.Rating), a |> Seq.length)
            |> Seq.map( fun (id,r,c) -> id, float(r)/float(c))
            |> Seq.sortBy(fun (id, apr) -> id)
            |> Seq.toArray
```

Sending this to the REPL we see:

```
val averageReviews : (int * float) [] =
  [|(749, 3.9); (750, 3.977272727); (751, 3.93877551); (752, 4.02173913);
    (753, 3.939393939); (754, 3.965517241); (755, 3.628571429);
    (756, 3.742857143); (757, 3.9375); (758, 3.845070423); (759,
3.483870968);
    (760, 4.035874439);
```

In this block of code, we are pulling down all the reviews. We are then grouping the reviews by product Id. From there, we can sum up the ratings and the count of the number of reviews (using Seq.length). We can then divide the total ratings amount by the number of reviews and get the average review for each product Id. Finally, we throw in a Seq.sortBy and pipe it to an array. All of this F# code should be familiar as it is very similar to how we manipulated data in *Chapter 2, AdventureWorks Regression, Chapter 3, More AdventureWorks Regression,* and *Chapter 4, Traffic Stops – Barking Up the Wrong Tree?*.

Next, let's create a data frame (sometimes called a *rectangle* of data if you are geometrically inclined) of prices for each product:

```
let listPrices =
    query {for p in context.Production.Product do
           where (p.ProductId |=| products)
           select p}
           |> Seq.map(fun p -> p.ProductId, p.ListPrice)
           |> Seq.sortBy(fun (id, lp) -> id)
           |> Seq.toArray
```

Sending that to the REPL, you should see the following:

```
val listPrices : (int * decimal) [] =
  [| (707, 34.9900M); (708, 34.9900M); (709, 9.5000M); (710, 9.5000M);
    (711, 34.9900M); (712, 8.9900M); (714, 49.9900M); (715, 49.9900M);
    (716, 49.9900M); (717, 1431.5000M); (718, 1431.5000M); (719,
1431.5000M);
    (722, 337.2200M); (723, 337.2200M); (725, 337.2200M); (726,
337.2200M);
    (727, 337.2200M)
```

This code does not introduce anything new. We pull down all of the products that are in our array, take the product Id and list price, sort it, and send it to an array. Finally, enter the following into the script file:

```
let averageOrders =
    query {for soh in context.Sales.SalesOrderHeader do
           join sod in context.Sales.SalesOrderDetail on
             (soh.SalesOrderId = sod.SalesOrderId)
           join c in context.Sales.Customer on
             (soh.CustomerId = c.CustomerId)
           where (c.CustomerId |=| customers)
           select (soh,sod)}
           |> Seq.map (fun (soh,sod) -> sod.ProductId,
             sod.OrderQty, soh.CustomerId)
           |> Seq.groupBy (fun (pid,q,cid) -> pid )
```

```
|> Seq.map (fun (pid,a) -> pid, a |> Seq.sumBy
   (fun (pid,q,cid) -> q), a
|> Seq.distinctBy (fun (pid,q,cid) -> cid))
|> Seq.map (fun (pid,q,a) -> pid,q, a |> Seq.length)
|> Seq.map (fun (pid,q,c) -> pid, float(q)/float(c))
|> Seq.sortBy (fun (id, ao) -> id)
|> Seq.toArray
```

Sending this to the REPL gives us the following:

```
val averageOrders : (int * float) [] =
  [|(707, 17.24786325); (708, 17.71713147); (709, 16.04347826);
    (710, 3.214285714); (711, 17.83011583); (712, 22.33941606);
    (714, 15.35576923); (715, 22.82527881); (716, 13.43979058);
    (717, 4.708737864); (718, 5.115789474); (719, 3.303030303);
```

This is a pretty sizable code block so it can look daunting. What we are doing is first pulling down all of the SalesOrderHeaders and SalesOrderDetails as a tuple select (soh, sod). We then pipe that set into a Seq.map that returns a sequence of a tuple that has three elements: ProductId, OrderQty, and CustomerId |> Seq.map(fun (soh,sod) -> sod.ProductId, sod.OrderQty, soh.CustomerId). From there we pipe those tuples into a groupBy for the ProductId |> Seq.groupBy(fun (pid,q,cid) -> pid). From there, we go a bit crazy. Take a look at the next line:

```
|> Seq.map(fun (pid,a) -> pid, a |> Seq.sumBy(fun (pid,q,cid) -> q), a
|> Seq.distinctBy(fun (pid,q,cid) -> cid))
```

Hopefully, you remember the discussion about GroupBy, so you realize that the input is a tuple of ProductId and an array of the three-item tuple of (ProductId, OrderQty, and CustomerId). We create a new three-item tuple that has ProductId, the sum of the OrderQty, and yet another tuple that has the CustomerId and a sequence of the distinct customerId items.

When we pipe this to the next line, we take the length of that last tuple (CustomerId, Array of CustomerIds) as that is the number of unique customers that ordered the product. The three-item tuple is ProductId, SumOfQuantityOrdered, and CountOfUniqueCustomersThatOrdered. Since that is a bit verbose, I used the standard tuple notation of (pid, q, c), where q is SumOfQuantityOrdered and c is CountOfUniqueCustomersThatOrdered. This tuple is then piped to the following:

```
|> Seq.map(fun (pid,q,c) -> pid, float(q)/float(c))
```

We can now get the average number of orders for each product. We then finish off with a sort and send it to an array. We now have three arrays of tuples:

```
averageOrders: ProductId, AverageNumberOfOrders
averageReviews: ProductId, AverageReviews
listPrices: ProductId, PriceOfProduct
```

Ideally, we can then combine these into one array that has `ProductId`, `AverageNumberOfOrders`, `AverageReviews`, and `PriceOfProduct`. To do that, you might think that we can just zip these three arrays up. Go into the script and enter the following:

```
Seq.zip3 averageOrders  averageReviews  listPrices
```

When you send it to the FSI, you will see something disappointing:

```
val it : seq<(int * float) * (int * float) * (int * decimal)> =
  seq
    [((707, 17.24786325), (749, 3.9), (707, 34.9900M));
     ((708, 17.71713147),
```

The arrays are not matching up. Apparently, some products do not have any ratings. What we need is a way to join these three arrays into one array and have the join occur on the `ProductId`. Although we could go back and play around with our `where` clauses in the LINQ expressions, there is an alternative way.

Deedle

Go into the script file and enter the following code:

```
#load "../packages/FsLab.0.3.17/FsLab.fsx"
open Foogle
open Deedle
open FSharp.Data
```

As we did earlier, you will have to make sure the version numbers match. When you send it to the REPL, you will see the following:

```
[Loading F:\Git\MLDotNet\Book Chapters\Chapter05\TypeProviders.Solution\
packages\FsLab.0.3.10\FsLab.fsx]

namespace FSI_0009.FsLab
  val server : Foogle.SimpleHttp.HttpServer option ref
  val tempDir : string
  val pid : int
  val counter : int ref
```

```
val displayHtml : html:string -> unit
namespace FSI_0009.FSharp.Charting
  type Chart with
    static member
      Line : data:Deedle.Series<'K,#FSharp.Charting.value> * ?Name:string *
             ?Title:string * ?Labels:#seq<string> * ?Color:Drawing.Color *
```

What we have done is loaded **Deedle**. Deedle is a neat library created for time-series analysis. Let's see if Deedle can help us with our unbalanced array issue. The first thing we want to do is to take our array of tuples and turn them into data frames. Enter this into the script:

```
let averageOrders' = Frame.ofRecords averageOrders
let listPrices' = Frame.ofRecords listPrices
let averageReviews' = Frame.ofRecords averageReviews
```

Sending this to the FSI, you will see something like the following:

```
       Item1  Item2
0  -> 749    3.9
1  -> 750    3.97727272727273
2  -> 751    3.93877551020408
3  -> 752    4.02173913043478
4  -> 753    3.9393939393939
```

Let's rename `Item1` and `Item2` to something that has a bit more meaning and make the first vector of the fame the primary key of the frame. Enter the following into the script file:

```
let orderNames = ["ProductId"; "AvgOrder"]
let priceNames = ["ProductId"; "Price"]
let reviewNames = ["ProductId"; "AvgReview"]

let adjustFrame frame headers =
    frame |> Frame.indexColsWith headers
          |> Frame.indexRowsInt "ProductId"
          |> Frame.sortRowsByKey

let averageOrders'' = adjustFrame averageOrders' orderNames
let listPrices'' = adjustFrame listPrices' priceNames
let averageReviews'' = adjustFrame averageReviews' reviewNames
Sending that to the REPL, should see something like:
val averageReviews'' : Frame<int,string> =
```

```
        AvgReview
749 -> 3.9
750 -> 3.97727272727273
751 -> 3.93877551020408
```

This code should be fairly self-explanatory. We are creating a function called `adjustFrame` that takes in two arguments: a data frame and an array of strings that will become the header values. We apply the headers via the first pipe, make the first column (`ProductId`) the `primaryKey` via the second pipe, and then sort the frame via the third pipe. We then apply this function to our three data frames: orders, prices, and reviews. Notice that we are using the tick notation.

From there, we can now combine the frames based on their key. Go to the script file and add this:

```
averageOrders'' |> Frame.join JoinKind.Inner listPrices''
                |> Frame.join JoinKind.Inner averageReviews''
```

Sending this to the FSI, you should see the following:

```
        AvgReview          Price     AvgOrder
749 -> 3.9                 3578.2700 4.47457627118644
750 -> 3.97727272727273   3578.2700 4.72727272727273
751 -> 3.93877551020408   3578.2700 4.875
752 -> 4.02173913043478
```

Cool huh? Deedle is a very powerful library that you can use in a variety of scenarios.

Going back to our original task, we now have two different ways to pull data out from a database and transform it. When you do a side-by-side comparison of the ADO.NET SQL ways and the type-provider approach, there are some pretty strong arguments to be made to use the type provider method. First, `SqlDataProvider` is designed for most of the popular relational databases out there. If you moved your **AdventureWorks** database from MS SQL Server to MySql, all you would have to change is the connection string and all the code would be the same. Second, consider that there is no SQL in the type provider implementation. Instead, we are using an F# computational expression to pick what tables and what records we want. This means we don't have to know any SQL and we have even more portability. If we move our AdventureWorks database to a NoSQL database like Mongo or DocumentDb, we would have to swap out a type provider and then change our connection string. Finally, consider our approach to the data using the type provider. We do not have to build any classes ahead of time to put our data into, as types are automatically generated for us.

Also, since we are bringing down small chunks of data to the client that are then transformed, we can run each step of our though process independently. I can't emphasize how important that is; we are extracting and transforming the data with small viewable steps that align with our thought process. We can spend our mental energy and time focusing on the problem at hand and not wading through the syntax of a language we may or may not be comfortable with. The downside of the type provider method is that it may be slower than the ADO.NET approach because there is less opportunity to hand-adjust query optimization. In this case, we are doing ad hoc data exploration and analysis on a small dataset so the performance differences are minor. However, even if it was a large dataset, I would still follow the software engineering mantra of, "Make it right. Then make it fast."

MicrosoftSqlProvider

Before we leave our discussion on type providers, I want to show another type provider that is built upon Entity Framework 7 that has a lot of promise, especially when you want to start using type providers as a replacement to your current ORM. It is called the `EntityFramework.MicrosoftSqlServer` type provider.

Go back to Visual Studio, open the package manager console and enter the following:

```
PM> Install-Package FSharp.EntityFramework.MicrosoftSqlServer –Pre
```

Next, go to your script file and enter the following:

```
#I @"..\packages"
#r @"EntityFramework.Core.7.0.0-rc1-final\lib\net451\EntityFramework.
Core.dll"
#r @"EntityFramework.MicrosoftSqlServer.7.0.0-rc1-final\lib\net451\
EntityFramework.MicrosoftSqlServer.dll"
#r @"EntityFramework.Relational.7.0.0-rc1-final\lib\net451\
EntityFramework.Relational.dll"
#r @"Inflector.1.0.0.0\lib\net45\Inflector.dll"
#r @"Microsoft.Extensions.Caching.Abstractions.1.0.0-rc1-final\lib\
net451\Microsoft.Extensions.Caching.Abstractions.dll"
#r @"Microsoft.Extensions.Caching.Memory.1.0.0-rc1-final\lib\net451\
Microsoft.Extensions.Caching.Memory.dll"
#r @"Microsoft.Extensions.Configuration.1.0.0-rc1-final\lib\net451\
Microsoft.Extensions.Configuration.dll"
#r @"Microsoft.Extensions.Configuration.Abstractions.1.0.0-rc1-final\
lib\net451\Microsoft.Extensions.Configuration.Abstractions.dll"
#r @"Microsoft.Extensions.Configuration.Binder.1.0.0-rc1-final\lib\
net451\Microsoft.Extensions.Configuration.Binder.dll"
#r @"Microsoft.Extensions.DependencyInjection.1.0.0-rc1-final\lib\
net451\Microsoft.Extensions.DependencyInjection.dll"
```

```
#r @"Microsoft.Extensions.Logging.1.0.0-rc1-final\lib\net451\
Microsoft.Extensions.Logging.dll"
#r @"Microsoft.Extensions.Logging.Abstractions.1.0.0-rc1-final\lib\
net451\Microsoft.Extensions.Logging.Abstractions.dll"
#r @"Microsoft.Extensions.OptionsModel.1.0.0-rc1-final\lib\net451\
Microsoft.Extensions.OptionsModel.dll"
#r @"Microsoft.Extensions.Primitives.1.0.0-rc1-final\lib\net451\
Microsoft.Extensions.Primitives.dll"
#r @"Remotion.Linq.2.0.1\lib\net45\Remotion.Linq.dll"
#r @"System.Collections.Immutable.1.1.36\lib\portable-
net45+win8+wp8+wpa81\System.Collections.Immutable.dll"
#r @"System.Diagnostics.DiagnosticSource.4.0.0-beta-23516\lib\
dotnet5.2\System.Diagnostics.DiagnosticSource.dll"
#r @"Ix-Async.1.2.5\lib\net45\System.Interactive.Async.dll"

#r "../packages/Microsoft.Extensions.DependencyInjection.
Abstractions.1.0.0-rc1-final/lib/net451/Microsoft.Extensions.
DependencyInjection.Abstractions.dll"
#r @"FSharp.EntityFramework.MicrosoftSqlServer.0.0.2.0-alpha\lib\
net451\FSharp.EntityFramework.MicrosoftSqlServer.dll"
```

Yes, I know that is a lot, but you only have to enter this once and you don't have to bring it over to your .fs file. If you don't want to copy and paste this code over to your script, you can just install all of Entity Framework, and these packages will be available. In any event, enter the following into the script file:

```
open System
open System.Data.SqlClient
open Microsoft.Data.Entity
open FSharp.Data.Entity

[<Literal>]
let connectionString = "data source=nc54a9m5kk.database.windows.
net;initial catalog=AdventureWorks2014; user id= PacktReader;password=
P@cktM@chine1e@rning;"

type AdventureWorks = SqlServer<connectionString, Pluralize = true>
let context = new AdventureWorks()
Sending this to the REPL will give you this:
    nested type Sales.SpecialOffer
    nested type Sales.SpecialOfferProduct
    nested type Sales.Store
    nested type dbo.AWBuildVersion
    nested type dbo.DatabaseLog
    nested type dbo.ErrorLog
  end
val context : AdventureWorks
```

Go back to the script file and enter the following:

```
let salesOrderQuery =
    query { for soh in context.``Sales.SalesOrderHeaders`` do
            join sod in context.``Sales.SalesOrderDetails`` on
                (soh.SalesOrderID = sod.SalesOrderID)
            where (soh.OrderDate > DateTime(2013,5,1))
            select(soh)} |> Seq.head
```

When you send this to the FSI, you will see the `SalesOrderheader` Entity Framework type in all its glory:

```
FK_SalesOrderHeader_Address_BillToAddressID = null;

FK_SalesOrderHeader_CreditCard_CreditCardID = null;

FK_SalesOrderHeader_CurrencyRate_CurrencyRateID = null;

FK_SalesOrderHeader_Customer_CustomerID = null;

FK_SalesOrderHeader_SalesPerson_SalesPersonID = null;

FK_SalesOrderHeader_SalesTerritory_TerritoryID = null;

FK_SalesOrderHeader_ShipMethod_ShipMethodID = null;

Freight = 51.7855M;

ModifiedDate = 5/9/2013 12:00:00 AM;

OnlineOrderFlag = true;

OrderDate = 5/2/2013 12:00:00 AM;

PurchaseOrderNumber = null;

RevisionNumber = 8uy;

SalesOrderDetail = null;

SalesOrderHeaderSalesReason = null;

SalesOrderID = 50788;

SalesOrderNumber = "SO50788";

SalesPersonID = null;

ShipDate = 5/9/2013 12:00:00 AM;

ShipMethodID = 1;

ShipToAddressID = 20927;

Status = 5uy;

SubTotal = 2071.4196M;

TaxAmt = 165.7136M;

TerritoryID = 4;

TotalDue = 2288.9187M;

rowguid = 74fca7f8-654b-432f-95fb-0dd42b0e3cf1;}
>
```

The implications are that anything you do with Entity Framework, you can do with the type provider—with no upfront code. No templates, no designers, no nothin'.

Let's press on and see how the type provider handles null. Go into the script and enter the following:

```
let salesOrderQuery' =
    query { for soh in context.``Sales.SalesOrderHeaders`` do
            join sod in context.``Sales.SalesOrderDetails`` on
              (soh.SalesOrderID = sod.SalesOrderID)
            join p in context.``Production.Products`` on
              (sod.ProductID = p.ProductID)
            where (soh.OrderDate > DateTime(2013,5,1) &&
            p.ProductSubcategoryID =  new System.Nullable<int>(1))
            select(soh)} |> Seq.head
salesOrderQuery'
```

When you send this to the FSI, you will see something like the following:

```
        SalesPersonID = null;
        ShipDate = 5/9/2013 12:00:00 AM;
        ShipMethodID = 1;
        ShipToAddressID = 20927;
        Status = 5uy;
        SubTotal = 2071.4196M;
        TaxAmt = 165.7136M;
        TerritoryID = 4;
        TotalDue = 2288.9187M;
        rowguid = 74fca7f8-654b-432f-95fb-0dd42b0e3cf1;}
>
```

Notice that we have to use `System.Nullable<int>` in the `where` condition to account for the fact that `ProductSubcategoyID` is nullable on the database. This leads to one small *gotcha* with using the type provider. You can't use the out of the box `|=|` operator to search for an array of values. For example, if you sent the following to the REPL:

```
let salesOrderQuery''' =
  query { for soh in context.``Sales.SalesOrderHeaders`` do
            join sod in context.``Sales.SalesOrderDetails`` on
              (soh.SalesOrderID = sod.SalesOrderID)
            join p in context.``Production.Products`` on
              (sod.ProductID = p.ProductID)
            where (soh.OrderDate > DateTime(2013,5,1) &&
              p.ProductSubcategoryID |=| [|1;2;3|])
            select(soh)} |> Seq.head
```

You will get the following back:

```
SqlServerProviders.fsx(199,105): error FS0001: This expression was
expected to have type
    Nullable<int>
> but here has type
    int
```

We now need to create an array of nullable ints. Will that work?

```
let produceSubcategories = [|new System.Nullable<int>(1); new System.
Nullable<int>(2); new System.Nullable<int>(3)|]

let salesOrderQuery''' =
query { for soh in context.``Sales.SalesOrderHeaders`` do
        join sod in context.``Sales.SalesOrderDetails`` on (soh.
SalesOrderID = sod.SalesOrderID)
        join p in context.``Production.Products`` on (sod.ProductID =
p.ProductID)
        where (soh.OrderDate > DateTime(2013,5,1) &&
p.ProductSubcategoryID |=| produceSubcategories)
        select(soh)} |> Seq.head
```

Alas, no:

```
System.ArgumentException: The input sequence was empty.
Parameter name: source
    at Microsoft.FSharp.Collections.SeqModule.Head[T](IEnumerable`1
source)
    at <StartupCode$FSI_0024>.$FSI_0024.main@() in F:\Git\MLDotNet\
Book Chapters\Chapter05\TypeProviders.Solution\TypeProviders\
SqlServerProviders.fsx:line 206
Stopped due to error
```

So there are a couple of ways out of this problem. Option number 1, is that you can create a function. Enter the following into your script file:

```
let isBikeSubcategory id =
    let produceSubcategories = [|new System.Nullable<int>(1);
    new System.Nullable<int>(2); new System.Nullable<int>(3)|]
    Array.contains id produceSubcategories

isBikeSubcategory(new System.Nullable<int>(1))
isBikeSubcategory(new System.Nullable<int>(6))
```

```
let salesOrderQuery''' =
    query { for soh in context.``Sales.SalesOrderHeaders`` do
            join sod in context.``Sales.SalesOrderDetails`` on
              (soh.SalesOrderID = sod.SalesOrderID)
            join p in context.``Production.Products`` on
              (sod.ProductID = p.ProductID)
            where (soh.OrderDate > DateTime(2013,5,1) &&
              isBikeSubcategory(p.ProductSubcategoryID))
            select(soh) } |> Seq.head
salesOrderQuery'''
```

Sending this to the FSI gives you the following:

```
Status = 5uy;
SubTotal = 2071.4196M;
TaxAmt = 165.7136M;
TerritoryID = 4;
TotalDue = 2288.9187M;
rowguid = 74fca7f8-654b-432f-95fb-0dd42b0e3cf1;}
```

```
>
```

There is no new code here. We created a function.

But wait! There's more! Go back to the script file and enter the following:

```
let produceSubcategories = [|new System.Nullable<int>(1);
new System.Nullable<int>(2); new System.Nullable<int>(3)|]
let (|=|) id a = Array.contains id a

let salesOrderQuery4 =
    query { for soh in context.``Sales.SalesOrderHeaders`` do
            join sod in context.``Sales.SalesOrderDetails`` on
              (soh.SalesOrderID = sod.SalesOrderID)
            join p in context.``Production.Products`` on
              (sod.ProductID = p.ProductID)
            where (soh.OrderDate > DateTime(2013,5,1) &&
              p.ProductSubcategoryID |=| produceSubcategories )
            select(soh) } |> Seq.head
salesOrderQuery4
```

So what is this line of code?

```
let (|=|) id a = Array.contains id a
```

It is a function named `|=|` that takes in two parameters: the `id` to search and the array that gets searched. This function is called an *infix* operator because we are assigning symbols to stand in for a more descriptive name. Consider how the `+` operator stands in for *Add*. With that infix operator in place, we can go back and make our syntax more intuitive here:

```
where (soh.OrderDate > DateTime(2013,5,1) && p.ProductSubcategoryID
|=| produceSubcategories )
```

There is one more option to consider: just ditching the extra function and inlining `Array.contains`. Go back to the script and enter this in:

```
let produceSubcategories = [|new System.Nullable<int>(1);
new System.Nullable<int>(2); new System.Nullable<int>(3)|]


let salesOrderQuery5 =
    query { for soh in context.``Sales.SalesOrderHeaders`` do
            join sod in context.``Sales.SalesOrderDetails`` on
              (soh.SalesOrderID = sod.SalesOrderID)
            join p in context.``Production.Products`` on
              (sod.ProductID = p.ProductID)
            where (soh.OrderDate > DateTime(2013,5,1) &&
              Array.contains p.ProductSubcategoryID
              produceSubcategories)
            select (soh)} |> Seq.head
salesOrderQuery5
```

Sending this to the REPL gives us the expected return:

```
ShipDate = 5/9/2013 12:00:00 AM;
ShipMethodID = 1;
ShipToAddressID = 20927;
Status = 5uy;
SubTotal = 2071.4196M;
TaxAmt = 165.7136M;
TerritoryID = 4;
TotalDue = 2288.9187M;
rowguid = 74fca7f8-654b-432f-95fb-0dd42b0e3cf1;}

>
```

So we have three different ways to handle the problem. Do we pick the named function, the in-fix operator, or the in-line function? In this case, I would pick the in-fix operator because we are replacing an existing operator that should work and makes the line the most readable. Others might disagree and you have to be prepared as a data scientist to be able to read other people's code, so it is good that you are familiar with all three ways.

SQL Server type provider wrap up

I have already highlighted two SQL type providers in this chapter. There are actually five different type providers that you can use when accessing SQL databases that I know of, and there are certainly more. When you first start using F#, you might be confused about which one to use. For your reference, here is my basic run down:

- `FSharp.Data.TypeProviders.SqlServerProvider`: This is a part of Visual Studio install, is supported by Microsoft, and no new development is going on. Since this is the end of life, you would not want to use this.

- `FSharp.Data.TypeProviders.EntityFrameworkProvider`: This is a part of Visual Studio install, is supported by Microsoft, and no new development is going on. It is good for vanilla databases.

- `FSharp.Data.SqlClient`: This was created by the community. It is a very stable way to pass SQL commands to the server. It does not support LINQ-style computational expressions. It is good for CRUD-based F# operations.

- `FSharp.Data.SqlProvider`: This was created by the community in pre-release, so there is some instability. It is very good for doing LINQ-style computation expressions. It supports different RDMS like Oracle, MySQL, and SQL Server.

- `FSharp.EntityFramework.MicrosoftSqlServer`: This was created by the community. It is in its very early stages, but holds tons of promise to be a great replacement to traditional ORM coding. It is good for doing LINQ-style computation expressions.

Non SQL type providers

Type providers are not just for relational database management systems. In fact, there are JSON type providers, XML type providers, CSV type providers, the list goes on. Let's take a look at a couple and see how we can use them to make some really interesting data frames based on heterogeneous data.

Go into Visual Studio and add a new script file called `NonSqlTypeProviders.fsx`. At the top, bring in all of the references that we'll be using and open up the needed libraries:

```
#load "../packages/FsLab.0.3.17/FsLab.fsx"

#I @"..\packages"
#r @"EntityFramework.Core.7.0.0-rc1-final\lib\net451\EntityFramework.
Core.dll"
#r @"EntityFramework.MicrosoftSqlServer.7.0.0-rc1-final\lib\net451\
EntityFramework.MicrosoftSqlServer.dll"
```

```
#r @"EntityFramework.Relational.7.0.0-rc1-final\lib\net451\
EntityFramework.Relational.dll"
#r @"Inflector.1.0.0.0\lib\net45\Inflector.dll"
#r @"Microsoft.Extensions.Caching.Abstractions.1.0.0-rc1-final\lib\
net451\Microsoft.Extensions.Caching.Abstractions.dll"
#r @"Microsoft.Extensions.Caching.Memory.1.0.0-rc1-final\lib\net451\
Microsoft.Extensions.Caching.Memory.dll"
#r @"Microsoft.Extensions.Configuration.1.0.0-rc1-final\lib\net451\
Microsoft.Extensions.Configuration.dll"
#r @"Microsoft.Extensions.Configuration.Abstractions.1.0.0-rc1-final\
lib\net451\Microsoft.Extensions.Configuration.Abstractions.dll"
#r @"Microsoft.Extensions.Configuration.Binder.1.0.0-rc1-final\lib\
net451\Microsoft.Extensions.Configuration.Binder.dll"
#r @"Microsoft.Extensions.DependencyInjection.1.0.0-rc1-final\lib\
net451\Microsoft.Extensions.DependencyInjection.dll"
#r @"Microsoft.Extensions.Logging.1.0.0-rc1-final\lib\net451\
Microsoft.Extensions.Logging.dll"
#r @"Microsoft.Extensions.Logging.Abstractions.1.0.0-rc1-final\lib\
net451\Microsoft.Extensions.Logging.Abstractions.dll"
#r @"Microsoft.Extensions.OptionsModel.1.0.0-rc1-final\lib\net451\
Microsoft.Extensions.OptionsModel.dll"
#r @"Microsoft.Extensions.Primitives.1.0.0-rc1-final\lib\net451\
Microsoft.Extensions.Primitives.dll"
#r @"Remotion.Linq.2.0.1\lib\net45\Remotion.Linq.dll"
#r @"System.Collections.Immutable.1.1.36\lib\portable-
net45+win8+wp8+wpa81\System.Collections.Immutable.dll"
#r @"System.Diagnostics.DiagnosticSource.4.0.0-beta-23516\lib\
dotnet5.2\System.Diagnostics.DiagnosticSource.dll"
#r @"Ix-Async.1.2.5\lib\net45\System.Interactive.Async.dll"
#r "../packages/Microsoft.Extensions.DependencyInjection.
Abstractions.1.0.0-rc1-final/lib/net451/Microsoft.Extensions.
DependencyInjection.Abstractions.dll"
#r @"FSharp.EntityFramework.MicrosoftSqlServer.0.0.2.0-alpha\lib\
net451\FSharp.EntityFramework.MicrosoftSqlServer.dll"

open System
open Foogle
open Deedle
open FSharp.Data
open System.Data.SqlClient
open Microsoft.Data.Entity
```

Send it to the REPL to make sure you have all of the needed libraries. In the script, add the following code to bring in data from our AdventureWorks SQL Server database. You will notice that I am piping straight to Deedle's dataframe:

```
[<Literal>]
let connectionString = "data source=nc54a9m5kk.database.windows.
net;initial catalog=AdventureWorks2014;user id=chickenskills@
nc54a9m5kk;password=sk1lzm@tter;"

type AdventureWorks = SqlServer<connectionString,
   Pluralize = true>
let context = new AdventureWorks()

let salesNames = ["Date"; "Sales"]
let salesByDay =
    query { for soh in context.``Sales.SalesOrderHeaders`` do
             join sod in context.``Sales.SalesOrderDetails`` on
              (soh.SalesOrderID = sod.SalesOrderID)
             where (soh.OrderDate > DateTime(2013,5,1))
             select(soh) }
        |> Seq.countBy(fun soh -> soh.OrderDate)
        |> Frame.ofRecords
        |> Frame.indexColsWith salesNames
        |> Frame.indexRowsDate "Date"
        |> Frame.sortRowsByKeySend it to the REPL to get this:
                         Sales
5/2/2013 12:00:00 AM   -> 9
5/3/2013 12:00:00 AM   -> 9
:                        ...
6/30/2014 12:00:00 AM -> 96
```

Go back to the script and add some data that is stored in a CSV file from Yahoo Finance. In this case, it is the change in daily stock price for the Dow Jones Industrial Average:

```
let stockNames = ["Date"; "PriceChange"]
type Stocks = CsvProvider<"http://ichart.finance.yahoo.com/table.
csv?s=^DJI">
let dow = Stocks.Load("http://ichart.finance.yahoo.com/table.
csv?s=^DJI")
let stockChangeByDay =
    dow.Rows |> Seq.map(fun r -> r.Date,
       (r.``Adj Close`` - r.Open)/r.Open)
              |> Frame.ofRecords
              |> Frame.indexColsWith stockNames
              |> Frame.indexRowsDate "Date"
              |> Frame.sortRowsByKey
```

Send it to the REPL to get the following:

```
type Stocks = CsvProvider<...>

val dow : CsvProvider<...>

val stockChangeByDay : Frame<int,string> =
```

```
                         PriceChange
1/29/1985 12:00:00 AM   -> 0.011661415911295950151506 2411
1/30/1985 12:00:00 AM   -> -0.0073147907201291486627914499
:                           ...
11/25/2015 12:00:00 AM -> -0.00041636276758741977102 5076
11/27/2015 12:00:00 AM -> 0.0004128690 819110368634773694
```

Go back to the script and add some data that is served up by an API in JSON format from Quandl. In this case, it is the number of sunspots recorded by the Royal Observatory in Belgium.

```
let sunspotNames = ["Date"; "Sunspots"]

type Sunspots = JsonProvider<"https://www.quandl.com/api/v3/datasets/
SIDC/SUNSPOTS_D.json?start_date=2015-10-01&end_date=2015-10-01">
let sunspots = Sunspots.Load("https://www.quandl.com/api/v3/datasets/
SIDC/SUNSPOTS_D.json?start_date=2013-05-01")
let sunspotsByDay =
    sunspots.Dataset.Data |> Seq.map(fun r -> r.DateTime, Seq.head
r.Numbers )
                            |> Frame.ofRecords
                            |> Frame.indexColsWith sunspotNames
                            |> Frame.indexRowsDate "Date"
                            |> Frame.sortRowsByKey
```

When you send it to the FSI, you should get something like the following:

```
val sunspotsByDay : Frame<DateTime,string> =
```

```
                         Sunspots
5/1/2013 12:00:00 AM    -> 142.0
5/2/2013 12:00:00 AM    -> 104.0
:                           ...
10/30/2015 12:00:00 AM -> 88.0
10/31/2015 12:00:00 AM -> 83.0
```

Finally, go back to the script and join all three data frames:

```
let dataFrame = salesByDay |> Frame.join JoinKind.Inner
    stockChangeByDay
                            |> Frame.join JoinKind.Inner
    sunspotsByDay
```

Sending that to the REPL gives:

```
val dataFrame : Frame<DateTime,string> =
```

	PriceChange	Sales	Sunspots
5/2/2013 12:00:00 AM	-> 0.0088858122275952653140731221	9	104.0
5/3/2013 12:00:00 AM	-> 0.0095997784626598973212920005	9	98.0
:	...	...	...
6/27/2014 12:00:00 AM	-> 0.00029319654567666616196704027	82	67.0
6/30/2014 12:00:00 AM	-> -0.0015363085597738848688182542	96	132.0

We'll leave the process of creating a model to see if there is a relationship among the Down Jones Price Change and the number of sunspots on the amount of Sales by Day up to the reader. Before you get too carried away, you might want to consider this website about data elements that have no relation but are correlated (http://tylervigen.com/spurious-correlations). I think this is my favorite one:

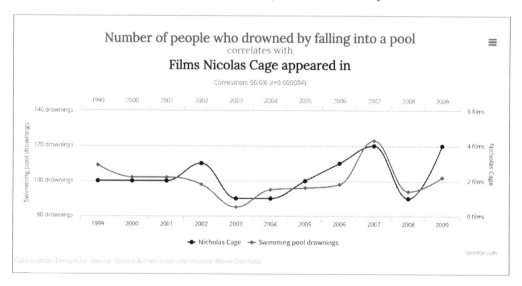

Combining data

Sometimes the data that you obtain from a source system is incomplete. Consider this dataset of crash locations that was obtained from the State Department of Transportation office:

Id	OnRoad	Miles	FromRoad	TowardRoad	Latitude	Longitude
46	PALACE GREEN	0.057	W LOCHMERE DR	KILDAIRE FARM RD	NULL	NULL
220	KILDAIRE FARM RD	2	SHANNON OAKS CIR	CARY PKY	NULL	NULL
240	US 1	0.564	KILDAIRE FARM RD	SE CARY PKY	NULL	NULL
363	1107 WALNUT ST	0.019	HUBBARD LANE	SE MAYNARD RD	NULL	NULL
814	KILDAIRE FARM RD	0.3	STEEP BANK DR	LOCH HIGHLANDS DR	NULL	NULL
878	BUCK JONES RD	3	WA,NUT ST	NOTTINGHAM DR	NULL	NULL
948	WALNUT ST	0.5	MEETING ST	DILLARD DR	NULL	NULL

Notice that latitude and longitude are missing and that location does not use a normal address/city/state pattern. Rather, it is **OnRoad**, **Miles**, **FromRoad**, and **TowardRoad**. Unfortunately, this is fairly common when getting data from public entities—systems may have been built before lat/lon became mainstream and the system's addressing might be designed to only work inside the system. This means we need a way to figure out the latitude and longitude from this atypical addressing.

If you pull the source code down from the site, you will see a couple of script files. The first is called `BingGeocode`. This is a script that goes out to the Bing maps API and returns a geolocation for a given address. The key thing is that, although Bing does not recognize **OnRoad/FromRoad/TowardRoad**, it does recognize cross streets. Therefore, we can take a sample from the crash dataset of incidents that happened at or near intersections—which we can determine from the **OnRoad/FromRoad** as long as the **Miles** value is fairly low. In fact, 90 percent of the records are within a quarter mile of an intersection.

If you inspect the code, you will see that there is nothing particularly new here. We use the JSON type provider to make the call to Bing, and we parse the results, using the `Option` type to return none or some Geolocation. If you want to run this on your machine, we will need to sign up for the Bing Map API developer program here (https://www.bingmapsportal.com/) and put your value into the `apiKey`:

```
#r "../packages/FSharp.Data.2.2.5/lib/net40/FSharp.Data.dll"

open System.IO
open System.Text
```

```
open FSharp.Data

[<Literal>]
let sample = "..\Data\BingHttpGet.json"
type Context = JsonProvider<sample>

let getGeocode address =
    let apiKey = "yourApiKeyHere"
    let baseUri = "http://dev.virtualearth.net/REST/v1/Locations?q=" +
address + "&o=json&key=" + apiKey
    let searchResult = Context.Load(baseUri)
    let resourceSets = searchResult.ResourceSets
    match resourceSets.Length with
    | 0 -> None
    | _ -> let resources = resourceSets.[0].Resources
            match resources.Length with
            | 0 -> None
            | _ -> let resource = resources.[0]
                    Some resource.GeocodePoints

let address = "1%20Microsoft%20Way%20Redmond%20WA%2098052"
let address' = "Webser st and Holtz ln Cary,NC"

getGeocode address'
```

In the solution, there is another script file that does the actual heavy lifting of pulling the original crash data from the database, updating it with the latitude and longitude, and then putting it back into the database. This script file is called UpdateCrashLatLon.fsx. If you look at the code, the first part pulls down crashes that happened in the same town as the traffic stops and occurred within a quarter mile of an intersection. It then creates an address string that is passed to the Bing geocode file and creates a frame with the ID and the latitude and longitude. We then filter that Array with only the values that returned as some:

```
#r "../packages/FSharp.Data.2.2.5/lib/net40/FSharp.Data.dll"
#r "System.Data.Entity.dll"
#r "FSharp.Data.TypeProviders.dll"
#r "System.Data.Linq.dll"
#load "BingGeocode.fsx"

open System
open System.Data.Linq
open System.Data.Entity
open Microsoft.FSharp.Data.TypeProviders
```

```
[<Literal>]
let connectionString = "data
source=nc54a9m5kk.database.windows.net;initial
catalog=Traffic;user
id=chickenskills@nc54a9m5kk;password=sk1lzm@tter;"

type EntityConnection = SqlEntityConnection<connectionString,Plurali
ze = true>
let context = EntityConnection.GetDataContext()

type Crash = {Id: int; OnRoad:string; FromRoad:string }

let trafficCrashes =
    context.dbo_TrafficCrashes
    |> Seq.filter(fun tc -> tc.MunicipalityId = Nullable<int>(13))
    |> Seq.filter(fun tc -> (float)tc.Miles <= 0.25)
    |> Seq.map(fun tc -> {Id=tc.Id; OnRoad=tc.OnRoad; FromRoad=tc.
FromRoad})
    |> Seq.toArray

let trafficCrashes' =
    trafficCrashes
    |> Array.map(fun c -> c.Id, c.OnRoad + " and " + c.FromRoad +
      " Cary,NC")
    |> Array.map(fun (i,l) -> i, BingGeocode.getGeocode(l))

let trafficCrashes'' =
    trafficCrashes'
    |> Array.filter(fun (i,p) -> p.IsSome)
    |> Array.map(fun (i,p) -> i, p.Value.[0].Coordinates.[0],
      p.Value.[0].Coordinates.[1])
```

There is one new line of code in this script: `#load "BingGeocode.fsx"`. This adds
a reference to the script file we already created, so we can go ahead and invoke the
`getGeocode()` function.

Before we update the database with our data, I wrote a script to write the data to the
local disk:

```
//Write so we can continue to work without going to Bing again
//They throttle so you really only want to go there once
open System.IO
let baseDirectory = System.IO.DirectoryInfo(__SOURCE_DIRECTORY__)
let dataDirectory = baseDirectory.Parent.Parent.FullName + @"\Data"
```

```
use outFile = new StreamWriter(dataDirectory + @"\crashGeocode.csv")
trafficCrashes'' |> Array.map (fun (i,lt,lg) -> i.ToString() ,lt.
ToString(), lg.ToString())
                 |> Array.iter (fun (i,lt,lg) -> outFile.
WriteLine(sprintf "%s,%s,%s" i lt lg))
outFile.Flush
outFile.Close()
```

As the comment says, Bing throttles how many requests you can make per hour. The last thing you want is to have to re-query Bing because you are experimenting with the data and get a 401 error back because you are at your limit. Rather, it is much better to bring it local once and work off a local copy.

With the data local, we can then pull down each record from the database that we want to update, update the lat/long, and write it back to the database:

```
type Crash' = {Id: int; Latitude: float; Longitude: float}

let updateDatabase (crash:Crash') =
    let trafficCrash =
        context.dbo_TrafficCrashes
        |> Seq.find(fun tc -> tc.Id = crash.Id)
    trafficCrash.Latitude <- Nullable<float>(crash.Latitude)
    trafficCrash.Longitude <- Nullable<float>(crash.Longitude)
    context.DataContext.SaveChanges() |> ignore

open FSharp.Data
type CrashProvider = CsvProvider<"../Data/crashGeocode.csv">
let crashes =
    CrashProvider.Load("../Data/crashGeocode.csv").Rows
    |> Seq.map(fun r -> {Id=r.id; Latitude=float r.latitude;
      Longitude= float r.longitude})
    |> Seq.toArray
    |> Array.iter(fun c -> updateDatabase(c))
```

Parallelism

I want to show you one more trick that will greatly speed up your data extraction— parallelism. My machine has four cores, but only one core is being used in the prior example when making the API calls to Bing. It would be much faster if I could use all of the cores and make the requests in parallel. F# makes this a snap. As a demonstration, I re-queried Bing for the first 200 crash records and wrote the time out to the FSI:

```
let trafficCrashes =
    context.dbo_TrafficCrashes
    |> Seq.filter (fun tc -> tc.MunicipalityId =
```

```
        Nullable<int>(13))
    |> Seq.filter (fun tc -> (float)tc.Miles <= 0.25)
    |> Seq.map (fun tc -> {Id=tc.Id; OnRoad=tc.OnRoad;
       FromRoad=tc.FromRoad})
    |> Seq.take 200
    |> Seq.toArray

open System.Diagnostics
let stopwatch = Stopwatch()
stopwatch.Start()
let trafficCrashes' =
    trafficCrashes
    |> Array.map (fun c -> c.Id, c.OnRoad + " and " + c.FromRoad +
       " Cary,NC")
    |> Array.map (fun (i,l) -> i, BingGeocode.getGeocode(l))

stopwatch.Stop()
printfn "serial - %A" stopwatch.Elapsed.Seconds
```

When I ran it, it took 33 seconds:

```
serial - 33
```

Next, I added this code:

```
stopwatch.Reset()

open Microsoft.FSharp.Collections.Array.Parallel

stopwatch.Start()
let pTrafficCrashes' =
    trafficCrashes
    |> Array.map (fun c -> c.Id, c.OnRoad + " and " + c.FromRoad +
       " Cary,NC")
    |> Array.Parallel.map (fun (i,l) -> i,
       BingGeocode.getGeocode(l))

stopwatch.Stop()
printfn "parallel - %A" stopwatch.Elapsed.Seconds
```

Notice that the only change was adding a reference to `Collections.Array.Parallel` and then considering the following line:

```
    |> Array.map (fun (i,l) -> i, BingGeocode.getGeocode(l))
```

Change this line to the following:

```
|> Array.Parallel.map (fun (i,l) -> i, BingGeocode.getGeocode(l))
```

When I ran it, I saw this in the FSI:

```
parallel - 12
```

So I got a 3x speed improvement by changing one line. Because F# was built from the ground-up with parallelism and async in mind, it is very easy to take advantage of these concepts. The other languages have these features bolted on and can be very cumbersome to use and often can lead to race conditions or worse.

There is one more thing to note when you are pulling mass data from a web service. Unless you explicitly code it, you have no real way of monitoring the progress. I often pop open Fiddler (`http://www.telerik.com/fiddler`) and monitor the HTTP traffic to see how things are progressing.

Fiddler Web Debugger				
File Edit Rules Tools View Help GET /book ▓ GeoEdge				
▓ WinConfig ◯ ⚡ Replay ✗ ▾ ▶ Go 🔽 Stream ▓ Decode	Keep: All sessions ▾			
#	Result	Protocol	Host	URL
64	200	HTTP	dev.virtualearth.net	/REST/v1/Locations?q=
65	200	HTTP	dev.virtualearth.net	/REST/v1/Locations?q=
66	200	HTTP	dev.virtualearth.net	/REST/v1/Locations?q=
67	200	HTTP	dev.virtualearth.net	/REST/v1/Locations?q=
68	200	HTTP	dev.virtualearth.net	/REST/v1/Locations?q=
69	200	HTTP	dev.virtualearth.net	/REST/v1/Locations?q=
70	200	HTTP	dev.virtualearth.net	/REST/v1/Locations?q=
71	200	HTTP	dev.virtualearth.net	/REST/v1/Locations?q=
72	200	HTTP	dev.virtualearth.net	/REST/v1/Locations?q=
73	200	HTTP	dev.virtualearth.net	/REST/v1/Locations?q=
74	200	HTTP	dev.virtualearth.net	/REST/v1/Locations?q=
75	200	HTTP	dev.virtualearth.net	/REST/v1/Locations?q=
76	200	HTTP	dev.virtualearth.net	/REST/v1/Locations?q=
77	200	HTTP	dev.virtualearth.net	/REST/v1/Locations?q=

JSON type provider – authentication

The JSON type provider is a very handy tool, but there is a limitation to its out of the box implementation—it assumes that the web service does not have any authentication or the authentication token is part of the query string. Some datasets are not like that—in fact most web services use headers for authentication. Fortunately, there is a way to code around this.

Consider this open dataset—the NOAA archives (http://www.ncdc.noaa.gov/ cdo-web/webservices/v2). If you look at the solution that comes with the chapter, there is a script file called GetWeatherData.fsx. In this script, I picked a single zip code for the town where the traffic stops and crashes occurred and pulled down the daily precipitation:

```
#r "System.Net.Http.dll"
#r "../packages/FSharp.Data.2.2.5/lib/net40/FSharp.Data.dll"

open System
open System.Net
open FSharp.Data
open System.Net.Http
open System.Net.Http.Headers
open System.Collections.Generic

[<Literal>]
let uri = "http://www.ncdc.noaa.gov/cdo-web/api/v2/data?datasetid
=GHCND&locationid=ZIP:27519&startdate=2012-01-01&enddate=2012-12-
31&limit=1000"
let apiToken = "yourApiTokenHere"
use client = new WebClient()
client.Headers.Add("token", apiToken)
let resultJson = client.DownloadString(uri)

[<Literal>]
let weatherSample = "..\Data\NOAAHttpGet.json"
type weatherServiceContext = JsonProvider<weatherSample>
let searchResult = weatherServiceContext.Parse(resultJson)
let results = searchResult.Results

let dailyPrecipitation =
    results
    |> Seq.where (fun r -> r.Value > 0)
    |> Seq.groupBy (fun r -> r.Date)
    |> Seq.map (fun (d,a) -> d, a |> Seq.sumBy (fun r -> r.Value))
    |> Seq.sortBy (fun (d,c) -> d)
```

There is one thing new here. I am using the JSON type provider but the authorization token needs to be in the header of the request. Since the JSON type provider does not allow you to set headers, you need to pull the data down via the System.Net.WebClient class (where you can set the auth token in the header) and then use the JSON type provider to parse the results. You can see that I am using Parse() and not Load() in the following line to accomplish that:

```
let searchResult = weatherServiceContext.Parse(resultJson)
```

Just like the geolocation data, I then pushed the data frame to disk because the number of requests are limited:

```
open System.IO
let baseDirectory = System.IO.DirectoryInfo(__SOURCE_DIRECTORY__)
let dataDirectory = baseDirectory.Parent.Parent.FullName +
  @"\Data"

use outFile = new StreamWriter(dataDirectory +
  @"\dailyPrecipitation.csv")
dailyPrecipitation
    |> Seq.map(fun (d,p) -> d.ToString(), p.ToString())
    |> Seq.iter(fun (d,p) ->
      outFile.WriteLine(sprintf "%s,%s" d p))

outFile.Flush
outFile.Close()
```

Also, like the data geolocation data, you can do this on your machine but you will need an `apiToken`. You can go to the NOAA developer website to apply for one. I also added the data as a table on the SQL Server so you don't have to pull the data from the source code to write the remaining code in the chapter. Go into the active `kmeans.fsx` script file and enter this to get the data from the database:

```
type DailyPercipitation = {WeatherDate: DateTime; Amount: int; }
let dailyWeather =
    context.dbo_DailyPercipitation
    |> Seq.map(fun dw -> {WeatherDate=dw.RecordDate;
      Amount=dw.Amount;})
    |> Seq.toArray
```

When you send it to the FSI, you will get the following:

```
type DailyPercipitation =
  {WeatherDate: DateTime;
   Amount: int;}
val dailyWeather : DailyPercipitation [] =
  [|{WeatherDate = 1/9/2012 12:00:00 AM;
     Amount = 41;};
    {WeatherDate = 1/10/2012 12:00:00 AM;
     Amount = 30;};
    {WeatherDate = 1/11/2012 12:00:00 AM;
     Amount = 5;};
```

```
{WeatherDate = 1/12/2012 12:00:00 AM;
 Amount = 124;};
{WeatherDate = 1/13/2012 12:00:00 AM;
 Amount = 5;};
{WeatherDate = 1/21/2012 12:00:00 AM;
...
```

Summary

If you ask a data scientist what they like least about their day, they will tell you meetings, building slide decks, and munging data in no particular order. Although F# type providers can't help you with meetings and building slide decks, it can decrease the amount of time spent obtaining and cleaning data. Although not completely frictionless, type providers can help you with relational and non-relational data stores and enable you to spend more time with the "fun" parts of data science. Speaking of which, let's jump back into the fun with KNN and Naïve Bayes modeling.

6
AdventureWorks Redux – k-NN and Naïve Bayes Classifiers

Let's jump back to AdventureWorks and put our software engineer hat back on. A couple weeks after your successful implementation of a model to improve high-margin bike sales to individual customers, the CEO comes to your desk and says, "Can you help us with a problem? If you were not aware, we started out as a bike-only company. Then, in May of 2013, we added additional merchandise to our product offering. Although it went well in the beginning, we seem to have plateaued. We want to try to push a bit harder in this area. Through some basic PowerBI reporting, we see that anywhere from 86 percent to 88 percent of the customers who buy a bike also buy additional merchandise at the time of purchase."

Year Month	Cross	Solo	Total	%Cross
201305	25	295	320	7.8%
201306	429	69	498	86.1%
201307	441	56	497	88.7%
201308	525	83	608	86.3%
201309	536	68	604	88.7%
201310	649	100	749	86.6%
201311	868	136	1,004	86.5%
201312	698	99	797	87.6%
201401	800	97	897	89.2%
201402	702	96	798	88.0%
201403	891	135	1,026	86.8%

Year Month	Cross	Solo	Total	%Cross
201404	965	121	1,086	88.9%
201405	1,034	152	1,186	87.2%
TOTAL	8,563	1,507	10,070	85.0%

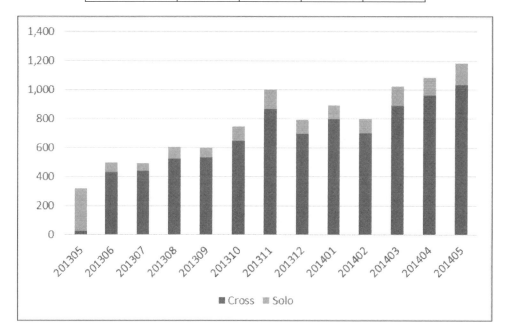

The CEO continues, "We would love to be able to get that up above 90 percent. We launched an expensive marketing campaign, but it really didn't move the needle. Is there any way you can help us be more focused and identify those people on the fence for cross-selling opportunities?"

You say, "Sure," and immediately start thinking of a way to implement her instructions. Perhaps if you could identify some unique characteristics of those customers who buy additional merchandise compared to those customers who do not, a more targeted method might be implemented to get more people to buy additional merchandise. You immediately think of classification models like **K-Nearest Neighbor (k-NN)** and **Naïve Bayes**. Since you are not sure which one might work, you decide to try them both out.

k-Nearest Neighbors (k-NN)

k-NN stands for k-Nearest Neighbors and is one of the most basic classification models available. Since a picture is worth a thousand words, let's take a look at k-NN from a graphical perspective. Consider a group of students who spent some amount of time studying and also drinking beers the night before the exam. On a graph, it looks like this:

If I added a seventh student to the graph like this, would you think that the student passed or failed the exam?

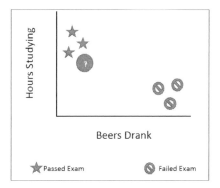

You would likely say they are a star—they passed the exam. If I asked you why, you would probably say that are more like the other stars. This kind of mental processing is very much how our minds work—if everyone in your neighborhood buys a Japanese car and thinks it has high quality, you are more likely to buy one too if you are looking for a high quality car. In fact, much of marketing is based on the k-NN theory.

Unlike the brain, which makes associations effortlessly, k-NN actually uses some math to classify. Going back to our seventh student, k-NN would put them in the passing students' group because the distance it is from the other passing students is short relative to the distance from the failing students:

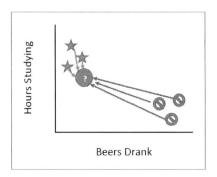

In fact, one of the simplest k-NN implementations is to take the average of all of the items of the category (five hours of studies and drinking one beer for the stars, on average) and measure that distance to the new item. Hopefully, the name k-NN makes sense now—for a given new item K, what are its nearest neighbors?

k-NN example

Let's take a look at k-NN in action using **Accord.NET**. Open up Visual Studio and create a new Visual F# Windows Library project called `Classification`:

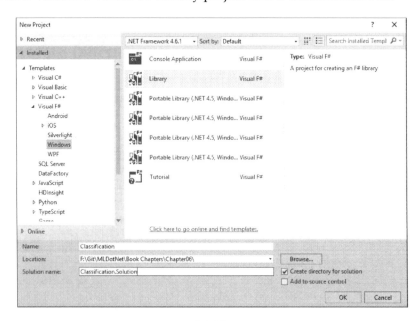

Go into the `Script.fsx` file and remove all of its contents. Rename `Scipt.fsx` to `k-NNAccord.fsx`. Open up **NuGet Package Manager** console and enter this:

```
PM> install-package Accord.MachineLearning
```

Go back to your script and enter in the following code:

```
#r "../packages/Accord.3.0.2/lib/net40/Accord.dll"
#r "../packages/Accord.Math.3.0.2/lib/net40/Accord.Math.dll"
#r "../packages/Accord.MachineLearning.3.0.2/lib/net40/Accord.
MachineLearning.dll"

open Accord
open Accord.Math
open Accord.MachineLearning

let inputs = [|[|5.0;1.0|];[|4.5;1.5|];[|5.1;0.75|];[|1.0;3.5|];[|0.5;
4.0|];[|1.25;4.0|]|]
let outputs = [|1;1;1;0;0;0|]

let classes = 2
let k = 3
let knn = new KNearestNeighbors(k, classes, inputs, outputs)
```

Send this to the REPL to see the following:

```
val inputs : float [] [] =
  [|[|5.0; 1.0|]; [|4.5; 1.5|]; [|5.1; 0.75|]; [|1.0; 3.5|]; [|0.5;
4.0|];
    [|1.25; 4.0|]|]
val outputs : int [] = [|1; 1; 1; 0; 0; 0|]
val classes : int = 2
val k : int = 3
val knn : KNearestNeighbors
```

Most of this code should look familiar to you by now. The inputs represent six students with two characteristics: how many hours they spent studying the night before an exam and how much beer they drank. The outputs represent whether they passed the exam: 1 if they passed, 0 if they did not. The class's value tells Accord that there are two types of values to consider. In this case, those values are the hours spent in studying and the quantity of beer consumed. The k value tells Accord how many data points we want to use for the calculation for each class. If we changed that to 4, then we would have included one failing student with the three passing students (and vice versa), which would have watered down our result.

Go back to the script and enter these lines that represent the seventh student:

```
let input = [|5.0;0.5|]
let output = knn.Compute input
```

When you send it to the FSI, you will see that student number 7 will most likely pass the exam:

```
val input : float [] = [|5.0; 0.5|]

val output : int = 1
```

As I mentioned earlier, k-NN is one of the most basic machine learning models you can use, but in certain circumstances it can be surprisingly powerful. One of the more common adjustments to k-NN is weighing the distance from the neighbors. The closer a point is to the neighbors, the more weight that distance gets. The biggest criticism of k-NN is that it can overweigh if there are many observations that center around one point, so it is important to have a balanced dataset, if possible.

Naïve Bayes

Naïve Bayes is a classification model that attempts to predict if an entity belongs to a series of predefined sets. When you aggregate all the sets together, you have a pretty good estimation of the final result. In order to illustrate, let's go back to the tennis example that we used when talking about decision trees.

We have the following observations for two weeks:

Day	Outlook	Temperature	Humidity	Wind	PlayTennis?
0	sunny	Hot	High	weak	No
1	sunny	Hot	High	strong	No
2	overcast	Hot	High	weak	Yes
3	rain	Mild	High	weak	Yes
4	rain	Cool	Normal	weak	Yes
5	rain	Cool	Normal	strong	No
6	overcast	Cool	Normal	strong	Yes
7	sunny	Mild	High	weak	No
8	sunny	Cool	Normal	weak	yes
9	rain	Mild	Normal	weak	yes
10	sunny	Mild	Normal	strong	yes
11	overcast	Mild	High	strong	yes
12	overcast	Hot	Normal	weak	yes
13	rain	Mild	High	strong	no

For each one of the classes, let's break down whether they wound up playing tennis that day and then do a percentage for each possibility:

ID	Outlook	Yes	No	% Yes	% No
0	sunny	2	3	0.22	0.60
1	overcast	4	0	0.44	0.00
2	rain	3	2	0.33	0.40
	Total	9	5	1.00	1.00

ID	Temperature	Yes	No	% Yes	% No
0	hot	2	2	0.22	0.40
1	mild	4	2	0.44	0.40
2	cool	3	1	0.33	0.20
	Total	9	5	1.00	1.00

ID	Humidity	Yes	No	% Yes	% No
0	high	3	4	0.33	0.80
1	normal	6	1	0.67	0.20
	Total	9	5	1.00	1.00

ID	Wind	Yes	No	% Yes	% No
0	weak	6	2	0.67	0.40
1	strong	3	3	0.33	0.60
	Total	9	5	1.00	1.00

ID	Final	Yes	No	% Yes	% No
0	Play	9	5	0.64	0.36

With these grids available, we can then predict if a person will or will not play tennis for a series of conditions. For example, will a person play on a sunny, cool day with high humidity and strong winds? We can pull the percentages from each grid:

		Yes	No
Outlook	sunny	0.222	0.600
Temperature	cool	0.333	0.200
Humidity	high	0.333	0.800
Wind	strong	0.333	0.600
	final	0.643	0.357

And then the values can be multiplied together for each possibility:

- Probability of Yes = 0.222 * 0.333 * 0.333 * 0.333 * 0.643 = 0.005
- Probability of No = 0.600 * 0.200 * 0.800 * 0.600 * 0.357 = 0.021

You can see that there is a higher percentage not playing than playing. We can also take the two percentages and compare them to each other like this:

0.005 + 0.021 = 0.026

0.005/0.026 = 0.205 and 0.021/0.026 = 0.795

There is about a 20 percent chance of playing tennis and 80 percent chance of not playing.

Naïve Bayes in action

Let's see how Accord.NET calculates a Naïve Bayes model. Go to Visual Studio and add a new script file called `NaiveBayesAccord.fsx`:

In that script, add the following code:

```
#r "../packages/Accord.3.0.2/lib/net40/Accord.dll"
#r "../packages/Accord.Math.3.0.2/lib/net40/Accord.Math.dll"
#r "../packages/Accord.Statistics.3.0.2/lib/net40/Accord.Statistics.
dll"
#r "../packages/Accord.MachineLearning.3.0.2/lib/net40/Accord.
MachineLearning.dll"

open Accord
open Accord.Math
open Accord.Statistics
open Accord.MachineLearning.Bayes

let inputs = [|[|0;0;0;0|];[|0;0;0;1|];[|1;0;0;0|];
               [|2;1;0;0|];[|2;2;1;0|];[|2;2;1;1|];
               [|1;2;1;1|];[|0;1;0;0|];[|0;2;1;0|];
               [|2;1;1;0|];[|0;2;1;1|];[|1;1;0;1|];
               [|1;0;1;0|];[|2;1;0;1|]|]

let outputs = [|0;0;1;1;1;0;1;0;1;1;1;1;1;0|]

let symbols = [|3;3;2;2|]
```

When you send them to the FSI, you will see the following:

```
val inputs : int [] [] =
   [| [|0; 0; 0; 0|]; [|0; 0; 0; 1|]; [|1; 0; 0; 0|]; [|2; 1; 0; 0|];
      [|2; 2; 1; 0|]; [|2; 2; 1; 1|]; [|1; 2; 1; 1|]; [|0; 1; 0; 0|];
      [|0; 2; 1; 0|]; [|2; 1; 1; 0|]; [|0; 2; 1; 1|]; [|1; 1; 0; 1|];
      [|1; 0; 1; 0|]; [|2; 1; 0; 1|] |] |]
```

>

```
val outputs : int [] = [|0; 0; 1; 1; 1; 0; 1; 0; 1; 1; 1; 1; 1; 0|]
```

>

```
val symbols : int [] = [|3; 3; 2; 2|]
```

The inputs are the values turned into integers. Consider the following example:

Outlook	ID
Sunny	0
Overcast	1
Rain	2
Temperature	**ID**
Hot	0
Mild	1
Cool	2
Humidity	**ID**
High	0
Normal	1
Wind	**ID**
Weak	0
Strong	1

The position in each array is *[outlook;temperature;humidity;wind]*.

The outputs are the result values turned into integers:

Play	ID
No	0
Yes	1

The symbols value is an array that tells Accord the total number of possible values for each feature. For example, the first position is for outlook and there are three possible values: (0, 1, 2).

Go back to the script and add in the Naïve Bayes calculation:

```
let bayes = new Accord.MachineLearning.Bayes.NaiveBayes(4,symbols)
let error = bayes.Estimate(inputs, outputs)
```

Sending to the REPL gives the following:

```
val bayes : Bayes.NaiveBayes
val error : float = 0.1428571429
```

The error is calculated by Accord re-running its estimate several times and comparing the actual to the expected. A good way of interpreting the error is that the lower the number is better, and the domain dictates if the actual number is "good enough". For example, a 14 percent error is great for social experiments, where humans are capable for random and unpredictable behaviors. Conversely, a 14 percent error rate for predicting airplane engine failure would not be considered acceptable.

Finally, let's see a prediction for sunny outlook, mild temperature, normal humidity, and weak wind. Go to the script and add this:

```
let input = [|0;1;1;0|]
let output = bayes.Compute(input)
```

Sending to the REPL gives us the following:

```
val input : int [] = [|0; 1; 1; 0|]
val output : int = 1
```

So we will be playing tennis on that day.

One thing to keep in mind while using Naïve Bayes

Created in the 1950s, Naïve Bayes is a highly effective classification model that has stood the test of time. In fact, many spam filters today still use, in part, Naïve Bayes. The biggest advantages of using Naïve Bayes are its simplicity and its ability to, well, be right. The biggest downside is the key assumption that every x variable is completely and utterly independent. If there is any chance that the x variables are collinear, Naïve Bayes breaks down. Also, Naïve Bayes, historically, has been applied to datasets that are Gaussian—that it follows a bell curve. If you are not familiar with a bell curve, it is a distribution of data where the most observations occur in the middle values with the outliers to both sides of the middle having roughly the same number of observations. Here is an example:

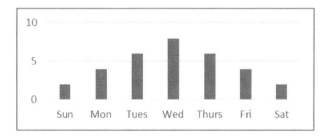

In contrast, a skewed distribution has the most observations at one end or the other:

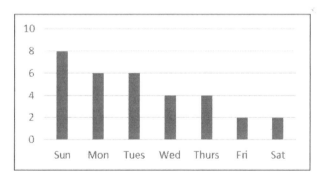

When you use Naïve Bayes, you will have to make sure the distribution you select matches your data. Let's now see if k-NN and/or Naïve Bayes can help us with AdventureWorks.

AdventureWorks

In this section, we are going to take the knowledge that we gained in *Chapter 5, Time Out – Obtaining Data*, to extract and transform data and apply both k-NN and Naïve Bayes machine learning models. Let's see if none, one, or both methodologies will help us increase cross-sales.

Getting the data ready

Go into Visual Studio and add another script called `AdventureWorks.fsx`. Open up the script, remove all of the contents, and open **NuGet Package Manager** console. In the package manager, run the following lines:

```
PM> Install-Package FSharp.EntityFramework.MicrosoftSqlServer -Pre

PM> Install-Package fslab

PM> Install-Package FSharp.Data.SqlClient

PM> Install-Package Microsoft.SqlServer.Types
```

Go back to the script file and add the following references:

```
#I "../packages"

#r "EntityFramework.Core.7.0.0-rc1-final/lib/net451/EntityFramework.
Core.dll"
#r "EntityFramework.MicrosoftSqlServer.7.0.0-rc1-final/lib/net451/
EntityFramework.MicrosoftSqlServer.dll"
#r "EntityFramework.Relational.7.0.0-rc1-final/lib/net451/
EntityFramework.Relational.dll"
#r "Inflector.1.0.0.0/lib/net45/Inflector.dll"
#r "Microsoft.Extensions.Caching.Abstractions.1.0.0-rc1-final/lib/
net451/Microsoft.Extensions.Caching.Abstractions.dll"
#r "Microsoft.Extensions.Caching.Memory.1.0.0-rc1-final/lib/net451/
Microsoft.Extensions.Caching.Memory.dll"
#r "Microsoft.Extensions.Configuration.1.0.0-rc1-final/lib/net451/
Microsoft.Extensions.Configuration.dll"
#r "Microsoft.Extensions.Configuration.Abstractions.1.0.0-rc1-final/
lib/net451/Microsoft.Extensions.Configuration.Abstractions.dll"
#r "Microsoft.Extensions.Configuration.Binder.1.0.0-rc1-final/lib/
net451/Microsoft.Extensions.Configuration.Binder.dll"
#r "Microsoft.Extensions.DependencyInjection.1.0.0-rc1-final/lib/
net451/Microsoft.Extensions.DependencyInjection.dll"
#r "Microsoft.Extensions.Logging.1.0.0-rc1-final/lib/net451/Microsoft.
Extensions.Logging.dll"
#r "Microsoft.Extensions.Logging.Abstractions.1.0.0-rc1-final/lib/
net451/Microsoft.Extensions.Logging.Abstractions.dll"
```

```
#r "Microsoft.Extensions.OptionsModel.1.0.0-rc1-final/lib/net451/
Microsoft.Extensions.OptionsModel.dll"
#r "Microsoft.Extensions.Primitives.1.0.0-rc1-final/lib/net451/
Microsoft.Extensions.Primitives.dll"
#r "Remotion.Linq.2.0.1/lib/net45/Remotion.Linq.dll"
#r "System.Collections.Immutable.1.1.36/lib/portable-
net45+win8+wp8+wpa81/System.Collections.Immutable.dll"
#r "System.Diagnostics.DiagnosticSource.4.0.0-beta-23516/lib/
dotnet5.2/System.Diagnostics.DiagnosticSource.dll"
#r "System.Xml.Linq.dll"
#r "Ix-Async.1.2.5/lib/net45/System.Interactive.Async.dll"
#r "FSharp.EntityFramework.MicrosoftSqlServer.0.0.2.0-alpha/lib/
net451/FSharp.EntityFramework.MicrosoftSqlServer.dll"


#r "../packages/Microsoft.Extensions.DependencyInjection.
Abstractions.1.0.0-rc1-final/lib/net451/Microsoft.Extensions.
DependencyInjection.Abstractions.dll"
#r "../packages/FSharp.Data.SqlClient.1.7.7/lib/net40/FSharp.Data.
SqlClient.dll"
#r "../packages/Microsoft.SqlServer.Types.11.0.2/lib/net20/Microsoft.
SqlServer.Types.dll"
#r "../packages/FSharp.Data.2.2.5/lib/net40/FSharp.Data.dll"


#r "../packages/Accord.3.0.2/lib/net40/Accord.dll"
#r "../packages/Accord.Math.3.0.2/lib/net40/Accord.Math.dll"
#r "../packages/Accord.MachineLearning.3.0.2/lib/net40/Accord.
MachineLearning.dll"
#r "../packages/Accord.Statistics.3.0.2/lib/net40/Accord.Statistics.
dll"


open System
open FSharp.Data
open FSharp.Data.Entity
open Microsoft.Data.Entity


open Accord
open Accord.Math
open Accord.Statistics
open Accord.MachineLearning
open Accord.Statistics.Filters
open Accord.Statistics.Analysis
open Accord.MachineLearning.Bayes
open Accord.Statistics.Models.Regression
open Accord.Statistics.Models.Regression.Fitting
```

Next add the following lines of code:

```
[<Literal>]
let connectionString = "data source=nc54a9m5kk.database.windows.
net;initial catalog=AdventureWorks2014;user id=PacktReader;password=P@
cktM@chine1e@rning;"
type AdventureWorks = SqlServer<connectionString, Pluralize = true>
let context = new AdventureWorks()
```

If you remember from *Chapter 5, Time Out – Obtaining Data*, this is creating our type provider to pull data from the database. Send everything so far to the REPL to see the following:

```
    nested type Sales.SalesTerritoryHistory
    nested type Sales.ShoppingCartItem
    nested type Sales.SpecialOffer
    nested type Sales.SpecialOfferProduct
    nested type Sales.Store
    nested type dbo.AWBuildVersion
    nested type dbo.DatabaseLog
    nested type dbo.ErrorLog
  end
val context : AdventureWorks
```

Go back to the script and add this:

```
let (|=|) id a = Array.contains id a
let productSubcategories = [|new System.Nullable<int>(1); new System.
Nullable<int>(2); new System.Nullable<int>(3)|]
```

Sending this to the FSI gives the following:

```
val ( |=| ) : id:'a -> a:'a [] -> bool when 'a : equality
val productSubcategories : Nullable<int> [] = [|1; 2; 3|]
```

This is also from *Chapter 5, Time Out – Obtaining Data*; we are overriding the in operator to handle null values in the database.

Go back to the script and add the following code:

```
let orderCustomers =
    query { for soh in context.``Sales.SalesOrderHeaders`` do
            join sod in context.``Sales.SalesOrderDetails`` on
            (soh.SalesOrderID = sod.SalesOrderID)
            join p in context.``Production.Products`` on
            (sod.ProductID = p.ProductID)
            join c in context.``Sales.Customers`` on
            (soh.CustomerID = c.CustomerID)
```

```
where (soh.OrderDate > DateTime(2013,5,1) &&
p.ProductSubcategoryID |=| productSubcategories &&
c.StoreID  = System.Nullable<int>())
select(soh.SalesOrderID,c.CustomerID)} |> Seq.toArray
```

Sending this to the REPL, we get:

```
val orderCustomers : (int * int) [] =
  [|(50788, 27575); (50789, 13553); (50790, 21509); (50791, 15969);
    (50792, 15972); (50793, 14457); (50794, 27488); (50795, 27489);
    (50796, 27490); (50797, 17964); (50798, 17900); (50799, 21016);
    (50800, 11590); (50801, 15989); (50802, 14494); (50803, 15789);
    (50804, 24466); (50805, 14471); (50806, 17980); (50807, 11433);
    (50808, 115
```

Even though we haven't seen this exact code before, we have seen code that is pretty close. In this block, we are creating a computational expression. We are joining together the `SalesOrderHeader`, `SalesOrderDetail`, `Products`, and `Customer` tables so we can select only the records we are interested in for this analysis. This would be: all bike sales to individual customers after May 1, 2013. Notice that we are returning two integers as a tuple: the `SalesOrderId` and the `CustomerId`.

Go back to the script and add the following code block:

```
let salesOrderIds = orderCustomers |> Array.distinctBy(fun (soid,coid)
                                                       -> soid)
                                   |> Array.map(fun (soid,cid)
                                                -> soid)
```

Sending this to the FSI gives us the following:

```
val salesOrderIds : int [] =
  [|50788; 50789; 50790; 50791; 50792; 50793; 50794; 50795; 50796; 50797;
    50798; 50799; 50800; 50801; 50802; 50803; 50804; 50805; 50806; 50807;
    50808; 50809
```

As you can probably tell, this creates an array of unique `CustomerIds`. Since a customer might have bought two bikes, they might have two `SalesOrderIds` so we need to call the `distinctBy` high-ordered function.

Go back to the script and enter this:

```
let orderDetailCounts =
    query { for soh in context.``Sales.SalesOrderHeaders`` do
            join sod in context.``Sales.SalesOrderDetails`` on
            (soh.SalesOrderID = sod.SalesOrderID)
```

```
join p in context.``Production.Products`` on
(sod.ProductID = p.ProductID)
join c in context.``Sales.Customers`` on
(soh.CustomerID = c.CustomerID)
where (sod.SalesOrderID |=| salesOrderIds)
select(sod.SalesOrderID, sod.SalesOrderDetailID) }
|> Seq.countBy(fun (soid, sodid) -> soid)
|> Seq.toArray
```

Send this to the FSI to get this (it takes a couple of seconds):

```
val orderDetailCounts : (int * int) [] =
  [|(50788, 1); (50789, 1); (50790, 1); (50791, 1); (50792, 1);
(50793, 1);
    (50794, 1); (50795, 1); (50796, 1); (50797, 1); (50798, 1);
(50799, 1);
    (50800, 1); (50801, 1); (50802, 1); (50803, 1); (50804, 1);
(50805, 1);
    (50806, 1); (50807
```

This is a similar query to the first one. Here we are joining together the same four tables and then selecting both the `SalesOrderId` and the `SalesOrderDetailId` for the customers we have already identified. We then apply the `countBy` high-order function to count up all of the details for each order. If there is only one `OrderDetailId`, then only the bike was purchased. If there is more than one, then the customer purchased items along with the bike.

We now have to pull individual details for a given customer. Since the database is in third normal form, these details are scattered across many tables. Instead of generating a pretty nasty expression, let's use the built-in view that has already been created in the database: `vIndividualCustomer`.

The catch is that the EF type provider cannot handle views at the time of this writing. The answer to this problem is another type provider.

Go to the script and enter this:

```
[<Literal>]
let commandText = "Select * from [Sales].[vIndividualCustomer]"
let command = new SqlCommandProvider<commandText,connectionString>()
let output = command.Execute()
let customers = output |> Seq.toArray
```

Sending this to the REPL, you can see the following:

```
val commandText : string = "Select * from [Sales].[vIndividualCustomer]"
val command : SqlCommandProvider<...>
val output : Collections.Generic.IEnumerable<SqlCommandProvider<...>.Reco
rd>
val customers : SqlCommandProvider<...>.Record [] =
  [|{ BusinessEntityID = 9196; Title = None; FirstName = "Calvin";
MiddleName = Some "A"; LastName = "Raji"; Suffix = None; PhoneNumber
= Some "230-555-0191"; PhoneNumberType = Some "Cell"; EmailAddress =
Some "calvin20@adventure-works.com"; EmailPromotion = 2; AddressType =
"Shipping"; AddressLine1 = "5415 San Gabriel Dr."; AddressLine2 = None;
City = "Bothell"; StateProvinceName = "Washington"; PostalCode = "98011";
CountryRegionName = "United States"; Demographics = Some

  "<IndividualSurvey xmlns="http://schemas.microsoft.com/
sqlserver/2004/07/adventure-works/IndividualSurvey"><TotalPurchas
eYTD>-13.5</TotalPurchaseYTD><DateFirstPurchase>2003-02-06Z</Date
FirstPurchase><BirthDate>1963-06-14Z</BirthDate><MaritalStatus>M</
MaritalStatus><YearlyIncome>50001-75000</YearlyIncome><Gender>M</
Gender><TotalChildren>4</TotalChildren><NumberChildrenAtHome>2</NumberCh
ildrenAtHome><Education>Bachelors </Education><Occupation>Professional</
Occupation><HomeOwnerFlag>1</HomeOwnerFlag><NumberCarsOwned>2</NumberCars
Owned><CommuteDistance>2-5 Miles</CommuteDistance></IndividualSurvey>" };

    { BusinessEntityID
```

Each record is a beast! It looks like the database has a field called `IndividualSurvey` that contains data about some of the customers that was collected on a survey. Interestingly, they decide to store it as XML. I think this proves the axiom that if given a datatype, developers will use it, whether it make sense or not. In any event, how are we going to parse this XML? I'll give you a hint: it rhymes with *hype divider*. That's right, the XML type provider. Go back to the script and add this code:

```
[<Literal>]
let sampleXml = """<IndividualSurvey xmlns="http://schemas.microsoft.
com/sqlserver/2004/07/adventure-works/IndividualSurvey"><TotalPurc
haseYTD>-13.5</TotalPurchaseYTD><DateFirstPurchase>2003-02-06Z</Dat
eFirstPurchase><BirthDate>1963-06-14Z</BirthDate><MaritalStatus>M</
MaritalStatus><YearlyIncome>50001-75000</YearlyIncome><Gender>M</
Gender><TotalChildren>4</TotalChildren><NumberChildrenAtHome>2</Num
berChildrenAtHome><Education>Bachelors </Education><Occupation>Prof
essional</Occupation><HomeOwnerFlag>1</HomeOwnerFlag><NumberCarsOwn
ed>2</NumberCarsOwned><CommuteDistance>2-5 Miles</CommuteDistance></
IndividualSurvey>"""
#r "System.Xml.Linq.dll"
type IndividualSurvey = XmlProvider<sampleXml>
```

```
let getIndividualSurvey (demographic:Option<string>) =
    match demographic.IsSome with
    | true -> Some (IndividualSurvey.Parse(demographic.Value))
    | false -> None
```

Sending this to the REPL gives us the following:

```
type IndividualSurvey = XmlProvider<...>
val getIndividualSurvey :
  demographic:Option<string> -> XmlProvider<...>.IndividualSurvey option
```

The XML type provider takes a representative sample to generate the types. In this case, sampleXML is being used to generate the types. With this type provider handling the heavy lifting of parsing the XML for us, we can now create a data structure for each CustomerId and their demographic information in an easy-to-use format.

Go back to the script and enter this:

```
let customerDemos = customers |> Array.map(fun c -> c.BusinessEntityID
  ,getIndividualSurvey(c.Demographics))
                                |> Array.filter(fun (id,s) -> s.IsSome)
                                |> Array.map(fun (id,s) -> id, s.Value)
                                |> Array.distinctBy(fun (id,s) -> id)
```

Sending this to the FSI gives us the following:

```
</IndividualSurvey>);
   (2455,
    <IndividualSurvey xmlns="http://schemas.microsoft.com/
sqlserver/2004/07/adventure-works/IndividualSurvey">
  <TotalPurchaseYTD>26.24</TotalPurchaseYTD>
  <DateFirstPurchase>2004-01-24Z</DateFirstPurchase>
  <BirthDate>1953-04-10Z</BirthDate>
  <MaritalStatus>M</MaritalStatus>
  <YearlyIncome>25001-50000</YearlyIncome>
  <Gender>F</Gender>
  <TotalChildren>2</TotalChildren>
  <NumberChildrenAtHome>0</NumberChildrenAtHome>
  <Education>Bachelors </Education>
  <Occupation>Management</Occupation>
  <HomeOwnerFlag>1</HomeOwnerFlag>
  <NumberCarsOwned>1</NumberCarsOwned>
```

```
    <CommuteDistance>5-10 Miles</CommuteDistance>
</IndividualSurvey>);
    ...|]
```

There is not much new code here. Since we have to take into account customers that do not have demographic information recorded, we are using `Option` types. If there is demographic information, a `Some` is returned with the values. If not, a `None` is returned. We then filter that to only give us the customers with demographic records and distinct is called to make sure that we have only one record per customer.

With the customer demographic ready, we can now build a final data frame that contains all of the information we need. Go back to the script file and enter this:

```
let getDemoForCustomer customerId =
    let exists = Array.exists(fun (id,d) -> id = customerId)
    customerDemos
    match exists with
    | true -> Some (customerDemos
                        |> Array.find(fun (id,d) -> id = customerId)
                        |> snd)
    | false -> None

let orderCustomerDemo =
    orderCustomers
    |> Array.map(fun oc -> oc, getDemoForCustomer(snd oc))
                            |> Array.map(fun (oc,d) -> fst oc,
                                        snd oc, d)
                            |> Array.filter(fun (oid,cid,d) ->
                                        d.IsSome)
                            |> Array.map(fun (oid,cid,d) ->
                                        oid,cid,d.Value)
```

Sending this to the FSI, you can see the following:

```
</IndividualSurvey>);
    (50949, 19070,
    <IndividualSurvey xmlns="http://schemas.microsoft.com/
sqlserver/2004/07/adventure-works/IndividualSurvey">
  <TotalPurchaseYTD>27.7</TotalPurchaseYTD>
  <DateFirstPurchase>2003-08-20Z</DateFirstPurchase>
  <BirthDate>1966-07-08Z</BirthDate>
  <MaritalStatus>S</MaritalStatus>
  <YearlyIncome>greater than 100000</YearlyIncome>
  <Gender>F</Gender>
```

```
<TotalChildren>2</TotalChildren>

<NumberChildrenAtHome>2</NumberChildrenAtHome>

<Education>Bachelors </Education>

<Occupation>Management</Occupation>

<HomeOwnerFlag>0</HomeOwnerFlag>

<NumberCarsOwned>4</NumberCarsOwned>

<CommuteDistance>0-1 Miles</CommuteDistance>
</IndividualSurvey>);
    ... |]
```

We now have a tuple with three elements: `OrderId`, `CustomerId`, and the demographic information. Note that the output still shows the demographic information as XML though we will be able to see in a second that indeed, those elements are part of the demographic type.

Go into the script file and enter this:

```
let getMultiOrderIndForOrderId orderId =
    orderDetailCounts
    |> Array.find(fun (oid,c) -> oid = orderId)
    |> snd > 1

let orders =
    orderCustomerDemo
    |> Array.map(fun (oid,cid,d) -> oid,
                 getMultiOrderIndForOrderId(oid), d)
```

Sending this to the REPL gives us the following:

```
(50949, false,

 <IndividualSurvey xmlns="http://schemas.microsoft.com/
sqlserver/2004/07/adventure-works/IndividualSurvey">

 <TotalPurchaseYTD>27.7</TotalPurchaseYTD>

 <DateFirstPurchase>2003-08-20Z</DateFirstPurchase>

 <BirthDate>1966-07-08Z</BirthDate>

 <MaritalStatus>S</MaritalStatus>

 <YearlyIncome>greater than 100000</YearlyIncome>

 <Gender>F</Gender>

 <TotalChildren>2</TotalChildren>

 <NumberChildrenAtHome>2</NumberChildrenAtHome>

 <Education>Bachelors </Education>
```

```
<Occupation>Management</Occupation>

<HomeOwnerFlag>0</HomeOwnerFlag>

<NumberCarsOwned>4</NumberCarsOwned>

<CommuteDistance>0-1 Miles</CommuteDistance>
</IndividualSurvey>);

   ...|]
```

getMultiOrderIndForOrderId is a function that takes in the orderId and finds the record in the orderDetailsCounts frame. If there is more than one, it returns true. If there is only one order (just the bike), it returns false.

With that function, we can create a tuple that has orderId, multiOrderind, and the demographics. I think we are ready to start doing some modeling! Before we start, we need to ask ourselves one question: what values do we want to use? The *y* variable is clear—the multiOrderInd. But which one of the demographic values do we want to plug into our model as *x* variables? Since we want to change our website to account for the model results, we probably need variables that are usable on the site. Some features like BirthDate are available if the person logs into our site via their Facebook or Google accounts, those accounts have that information accurately populated and the user agrees to let our site access that information. Those are big *ifs*. Alternatively, we might be able to use the inferred analytics via the cookies that advertisers place on the user's device, but that is also an imprecise measure, depending on the feature used. It is better to design our model assuming that any information that will be input to the model will be accurately self-reported, and let's give the user an incentive to accurately self-report. This means education, yearly income, and other sensitive measures are out. Let's look at the gender and marital status, which we should be able to get from the user, if asked correctly. So our model will be *MultiOrder = Gender + MartialStatus + E*.

Go to the script and enter this:

```
let getValuesForMartialStatus martialStatus =
    match martialStatus with
    | "S" -> 0.0
    | _ -> 1.0

let getValuesForGender gender =
    match gender with
    | "M" -> 0.0
    | _ -> 1.0

let getValuesForMultiPurchaseInd multiPurchaseInd =
    match multiPurchaseInd with
    | true -> 1
    | false -> 0
```

Sending this to the REPL, we see the following:

```
val getValuesForMartialStatus : martialStatus:string -> float
val getValuesForGender : gender:string -> float
val getValuesForMultiPurchaseInd : multiPurchaseInd:bool -> int
```

Since Accord deals with input `float` values and output `int` values, we need a function to convert the features of our attributes (current as strings) to those types. If you want to make sure we have all of the cases covered, you can also send this to the FSI:

```
orders |> Array.distinctBy(fun (oid,ind,d) -> d.Gender)
       |> Array.map(fun (oid,ind,d) -> d.Gender)
//val it : string [] = [|"M"; "F"|]

orders |> Array.distinctBy(fun (oid,ind,d) -> d.MaritalStatus)
       |> Array.map(fun (oid,ind,d) -> d.MaritalStatus)
//val it : string [] = [|"M"; "S"|]
```

There is one danger with how the `getValues` function is written. If you remember from the previous chapter, dealing with missing values is an ongoing concern when doing any kind of modeling. The functions deal with the null issue by running away from it. Consider the `getValuesForGender` function:

```
let getValuesForGender gender =
    match gender with
    | "M" -> 0.0
    | _ -> 1.0
```

If a gender code comes in as UNK, YOMAMA, null, or any other string, it gets assigned the female code. This means we would be over reporting the number of females in our model. We can get away with that with this dataset because every record had values M or F, but if they did not, we would need a way to handle the incorrect values. In this case, I would create some code like this:

```
let mutable lastGender = "M"
let getValuesForGender gender =
    match gender, lastGender with
    | "M",_ -> 0.0
    | "F",_ -> 1.0
    | _,"M" -> lastGender = "F"
             1.0
    | _,_ -> lastGender = "M"
           0.0
```

This would balance the inferred values equally across males and females. In any event, let's get to modeling.

k-NN and AdventureWorks data

Go back to the script and enter this:

```
let inputs = orders |> Array.map(fun (oid,ind,d) ->
[|getValuesForMartialStatus(d.MaritalStatus);
getValuesForGender(d.Gender)|])
let outputs = orders |> Array.map(fun (oid,ind,d) ->
getValuesForMultiPurchaseInd(ind))

let classes = 2
let k = 3
let knn = new KNearestNeighbors(k, classes, inputs, outputs)
```

Sending this to the REPL gives us the following:

```
    ...|]
val classes : int = 2

val k : int = 3

val knn : KNearestNeighbors
```

Now that we have our model set up, let's pass in the four possible scenarios. Go to the script and enter this:

```
knn.Compute([|0.0;0.0|])
knn.Compute([|1.0;0.0|])
knn.Compute([|0.0;1.0|])
knn.Compute([|1.0;1.0|])
```

Sending this to the FSI give us the following:

```
>
val it : int = 1
>
val it : int = 1
>
val it : int = 0
>
val it : int = 1
```

So it looks like single women are NOT buying multiple items.

Naïve Bayes and AdventureWorks data

Go back to the script and enter this:

```
let inputs' = orders |> Array.map(fun (oid,ind,d) ->
[|int(getValuesForMartialStatus(d.MaritalStatus));

int(getValuesForGender(d.Gender));|])
let outputs' = orders |> Array.map(fun (oid,ind,d) ->
getValuesForMultiPurchaseInd(ind))

let symbols = [|2;2|]

let bayes = new Accord.MachineLearning.Bayes.NaiveBayes(2,symbols)
let error = bayes.Estimate(inputs', outputs')
```

Sending that to the FSI gives us the following:

```
    ...|]
val symbols : int [] = [|2; 2|]
val bayes : NaiveBayes
val error : float = 0.148738812
```

So we have a Naïve Bayes with a 15 percent error. Not great, but let's press on. Enter in the same four options for gender/martialStatus in the script file:

```
bayes.Compute([|0;0|])
bayes.Compute([|1;0|])
bayes.Compute([|0;1|])
bayes.Compute([|1;1|])
```

When you send it to the REPL, you will get the following:

```
val it : int = 1
>
val it : int = 1
>
val it : int = 1
>
val it : int = 1
>
```

Rut Row Raggy. Looks like we have a problem. In fact, we do. If you remember the previous description of using the Naïve Bayes model, it needs to have the values distributed along a bell curve to be effective. 90 percent of the bike purchases have a cross-sale — which means we are heavily skewed. No matter what kind of tweaks you do to the model, you can't get around the fact that you are multiplying by 0.9 to Yes for `multiPurchase`.

Making use of our discoveries

What should we do? We have a k-NN telling us that single women are not buying additional items and we have Naïve Bayes being no help at all. We could do some more classification models, but let's assume we feel good enough about our analysis and want to go to production with this model. How should we do that? A key issue to consider is that the model is based on some static data in one of our database tables that is not updated via the normal transactions of the company. This means we really don't need to retrain the model frequently. Another problem we have is that we need to figure out the gender and marital status of the people ordering our bikes. Perhaps we are asking the wrong question. Instead of asking how to get the gender and marital status of the user, what if we already knew it? You may be thinking that we don't know because we haven't asked yet. But we might — based on the bike selected for purchase!

Getting the data ready

Go back into the script and enter this code block:

```
let customerProduct =
    query { for soh in context.``Sales.SalesOrderHeaders`` do
            join sod in context.``Sales.SalesOrderDetails`` on
            (soh.SalesOrderID = sod.SalesOrderID)
            join p in context.``Production.Products`` on
            (sod.ProductID = p.ProductID)
            join c in context.``Sales.Customers`` on
            (soh.CustomerID = c.CustomerID)
            where (sod.SalesOrderID |=| salesOrderIds)
            select(c.CustomerID, sod.ProductID) }
    |> Seq.toArray
```

Sending this to the REPL, we see the following:

```
val customerProduct : (int * int) [] =
  [|(27575, 780); (13553, 779); (21509, 759); (15969, 769); (15972, 760);
    (14457, 798); (27488, 763); (27489, 761); (27490, 770); (17964, 793);
    (17900,
```

Hopefully, this code should look pretty boring to you by now. It is creating a tuple of `customerId` and `ProductId` from all of the bike sales.

Go back to the script and enter this:

```
let getProductId customerId =
    customerProduct |> Array.find(fun (cid,pid) -> cid = customerId)
                    |> snd

let getSingleFemaleInd (martialStatus:string, gender:string) =
    match martialStatus, gender with
    | "S", "F" -> 1
    | _, _ -> 0

let customerDemo = orderCustomerDemo |> Array.map(fun (oid,cid,d) ->
cid, getSingleFemaleInd(d.MaritalStatus, d.Gender))
                                     |> Array.map(fun (cid,sfInd) ->
cid, getProductId(cid),sfInd)
```

Sending this to the REPL, we can see the following:

```
val getProductId : customerId:int -> int
val getSingleFemaleInd : martialStatus:string * gender:string -> int
val customerDemo : (int * int * int) [] =
  [| (13553, 779, 0); (15969, 769, 0); (15972, 760, 0); (14457, 798, 0);
     (17964, 793, 0);
```

This code block is shaping our data for Accord by creating a frame of tuples of `customerId`, `productId`, and `singleFemaleInd`. We are almost ready to throw this data at a model, but we still need to determine which model we want to use. We are trying to determine the probability of a customer being a single female based on the bike purchased. This seems like a question that is well-suited for a logistic regression (*Chapter 3, More AdventureWorks Regression*). The issue is that each bike needs to become a feature in this regression:

singleFemale = BikeId0 + BikeId1 + BikeId2 + BikeIdN + E

If you throw this code into your script and send it to the FSI, you will see we have 80 different bike IDs:

```
let numberOfBikeIds = customerDemo |> Array.map (fun (cid,pid,sfInd) ->
pid)
                                   |> Array.distinct
                                   |> Array.length
val numberOfBikeIds : int = 80
```

So how do we create an input of 80 features from the original frame? Certainly not by hand. Let's see if Accord can help us.

Expanding features

Open up the script you were using from the previous section and enter this:

```
let inputs'' = customerDemo |> Array.map(fun (cid,pid,sfInd) -> pid)
let outputs'' = customerDemo |> Array.map(fun (cid,pid,sfInd) ->
(float)sfInd)

let expandedInputs = Tools.Expand(inputs'')
```

Sending this to the REPL, we see the following:

```
val expandedInputs : float [] [] =
  [|[|0.0; 0.0; 0.0; 0.0; 0.0; 0.0; 0.0; 0.0; 0.0; 0.0; 0.0; 0.0; 0.0;
0.0;
     0.0; 0.0; 0.0; 0.0; 0.0; 0.0; 0.0; 0.0; 0.0; 0.0; 0.0; 0.0; 0.0;
0.0;
     0.0; 0.0
```

What we are doing is taking the `customerDemo` frame and selecting the `productId`. We are then sending that array to Accord's `Tools.Expand` method that explodes the array so that each value becomes its own feature. Graphically, it looks like this:

As you can guess after reading *Chapter 5, Time Out – Obtaining Data*, this is considered a sparse data frame. With the input and output ready, go back to the script file and enter this:

```
let analysis = new LogisticRegressionAnalysis(expandedInputs,
outputs'')
analysis.Compute() |> ignore
let pValue = analysis.ChiSquare.PValue
let coefficients = analysis.CoefficientValues
let coefficients' = coefficients |> Array.mapi(fun i c -> i,c)
                                 |> Array.filter(fun (i,c) -> c > 5.0)
```

Before you send this to the REPL, let me warn you. The reason we identify a sparse frame is that computing a regression on 80 features takes a while. So hit *ALT +ENTER* and go get a cup of coffee. From Starbucks. Across town. Eventually, you will get this back:

```
val analysis : Analysis.LogisticRegressionAnalysis
>
val it : unit = ()
>
val pValue : float = 1.0
val coefficients : float [] =
  [|-3.625805913; 1.845275228e-10; 7.336791927e-11; 1.184805489e-10;
    -8.762459325e-11; -2.16833771e-10; -7.952785344e-12; 1.992174635e-10;
    2.562929393e-11; -2.957572867e-11; 2.060678611e-10; -2.103176298e-11;
    -2.3
```

And when we filter at the coefficient table, we can see that there is one bike model that is favored by single women. Add this to your script file and send to the FSI:

```
let coefficients' = coefficients |> Array.mapi(fun i c -> i,c)
                                 |> Array.filter(fun (i,c) -> c > 5.0)

val coefficients' : (int * float) [] = [|(765, 15.85774698)|]

>
```

So perhaps when a person purchases item number 765, we try to give them an incentive to buy other products, either via a coupon or a really slick website experience. This is where an excellent UX person with a knowledgeable marketing person can pay dividends. Since I am neither, I will leave that exercise to the reader.

Summary

In this chapter, we took a look at two common machine learning classifiers: k-Nearest Neighbors and Naïve Bayes. We saw them both in action with our AdventureWorks dataset to see if we can increase cross sales. We saw that k-NN had some limited success and Naïve Bayes was not useful. We then used our old friend logistic regression to help us narrow down a specific bike model that can be used to promote cross sales. Finally, we considered that since the data is ad hoc, we can't implement any real-time training on our website. We would want to periodically run this analysis to see if our original findings continued to hold.

In the next chapter, we are going to take off our software engineer hat and put on our data scientist hat to see if we can do anything with that traffic stop data. We are going to look at augmenting the original dataset with another dataset and then using a couple of clustering models: k-means and PCA. See you on the next page!

7
Traffic Stops and Crash Locations – When Two Datasets Are Better Than One

If you remember from *Chapter 4, Traffic Stops – Barking Up the Wrong Tree?*, we used a decision tree to help us determine if a person received a ticket or a warning based on several seasonality factors like time of day, day of the week, and the like. Ultimately, we could not find a relationship. Your first inclination might be to throw out the dataset, which I think is a mistake because there might be data gold in them thar hills, but we are just using the wrong model. Also, if a single dataset is not profitable, I typically start augmenting that set with others to see if the combination of features will provide a more satisfactory answer. In this chapter, let's go back to our Code-4-Good group and see if we can both augment the traffic stop dataset and apply some different models that will help us formulate interesting questions and answers. Perhaps even if we are not asking the right questions, the computer can help us ask the right questions too.

Unsupervised learning

To this point in the book, we have used several different models to answer our questions: linear regression, logistic regression, and kNN to name a few. Although different in their methodology, they share a common thread; we told the computer the answer (called the dependent or *y* variable) and then provided a series of features (called independent or *x* variables) that can be associated with that answer. Consider the following diagram for example:

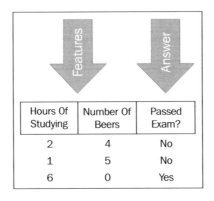

Hours Of Studying	Number Of Beers	Passed Exam?
2	4	No
1	5	No
6	0	Yes

We then presented the computer with some combination of independent variables that it had not seen before and asked it to guess the answer:

Hours Of Studying	Number Of Beers	Passed Exam?
5	1	?
2	8	?
4	4	?

We then compared to the known answers via the test and, if it did a good job guessing, we would use the model in production:

Hours Of Studying	Number Of Beers	Passed Exam?	Actual
5	1	Yes	Yes
2	8	No	No
4	4	Yes	No

This methodology of telling the computer the answer ahead of time is called *supervised learning*. The term *supervised* is used because we provide the computer an answer explicitly and then tell it which model to use.

There is another class of models that do not provide the answer to the computer. This class is called *unsupervised learning*. If your mental model of *unsupervised learning* is the chaos that engulfs a sixth grade class when a substitute teacher shows up the day before summer vacation, you are not far off. Okay, maybe not *that* bad. With unsupervised learning, we hand the computer a data frame of only attributes and ask it to tell us about the data. With that information, we can then narrow down the data that might help us make insightful business decisions. For example, let's say you send this data frame to the computer:

Hours Of Studying	Number Of Beers
2	4
1	5
6	0
5	1
2	8
4	4

It might tell you that the data seems to cluster in two areas:

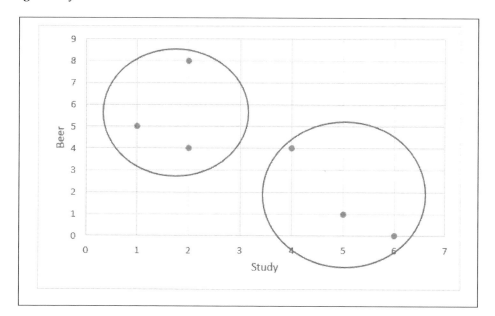

Although you might have eye-balled this relationship on this simple 2D data frame, the task becomes much harder, if not impossible, when adding more rows and features. In this chapter, we are going to use the k-means model to do this kind of clustering.

Also, we can use the computer to tell us what features are useful in a data frame and what features are just noise. For example, consider this dataset:

Hours Of Studying	Number Of Beers	StudyLocation
2	4	Dorm
1	5	Dorm
6	0	Dorm
5	1	Dorm
2	8	Dorm
4	4	Dorm

Will the inclusion of **StudyLocation** in our data frame lead to any insights? The answer is no, because the values are all the same. In this chapter, we are going to use **Principle Component Analysis (PCA)** to this kind of feature filtering; it will tell us what features are important and what can be safely removed.

k-means

As mentioned in the prior section, k-means is an unsupervised technique: observations are grouped based on mean of each cluster. Let's take a look at k-means in action. Open up Visual Studio and create a new Visual F# Windows Library Project. Rename the `Script.fsx` file to `kmeans.fsx`. Open up the **NuGet Package Manager** console and enter the following:

```
PM> install-package Accord.MachineLearning
```

Next, go to the script and replace all of the contents with this:

```
#r "../packages/Accord.3.0.2/lib/net40/Accord.dll"
#r "../packages/Accord.Math.3.0.2/lib/net40/Accord.Math.dll"
#r "../packages/Accord.Statistics.3.0.2/
lib/net40/Accord.Statistics.dll"
#r "../packages/Accord.MachineLearning.3.0.2/
lib/net40/Accord.MachineLearning.dll"

open Accord.MachineLearning
```

Next, let's create an array of different beverages that are served at our local restaurant:

```
let drinks = ["Boones Farm", 0;
               "Mad Dog", 1;
               "Night Train", 2;
               "Buckfast", 3;
               "Smirnoff", 4;
               "Bacardi", 5;
               "Johhnie Walker", 6;
               "Snow", 7;
               "Tsingtao", 8;
               "Budweiser", 9;
               "Skol", 10;
               "Yanjing", 11;
               "Heineken", 12;
               "Harbin", 13]
```

Sending this to the FSI, you will see the following:

```
val drinks : (string * int) list =
  [("Boones Farm", 0); ("Mad Dog", 1); ("Night Train", 2); ("Buckfast",
3);
   ("Smirnoff", 4); ("Bacardi", 5); ("Johhnie Walker", 6); ("Snow", 7);
   ("Tsingtao", 8); ("Budweiser", 9); ("Skol", 10); ("Yanjing", 11);
   ("Heineken", 12); ("Harbin", 13)]


>
```

Go back to the script and enter in some records of some patrons of the restaurant. We are using a float value because that is what Accord expects as an input.:

```
let observations = [|[|1.0;2.0;3.0|];[|1.0;1.0;0.0|];
                     [|5.0;4.0;4.0|];[|4.0;4.0;5.0|];[|4.0;5.0;5.0|];
                     [|6.0;4.0;5.0|];
                     [|11.0;8.0;7.0|];[|12.0;8.0;9.0|];
                     [|10.0;8.0;9.0|]|]
```

Sending that to the REPL gives us the following:

```
val observations : float [] [] =
  [|[|1.0; 2.0; 3.0|]; [|1.0; 1.0; 0.0|]; [|5.0; 4.0; 4.0|]; [|4.0; 4.0;
5.0|];
   [|4.0; 5.0; 5.0|]; [|6.0; 4.0; 5.0|]; [|11.0; 8.0; 7.0|];
   [|12.0; 8.0; 9.0|]; [|10.0; 8.0; 9.0|]|]
```

You will notice that there are nine different patrons and each had three drinks. Patron number 1 had a Boone's Farm, a Mad Dog, and a Night Train. With this data ready, let's run a k-means against it. Enter this into the script file:

```
let numberOfClusters = 3
let kmeans = new KMeans(numberOfClusters);
let labels = kmeans.Compute(observations)
```

When you send this to the FSI, you will see the following:

val numberOfClusters : int = 3

val kmeans : KMeans

val labels : int [] = [|0; 0; 1; 1; 1; 1; 2; 2; 2|]

This output takes each patron and assigns them to one of the three clusters. For example, Patrons number 1 and 2 are in cluster number 0. If we wanted more observations in each cluster, we could change the numberOfClusters like this:

```
let numberOfClusters = 2
let kmeans = new KMeans(numberOfClusters);
let labels = kmeans.Compute(observations)
```

And sending that to the FSI would give the following:

val numberOfClusters : int = 2

val kmeans : KMeans

val labels : int [] = [|1; 1; 1; 1; 1; 1; 0; 0; 0|]

Notice that the computer does not try to label or otherwise assign any value to each of the clusters. The data scientist would then need to assign a meaningful value, if one is possible. Go back to the script and change the numberOfClusters back to three and resend to the FSI. Looking at the input array, we can say that the cluster assigned 0 is for fortified wine drinkers, cluster 1 is for hard liquor drinkers, and cluster 2 is for beer drinkers. However, sometimes you may not be able to tell what each cluster means by eye-balling the input array. In that case, you can ask Accord for some (limited) help. Enter this into the script file:

```
kmeans.Clusters.[0]
```

Sending this to the FSI will give the following:

val it : KMeansCluster =

  Accord.MachineLearning.KMeansCluster

    {Covariance = [[4.3; 2.6; 3.2]

                [2.6; 2.266666667; 2.733333333]

                [3.2; 2.733333333; 3.866666667]];

```
Index = 0;
Mean = [|3.5; 3.333333333; 3.666666667|];
Proportion = 0.6666666667;}
```

Notice the mean is mid-threes, which is a low number as we are counting from 0 to 13. We could say that category 0's label should be *Buckfast*-like drinkers, which is generally correct.

Principle Component Analysis (PCA)

Another common task we can do with unsupervised learning is to help us throw out features that are not relevant. If you remember from the last chapter, we used a stepwise regression to determine the best features when building our model and then used Occum's Razor to toss insignificant features. One of the more common things you can do with PCA is use this unsupervised model as a way of picking the best features—the **principle components** of the frame.

Add another script file to your project and name it `pca.fsx`. Add in the following code:

```
#r "../packages/Accord.3.0.2/lib/net40/Accord.dll"
#r "../packages/Accord.Math.3.0.2/lib/net40/Accord.Math.dll"
#r "../packages/Accord.Statistics.3.0.2/
lib/net40/Accord.Statistics.dll"

open Accord.Statistics.Analysis


let sourceMatrix = [|[|2.5; 2.4|];[|0.5; 0.7|];[|2.2; 2.9|];
                     [|1.9; 2.2|];[|3.1; 3.0|];[|2.3; 2.7|];
                     [|2.0; 1.6|];
                     [|1.0; 1.1|];[|1.5; 1.6|]; [|1.1; 0.9|]|]
```

Sending this to the FSI gives the following:

```
val sourceMatrix : float [] [] =
  [|[|2.5; 2.4|]; [|0.5; 0.7|]; [|2.2; 2.9|]; [|1.9; 2.2|]; [|3.1; 3.0|];
    [|2.3; 2.7|]; [|2.0; 1.6|]; [|1.0; 1.1|]; [|1.5; 1.6|];
    [|1.1; 0.9|]|]
```

In this case, the `sourceMatix` is a list of students that studied for a certain number of hours for an exam and the number of beers that they consumed before the exam. For example, the first student studied 2.5 hours and drank 2.4 beers. Unlike similar examples you have seen in the book so far, you will notice that there is not a dependent variable (Y) in this frame. We don't know if these students passed or not. But with just these features, we can determine which ones would be the most useful for an analysis. You might be saying to yourself, "How is that possible?" Without going too much into the math, the PCA will look at the variance of each of the variables under a series of scenarios. If the variable can explain differences, it is given a higher score. If it cannot, it is given a lower one.

Let's see what PCA tells us about this dataset. Enter this code into the script:

```
let pca = new PrincipalComponentAnalysis(sourceMatrix, AnalysisMethod.
Center)
pca.Compute()
pca.Transform(sourceMatrix)
pca.ComponentMatrix
```

Sending this to the REPL, we will get the following:

```
val pca : PrincipalComponentAnalysis
val it : float [,] = [[0.6778733985; -0.7351786555]
                      [0.7351786555; 0.6778733985]]
```

You will notice that the output of the `ComponentMatrix` property is a 2 x 2 array with the complementary value as a cross. In formal terms, this jagged array is called an eigenvector and the contents of the array are called eigenvalues. If you start working deeply with PCA, you will need to come up to speed with what those words mean and the implications of the values. For our purposes here, we can safely ignore these values (unless you want to toss around the word, eigenvalue, at your next family gathering).

The important property that we do need to pay attention to with PCA is the component proportions. Go back to the script file and enter this:

```
pca.ComponentProportions
```

Sending this to the REPL gives the following:

```
val it : float [] = [|0.9631813143; 0.03681868565|]
```

These values are important for our analysis. Notice how adding these two values together amounts to 100 percent? These percentages tell you the amount of variance (and therefore the amount of usefulness) in the data frame. In this case, the hours of studying is 96 percent of the variance with the amount of beer being only 4 percent, so if we wanted to use this data in some kind of analysis, we would certainly pick the hours of studying and safely discard the beer drinking. Note that if we increased the range of beers being drunk, the percentages would shift and perhaps we would want to use both variables. This is a fairly simple example with two features. PCA really shines when you have lots and lots of features and you need to determine their usefulness.

Traffic stop and crash exploration

With the k-means and PCA theory under our belts, let's see what we can do with open data. If you remember, we had a dataset for traffic stops. Let's bring in two more datasets: the number of car crashes over the same time period, and also the amount of precipitation on the day of the crash/ticket.

Preparing the script and the data

In Visual Studio, create a new Visual F# Library Project called `Hack4Good.Traffic`:

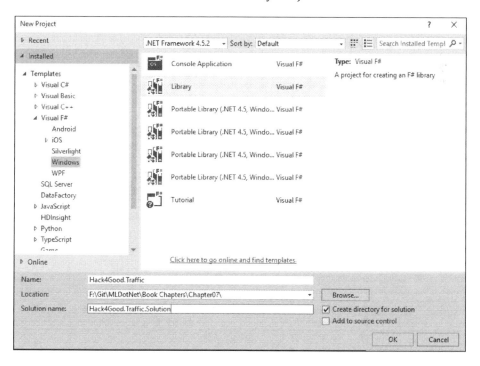

Once the project is created, rename the `Script.fsx` file to `Clustering.fsx`:

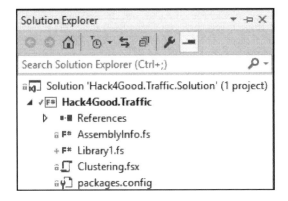

Next, open the NuGet Package Manager console and enter this:

```
PM> install-package Accord.MachineLearning
```

Inside `Clustering.fsx`, enter in the following code into the script:

```
#r "System.Data.Entity.dll"
#r "FSharp.Data.TypeProviders.dll"
#r "System.Data.Linq.dll"
#r "../packages/Accord.3.0.2/lib/net40/Accord.dll"
#r "../packages/Accord.Math.3.0.2/lib/net40/Accord.Math.dll"
#r "../packages/Accord.Statistics.3.0.2/
lib/net40/Accord.Statistics.dll"
#r "../packages/Accord.MachineLearning.3.0.2/
lib/net40/Accord.MachineLearning.dll"

open System
open System.Linq
open System.Data.Linq
open System.Data.Entity
open Accord.MachineLearning
open System.Collections.Generic
open Accord.Statistics.Analysis
open Microsoft.FSharp.Data.TypeProviders

[<Literal>]
let connectionString = "data source=nc54a9m5kk.database.windows.net;
initial catalog=Traffic;
user id=chickenskills@nc54a9m5kk;password=sk1lzm@tter;"
```

```
type Geolocation = {Latitude: float; Longitude: float}

type EntityConnection =
SqlEntityConnection<connectionString,Pluralize = true>
let context = EntityConnection.GetDataContext()
```

When you send this to the FSI, you will see the following:

```
val connectionString : string =
  "data source=nc54a9m5kk.database.windows.net;initial catalog=T"+
  [61 chars]
type Geolocation =
  {Latitude: float;
   Longitude: float;}
type EntityConnection =
  class
    static member GetDataContext : unit -> EntityConnection.ServiceTypes.
SimpleDataContextTypes.EntityContainer
      + 1 overload
    nested type ServiceTypes
  end
val context :
  EntityConnection.ServiceTypes.SimpleDataContextTypes.EntityContainer
```

With this prep code out of the way, let's bring down the stop data from the database. Put the following code into the script file:

```
//Stop Data
type TrafficStop = {StopDateTime: DateTime; Geolocation:
Geolocation; DispositionId: int}
let trafficStops =
    context.dbo_TrafficStops
    |> Seq.map(fun ts -> {StopDateTime = ts.StopDateTime.Value;
                          Geolocation = {Latitude =
                          Math.Round(ts.Latitude.Value,3);
                          Longitude =
                          Math.Round(ts.Longitude.Value,3)};
                          DispositionId = ts.DispositionId.Value})
    |> Seq.toArray
```

When you send it to the REPL, you will see the following:

```
type TrafficStop =
  {StopDateTime: DateTime;
   Geolocation: Geolocation;
   DispositionId: int;}
val trafficStops : TrafficStop [] =
  [|{StopDateTime = 6/30/2012 12:36:38 AM;
     Geolocation = {Latitude = 35.789;
                    Longitude = -78.829;};
     DispositionId = 7;}; {StopDateTime = 6/30/2012 12:48:38 AM;
                           Geolocation = {Latitude = 35.821;
                                          Longitude = -78.901;};
                           DispositionId = 15;};
    {StopDateTime = 6/30/2012 1:14:29 AM;
     Geolocation = {Latitude = 35.766;
```

All of this data should be familiar to you from *Chapter 4, Traffic Stops – Barking Up the Wrong Tree?*. The only real difference is that there is now a geolocation type that holds both latitude and longitude. Notice that we assign whatever values are in the database first in this line:

```
|> Seq.map(fun ts -> {StopDateTime = ts.StopDateTime.Value;
                      Geolocation = {Latitude =
                      Math.Round(ts.Latitude.Value,3);
                      Longitude =
                      Math.Round(ts.Longitude.Value,3)};
                      DispositionId = ts.DispositionId.Value})
```

Also, you will notice that we are making the values to three decimal point precision with the `Math.Round`. With this data local, let's bring in the crash data. Enter the following code into the script:

```
//Crash Data
type TrafficCrash = {CrashDateTime: DateTime;  Geolocation:
Geolocation; CrashSeverityId: int; CrashTypeId: int; }
let trafficCrashes=
    context.dbo_TrafficCrashes
    |> Seq.filter(fun tc -> tc.MunicipalityId = Nullable<int>(13))
    |> Seq.filter(fun tc -> not (tc.Latitude = Nullable<float>()))
    |> Seq.map(fun tc -> {CrashDateTime=tc.CrashDateTime.Value;
                          Geolocation = {Latitude =Math.Round
                          (tc.Latitude.Value,3);
```

```
                               Longitude=Math.Round(tc.Longitude.Value,3)};
                               CrashSeverityId=tc.CrashSeverityId.Value;
                               CrashTypeId =tc.CrashTypeId.Value})
        |> Seq.toArray
```

Sending this to the FSI gives us the following:

```
type TrafficCrash =
  {CrashDateTime: DateTime;
   Geolocation: Geolocation;
   CrashSeverityId: int;
   CrashTypeId: int;}
val trafficCrashes : TrafficCrash [] =
  [|{CrashDateTime = 12/30/2011 1:00:00 AM;
     Geolocation = {Latitude = 35.79;
                    Longitude = -78.781;};
     CrashSeverityId = 4;
     CrashTypeId = 3;}; {CrashDateTime = 12/30/2011 3:12:00 AM;
                         Geolocation = {Latitude = 35.783;
                                        Longitude = -78.781;};
                         CrashSeverityId = 3;
                         CrashTypeId = 24;};
```

We have one more dataset we want to use: the traffic conditions for each day. Enter the following into the script:

```
//Weather Data
type DailyPercipitation = {WeatherDate: DateTime; Amount: int; }
let dailyWeather =
    context.dbo_DailyPercipitation
    |> Seq.map(fun dw -> {WeatherDate=dw.RecordDate;
                          Amount=dw.Amount;})
    |> Seq.toArray
```

Sending this to the FSI gives us the following:

```
type DailyPercipitation =
  {WeatherDate: DateTime;
   Amount: int;}
val dailyWeather : DailyPercipitation [] =
  [|{WeatherDate = 1/9/2012 12:00:00 AM;
     Amount = 41;}; {WeatherDate = 1/10/2012 12:00:00 AM;
```

```
                         Amount = 30;}; {WeatherDate = 1/11/2012 12:00:00 AM;
                                     Amount = 5;};
     {WeatherDate = 1/12/2012 12:00:00 AM;
```

With these three datasets available, let's combine the traffic stop and traffic crash datasets together into a single data frame to see if there is anything going on with geolocation.

Geolocation analysis

Go to the script file and add the following:

```
let stopData =
    trafficStops
    |> Array.countBy(fun ts -> ts.Geolocation)
```

Sending this to the REPL gives us the following:

```
val stopData : (Geolocation * int) [] =
  [|({Latitude = 35.789;
     Longitude = -78.829;}, 178); ({Latitude = 35.821;
                                    Longitude = -78.901;}, 8);
    ({Latitude = 35.766;
     Longitu...
```

This code should look familiar to you by now; we are counting up the number of traffic stops by geolocation. For the first record, geopoint 35.789/-78.829 had 178 traffic stops.

Next, go back to the script and enter the following:

```
let crashData =
    trafficCrashes
    |> Array.countBy(fun tc -> tc.Geolocation)
```

Sending this to the REPL gives us the following:

```
val crashData : (Geolocation * int) [] =
  [|({Latitude = 35.79;
     Longitude = -78.781;}, 51); ({Latitude = 35.783;
```

This code is identical to the stop data; we are counting up the number of traffic crashes by geolocation. For the first record, geopoint 35.790/-78.781 had 51 traffic crashes.

Our next step is to combine these two datasets into a single data frame that we can send to Accord. As for most things in F#, let's use types and functions to achieve this. Go back to the script file and enter the following:

```
type GeoTraffic = {Geolocation:Geolocation; CrashCount: int;
StopCount: int}

let trafficGeo =
    Enumerable.Join(crashData, stopData,
                (fun crashData -> fst crashData),
                (fun stopData -> fst stopData),
                (fun crashData stopData -> { Geolocation = fst
                  crashData; StopCount = snd crashData ;
                  CrashCount = snd stopData }))
                |> Seq.toArray
```

When you send this to the FSI, you will see something like the following:

```
type GeoTraffic =
  {Geolocation: Geolocation;
   CrashCount: int;
   StopCount: int;}
val trafficGeo : GeoTraffic [] =
  [|{Geolocation = {Latitude = 35.79;
                    Longitude = -78.781;};
     CrashCount = 9;
     StopCount = 51;}; {Geolocation = {Latitude = 35.783;
                                       Longitude = -78.781;};
                 CrashCount = 16;
                 StopCount = 5;};
    {Geolocation = {Latitude = 35.803;
                    Longitude = -78.775;};
     CrashCount = 76;
     StopCount = 2;};
```

There is some new code here that can seem intimidating at first (at least, it was to me). We are using the LINQ class Enumerable's *Join* method to join the `crashData` and `stopData` together. The *Join* method takes in several parameters:

- The first dataset (in this case `crashData`).
- The second dataset (in this case `stopData`).

- A lambda that extracts the value from the first dataset, which we will use to join. In this case, the first item of the tuple, which is the geolocation value.

- A lambda that extracts the value from the second dataset, which we will use to join. In this case, the first item of the tuple, which is the geolocation value.

- A lambda that specifies what the output of the join operation will look like. In this case, it is the record type called `GeoTraffic` that we defined on the first line of this code block.

The key thing to realize about using the Join method is that it only keeps records that are in both datasets (an inner join to you SQL fans). This means if there is a geolocation that has one traffic ticket and no traffic stops, it is dropped from our analysis. If you want to do an outer join, there is the *GroupJoin* method that does this. Since we are only really interested in high-activity areas, an inner join seems more appropriate.

With our data frame created, we are now ready to send the data to Accord's k-means. If you remember, Accord's k-means wants the input to be a jagged array of floats. Therefore, we have one last transformation. Go to the script file and enter the following:

```
let kmeansInput =
    trafficGeo
    |> Array.map(fun cs -> [|float cs.CrashCount; float cs.StopCount
                           |])
```

Sending to the FSI, we get the following:

```
val kmeansInput : float [] [] =
  [|[|9.0; 51.0|]; [|16.0; 5.0|]; [|76.0; 2.0|]; [|10.0; 1.0|];
  [|80.0; 7.0|];
    [|92.0; 27.0|]; [|8.0; 2.0|]; [|104.0; 11.0|]; [|47.0; 4.0|];
    [|36.0; 16.0
```

Go back to the script file and enter the following:

```
let numberOfClusters = 3
let kmeans = new KMeans(numberOfClusters)
let labels = kmeans.Compute(kmeansInput.ToArray())
kmeans.Clusters.[0]
kmeans.Clusters.[1]
kmeans.Clusters.[2]
```

Sending to the REPL, we will get the following:

```
val numberOfClusters : int = 3

val kmeans : KMeans
```

```
val labels : int [] =
  [|1; 1; 0; 1; 0; 0; 1; 0; 0; 1; 0; 0; 0; 1; 1; 0; 1; 1; 0; 0; 0; 2; 1;
  0; 1;
    2; 0; 2;
```

Woot! We have a k-means working on our traffic data. If you inspect each of the clusters, you will see the following:

```
val it : KMeansCluster =
  Accord.MachineLearning.KMeansCluster
    {Covariance = [[533.856744; 25.86726804]
                   [25.86726804; 42.23152921]];
     Index = 0;
     Mean = [|67.50515464; 6.484536082|];
     Proportion = 0.1916996047;}
>
val it : KMeansCluster =
  Accord.MachineLearning.KMeansCluster
    {Covariance = [[108.806009; 8.231942669]
                   [8.231942669; 16.71306776]];
     Index = 1;
     Mean = [|11.69170984; 2.624352332|];
     Proportion = 0.7628458498;}
>
val it : KMeansCluster =
  Accord.MachineLearning.KMeansCluster
    {Covariance = [[5816.209486; -141.4980237]
                   [-141.4980237; 194.4189723]];
     Index = 2;
     Mean = [|188.8695652; 13.34782609|];
     Proportion = 0.04545454545;}
```

We have three clusters. I pulled the means and the proportions from each of the clusters and put them into a spreadsheet like this:

Crashes	Stops	% of records
67.5	6.48	20.2%
11.69	2.62	76.3%
188.87	13.35	4.5%

Looking at all the three clusters, it is notable that there are a lot more traffic crashes than stops. Also of interest is that the first and second cluster have about a 10:1 ratio of crashes to stops but the really high crash areas have a higher proportion of crashes to stops—about 14:1. It seems reasonable to conclude that there are a few high-crash areas in town and the police are very active there, but they could be even more active. I would name each cluster after their activity level: (low, medium, and high). If the geolocation was not in our data frame (a majority of the points in town), we could call that *no activity*.

Finally, enter this into the script file:

```
let trafficGeo' = Array.zip trafficGeo labels
```

Sending this to the FSI gives us the following:

```
val trafficGeo' : (GeoTraffic * int) [] =
  [|({Geolocation = {Latitude = 35.79;
                     Longitude = -78.781;};
      CrashCount = 9;
      StopCount = 51;}, 1); ({Geolocation = {Latitude = 35.783;
                                             Longitude = -78.781;};
                              CrashCount = 16;
                              StopCount = 5;}, 1);
```

We have seen `.zip` before. We are merging our data frame that contains the geolocation, number of stops, and number of crashes with the labels frame that came out k-means. Then we can look up a given geolocation and see its cluster assignment. For example, geolocation 35.790/-78.781 is in Cluster 1—or medium activity.

PCA

Now that we have a pretty good sense of the data via k-means, let's see if we can use PCA to uncover even more insights in our traffic data. Instead of location, let's look at date. As we found in *Chapter 4, Traffic Stops – Barking Up the Wrong Tree?*, using our decision tree, there was nothing we could conclude with different bins of date/time and our traffic tickets. Perhaps augmenting the stop data with crash and weather will lead to something.

Go back into the `Clustering.fsx` script file and enter the following:

```
let crashCounts =
    trafficCrashes
    |> Array.countBy(fun tc -> tc.CrashDateTime.DayOfYear)
```

Sending this to the FSI gives the following:

```
val crashCounts : (int * int) [] =
  [|(364, 10); (365, 3); (1, 2); (2, 3); (3, 12); (4, 5); (5, 3); (6, 1);
    (7, 9); (8, 6); (9, 10); (10, 6); (11, 9);
```

This code is very much like the code we already wrote when creating the `crashData` for k-means. In this case, we are counting up traffic crashes by `DayOfYear`. `DayOfYear` assigns each day of the year an index value. For example, January 1 gets a 1, January 2 gets a 2 and December 31 gets a 365 or 366, depending on if it is a leap year or not. Notice that it is one-based because `DateTime.DayOfYear` is one-based.

Go back into the script file and enter the following:

```
let stopCounts =
    trafficStops
    |> Array.countBy(fun ts -> ts.StopDateTime.DayOfYear)
```

Sending this to the FSI gives us the following:

```
val stopCounts : (int * int) [] =
  [|(182, 58); (183, 96); (184, 89); (185, 65); (38, 65);
```

As you can probably guess, this sums up the number of traffic stops by the day of the year. Pressing onward, go to the script file and enter the following:

```
let weatherData' =
    dailyWeather
    |> Array.map(fun w -> w.WeatherDate.DayOfYear, w.Amount)
```

Sending this to the REPL gives us the following:

```
val weatherData' : (int * int) [] =
  [|(9, 41); (10,` 30); (11, 5); (12, 124);
```

Just like crash and stop data, this creates a dataset with the amount of precipitation by day of year. You will notice that the data was already at the date level (sometimes called the level of atomicity), so an `Array.map` was used to transform the date; we don't need to use `countBy`.

With the initial datasets created, we now need a way to join all three together. The `Enumerable.Join` method that we used in the k-means example will not do here, so we will have to build our own joiner function. Go into the script file and enter the following:

```
let getItem dataSet item  =
    let found = dataSet |> Array.tryFind(fun sd -> fst(sd) = item)
```

```
        match found with
        | Some value -> snd value
        | None -> 0
```

When you send this to the FSI, you will get the following:

```
val getItem : dataSet:('a * int) [] -> item:'a -> int when 'a : equality
```

This is a pretty complicated function signature. It might help if I added parameter hints to the method as shown in the following code:

```
let getItem (dataSet:(int*int)[], item:int)  =
    let found = dataSet |> Array.tryFind(fun sd -> fst(sd) = item)
    match found with
    | Some value -> snd value
    | None -> 0
```

When you send this to the FSI, you will get the following:

```
val getItem : dataSet:(int * int) [] * item:int -> int
```

This should be slightly more accessible but less generic, which is fine because all of our datasets (crash, stops, and weather) are arrays of `int*int`. Reading the output, we see that `getItem` is a function that takes in one parameter named dataset that is an array of `int` tuples `(int * int)[]` and another parameter named item that is an int. The function then attempts to find the tuple in the array whose `fst` has the same value as the item. If it is found, it returns the second value of the tuple. If it does not find the item in the array, it returns `0`.

This function will work well for all three of our datasets (crash, stops, and weather) because all three only hold records for days they have observations. For traffic stops, this is not a problem because there was at least one traffic stop on each day of the year. However, there were 16 days where there were no traffic crashes recorded, so `stopData` has 350 records and there were over 250 days where there was not any precipitation, so `weatherData` only has 114 records.

Since the first way of creating `getItem` is more generic and idiomatic to F#, I will use it for the remaining part of the chapter. Both the examples are in the example script file that you can download.

Going back to the script, enter the following:

```
type TrafficDay = {DayNumber:int; CrashCount: int; StopCount: int;
RainAmount: int}

let trafficDates =
    [|1..366|]
```

```
|> Array.map(fun d -> {DayNumber=d;
                       CrashCount=getItem crashCounts d;
                       StopCount=getItem stopCounts d;
                       RainAmount=getItem weatherData' d})
```

When you send this to the REPL, you will see the following:

```
type TrafficDay =
  {DayNumber: int;
   CrashCount: int;
   StopCount: int;
   RainAmount: int;}
val trafficDates : TrafficDay [] =
  [|{DayNumber = 1;
     CrashCount = 2;
     StopCount = 49;
     RainAmount = 0;}; {DayNumber = 2;
                        CrashCount = 3;
                        StopCount = 43;
                        RainAmount = 0;};
```

The first line creates a record type that contains the number of crashes, stops, and precipitation for the day. I used rain as the field name because we rarely get snow in North Carolina and I want to rub it in to any reader who lives up north. Of course, when we do get snow, it is borderline Armageddon.

The next block of code is where we create our final data frame. First, an integer array is created with every day of the year. A mapper function is then applied that calls `getItem` three times for each item of the array: the first time for `crashData`, the second for stop data, and finally for weather data. The results are put into the `TrafficDay` record.

With the data frame setup, we are now ready for Accord. Go to the script file and enter the following:

```
let pcaInput =
    trafficDates
    |> Array.map(fun td -> [|float td.CrashCount; float td.StopCount;
    float td.RainAmount |])
```

When you send it to the REPL, you will get the following:

```
val pcaInput : float [] [] =
  [|[|2.0; 49.0; 0.0|]; [|3.0; 43.0; 0.0|]; [|12.0; 52.0; 0.0|];
    [|5.0; 102.0; 0.0|];
```

This is a jagged array that Accord wants. Go back to the script and enter the following:

```
let pca = new PrincipalComponentAnalysis(pcaInput, AnalysisMethod.
Center)
pca.Compute()
pca.Transform(pcaInput)
pca.ComponentMatrix
pca.ComponentProportions
```

When you send this to the REPL, you will get the following:

```
val pca : PrincipalComponentAnalysis
val it : unit = ()


>
val it : float [] [] =
  [|[|-43.72753865; 26.15506878; -4.671924583|];

val it : float [,] = [[0.00127851745; 0.01016388954; 0.999947529]
                      [0.01597172498; -0.999821004; 0.01014218229]
                      [0.9998716265; 0.01595791997; -0.001440623449]]
>
val it : float [] = [|0.9379825626; 0.06122702459; 0.0007904128341|]
>



>
```

This shows that 94 percent of the variance in our data frame is from crashes, not stops or the weather. This is interesting because common wisdom is that, once it rains (or <gasp> snows <gasp>) in North Carolina, traffic accidents spike. Although that might make a good press story, this one-year sample does not bear it out.

Analysis summary

We now have a couple of models that point to some interesting ideas:

- There are a few locations that account for most of the traffic crashes and tickets in town
- Weather is not as important as you might think

With this knowledge, we are ready to put machine learning to work for us.

The Code-4-Good application

Let's create a Windows application that helps people drive more safely. In addition, let's make the application "smart" so that it will progressively get more accurate. Let's start in Visual Studio with the project you have already created.

Machine learning assembly

Go into the **Solution Explorer** and rename `Library1.fs` to `TrafficML.fs`. Add a reference to `System.Data`, `System.Data.Entity`, `System.Data.Linq`, and `FSharp.Data.TypeProviders`:

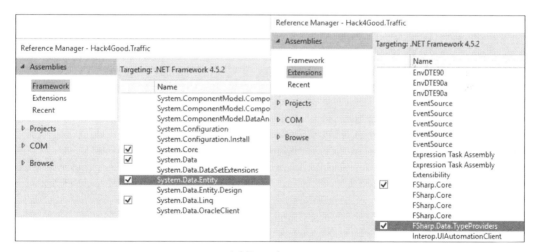

Adding references

Go into the `TrafficML.fs` file and enter the following code:

```
namespace Hack4Good.Traffic

open System
open System.Linq
open System.Data.Linq
```

```
open System.Data.Entity
open Accord.MachineLearning
open System.Collections.Generic
open Accord.Statistics.Analysis
open Microsoft.FSharp.Data.TypeProviders

type Geolocation = {Latitude: float; Longitude: float}
type private EntityConnection = SqlEntityConnection<"data
source=nc54a9m5kk.database.windows.net;initial catalog=Traffic;user
id=chickenskills@nc54a9m5kk;password=sk1lzm@tter;",Pluralize = true>
type TrafficStop = {StopDateTime: DateTime; Geolocation: Geolocation;
DispositionId: int}
type TrafficCrash = {CrashDateTime: DateTime;  Geolocation:
Geolocation; CrashSeverityId: int; CrashTypeId: int; }
type GeoTraffic = {Geolocation:Geolocation; CrashCount: int;
StopCount: int}
type GeoTraffic' = {Geolocation:Geolocation; CrashCount: int;
StopCount: int; Cluster: int}
```

I know it feels weird not to send code you just wrote to FSI, but there is no way of getting immediate feedback of the code you wrote in a compliable file. We will be addressing this in the next chapter when we talk TDD. Until then, just compile the project to make sure you are on the right track.

Back to the `TrafficML.fs` file, enter the following wall of code or copy it from the book's download:

```
type TrafficML(connectionString:string) =
    let context = EntityConnection.GetDataContext(connectionString)

        let trafficStops =
        context.dbo_TrafficStops
        |> Seq.map(fun ts -> {StopDateTime = ts.StopDateTime.Value;
                                Geolocation = {Latitude =Math.Round(ts.
                                        Latitude.Value,3);
                              Longitude=Math.Round(ts.Longitude.
                                            Value,3)};
                              DispositionId = ts.DispositionId.Value})
        |> Seq.toArray

    let trafficCrashes=
        context.dbo_TrafficCrashes
        |> Seq.filter(fun tc -> tc.MunicipalityId = Nullable<int>(13))
        |> Seq.filter(fun tc -> not (tc.Latitude = Nullable<float>()))
        |> Seq.map(fun tc -> {CrashDateTime=tc.CrashDateTime.Value;
```

```
                    Geolocation = {Latitude =Math.Round(tc.
                                        Latitude.Value,3);
                    Longitude=Math.Round(tc.Longitude.
                                        Value,3)};
                    CrashSeverityId=tc.CrashSeverityId.Value;
                    CrashTypeId =tc.CrashTypeId.Value})
        |> Seq.toArray

let stopData =
    trafficStops
    |> Array.countBy(fun ts -> ts.Geolocation)

let crashData =
    trafficCrashes
    |> Array.countBy(fun tc -> tc.Geolocation)

let trafficGeo =
    Enumerable.Join(crashData, stopData,
                (fun crashData -> fst crashData),
                (fun stopData -> fst stopData),
                (fun crashData stopData -> {
                    GeoTraffic.Geolocation = fst crashData;
                    StopCount = snd crashData ;
                    CrashCount = snd stopData }))
                |> Seq.toArray

let kmeansInput =
    trafficGeo
    |> Array.map(fun cs -> [|float cs.CrashCount;
                            float cs.StopCount |])

let numberOfClusters = 3
let kmeans = new KMeans(numberOfClusters)
let labels = kmeans.Compute(kmeansInput.ToArray())
let trafficGeo' = Array.zip trafficGeo labels
                |> Array.map(fun (tg,l) -> {Geolocation=tg.
                Geolocation;CrashCount=tg.CrashCount;
                StopCount=tg.StopCount;Cluster=l} )
```

This code is very similar to the k-means code we wrote in the `Clustering.fsx` script file. Notice that all the work of getting the data, shaping it, and running a k-means on it happens in the constructor of the `TrafficML` type. This means every time you create a new instance of the class from another location, you are making database calls and running the model. Also, notice that the connection string is hardcoded into the `SqlEntity` type provider for the type but then passed in via the constructor parameter when `GetDataContext()` is actually called. This allows you to move to code around environments (dev/test/prod). The downside is that you need to have your DEV environment exposed always so that the type is generated. One way to avoid this is to hardcode your Entity Framework `.edmx`/schema into the project.

Go back to the `TrafficML.fs` file and enter in the following function to the `TrafficML` type:

```
member this.GetCluster(latitude: float, longitude: float,
distance: float) =
    let geolocation = {Latitude=latitude; Longitude=longitude}
    let found = trafficGeo'
                |> Array.map(fun gt -> gt,
                (haversine gt.Geolocation geolocation))
                |> Array.filter(fun (gt,d) -> d < distance)
                |> Array.sortByDescending(fun (gt,d) ->
                gt.Cluster)
    match found.Length with
    | 0 -> -1
    | _ -> let first = found |> Array.head
           let gt = fst first
           gt.Cluster
```

This does a search of the geolocations. If there is a match, the cluster is returned. If there is no match, *a-1* is returned, signifying that there was not a match. We now have enough to make a first pass at creating a real time "smart" traffic application.

The UI

In the **Solution Explorer**, add a new Visual C# WPF Application:

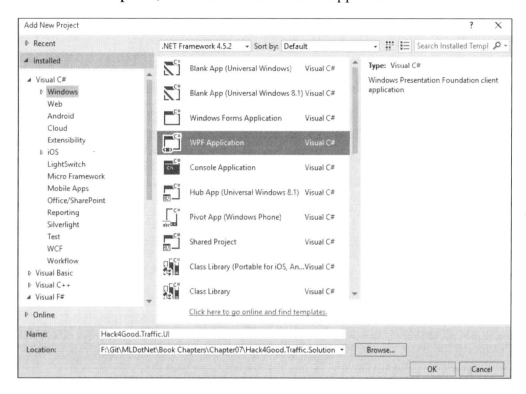

After the project is created, add a reference from the C# UI project to the F# one, `System.Configuration` and `System.Device`:

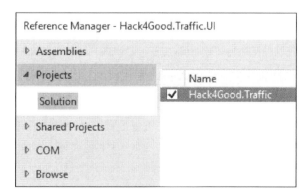

As a quick preparatory note, you are supposed to follow MVVM and command relay patterns when writing WFP applications which we will not cover in this book. This is a book about machine learning, not coddling humans via a delightful UI, so I code up enough of the UI just to get it to work. If you are interested in doing WPF following best practices, consider *Windows Presentation Foundation 4.5 Cookbook*.

Inside the UI project, open up the `MainWindow.xaml` file, locate the `Grid` element, and enter in this XAML inside the grid:

```
<Button x:Name="crashbutton" Content="Crash" Click="notifyButton_
Click" HorizontalAlignment="Left" Height="41" Margin="31,115,0,0"
VerticalAlignment="Top" Width="123"/>
<Button x:Name="stopButton" Content="Stop" Click="notifyButton_
Click" HorizontalAlignment="Left" Height="41" Margin="171,115,0,0"
VerticalAlignment="Top" Width="132"/>
<TextBlock x:Name="statusTextBlock" HorizontalAlignment="Left"
Height="100" Margin="31,10,0,0" TextWrapping="Wrap" Text="Current
Status: No Risk" VerticalAlignment="Top" Width="272"/>
```

Next, open up `MainWindow.xaml.cs` and enter the following `using` statements to the block of `using` at the top of the file:

```
using System.Configuration;
using System.Device.Location;
```

Your file should look like the following:

```
6     using System.Windows;
7     using System.Windows.Controls;
8     using System.Windows.Data;
9     using System.Windows.Documents;
10    using System.Windows.Input;
11    using System.Windows.Media;
12    using System.Windows.Media.Imaging;
13    using System.Windows.Navigation;
14    using System.Windows.Shapes;
15    using System.Configuration;
16    using System.Device.Location;
```

Inside the `MainWindow` class, enter three class-level variables:

```
TrafficML _trafficML = null;
GeoCoordinateWatcher _watcher = null;
String _connectionString = null;
```

Your file should look like the following:

```
public partial class MainWindow : Window
{
    TrafficML _trafficML = null;
    GeoCoordinateWatcher _watcher = null;
    String _connectionString = null;
```

Then, in the `MainWindow()` constructor, add in the following code below `InitializeComponent()`:

```
InitializeComponent();
_connectionString = ConfigurationManager.ConnectionStrings
["trafficDatabase"].ConnectionString;
_trafficML = new TrafficML(_connectionString);

_watcher = new GeoCoordinateWatcher(GeoPositionAccuracy.
High);
_watcher.PositionChanged += Watcher_PositionChanged;
bool started = this._watcher.TryStart(false, TimeSpan.
FromMilliseconds(2000));
StartUpdateLoop();
```

Your file should look like this:

```
public MainWindow()
{
    InitializeComponent();
    _connectionString = ConfigurationManager.ConnectionStrings["trafficDatabase"].ConnectionString;
    _trafficML = new TrafficML(_connectionString);

    _watcher = new GeoCoordinateWatcher(GeoPositionAccuracy.High);
    _watcher.PositionChanged += Watcher_PositionChanged;
    bool started = this._watcher.TryStart(false, TimeSpan.FromMilliseconds(2000));
    StartUpdateLoop();
}
```

Next, create the `Watcher_PositionChanged` method for the event handler:

```
private void Watcher_PositionChanged(object sender,
GeoPositionChangedEventArgs<GeoCoordinate> e)
{
    var location = e.Position.Location;
    var latitude = Double.Parse(location.Latitude.
    ToString("00.000"));
    var longitude = Double.Parse(location.Longitude.
    ToString("00.000"));

    var cluster = _trafficML.GetCluster(latitude, longitude);
    var status = "No Risk";
    switch(cluster)
    {
        case 0:
            status = "Low Risk";
            break;
        case 1:
            status = "Medium Risk";
            break;
        case 2:
            status = "High Risk";
            break;
        default:
            status = "No Risk";
            break;
    }
```

```
this.statusTextBlock.Text = "Current Status: " + status;

}
```

Next, create a loop to refresh the `MachineLearning` model every minute:

```
private async Task StartUpdateLoop()
{
    while (true)
    {
        await Task.Delay(TimeSpan.FromMinutes(1.0));
        _trafficML = await Task.Run(() => new
        TrafficML(_connectionString));
    }
}
```

Finally, add an event handler placeholder for the button clicks on the screen:

```
private void notifyButton_Click(object sender,
    RoutedEventArgs e)
{
    //TODO
}
```

If you collapse the code to definitions (*CTRL + M, L*), your code should look like the following:

```
public partial class MainWindow : Window
{
    TrafficML _trafficML = null;
    GeoCoordinateWatcher _watcher = null;
    String _connectionString = null;

    0 references | Jamie Dixon, 11 hours ago | 1 author, 3 changes
    public MainWindow()...

    1 reference | Jamie Dixon, 11 hours ago | 1 author, 2 changes
    private void Watcher_PositionChanged(object sender, GeoPositionChanged

    1 reference | 0 changes | 0 authors, 0 changes
    private async Task StartUpdateLoop()...

    2 references | 0 changes | 0 authors, 0 changes
    private void notifyButton_Click(object sender, RoutedEventArgs e)...
```

Next, go into **Solution Explorer**, right-click to add a new **Application Configuration** file:

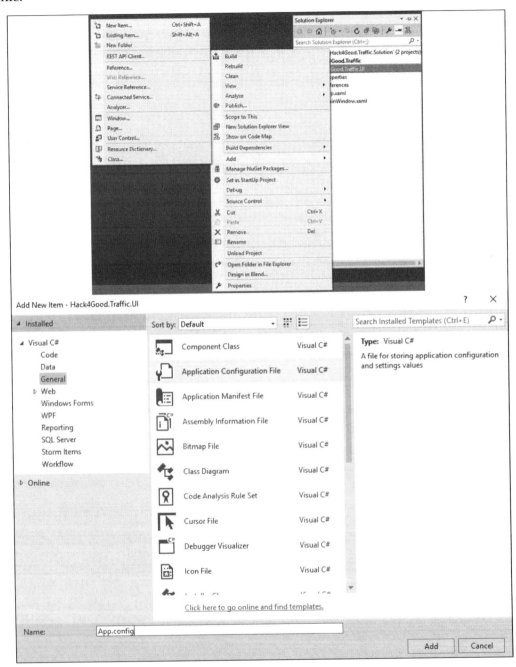

Adding new Application Configuration file

Inside that `app.config` file, replace the contents with this XML (replace the connection string with your connection string if you are using a local instance of the database):

```xml
<?xml version="1.0" encoding="utf-8" ?>
<configuration>
    <startup>
        <supportedRuntime version="v4.0" sku=
          ".NETFramework,Version=v4.5.2" />
    </startup>
  <connectionStrings>
    <add name="trafficDatabase"
        connectionString="data source=
          nc54a9m5kk.database.windows.net;initial catalog=Traffic;
        user id=chickenskills@nc54a9m5kk;password=sk1lzm@tter;" />
  </connectionStrings>
</configuration>
```

Go to **Solution Explorer** and make the UI project the startup project:

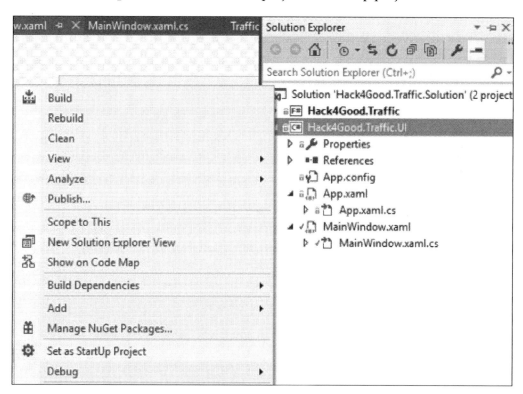

Compile your project. If all is well, try to run it. You should get a warning dialog like this:

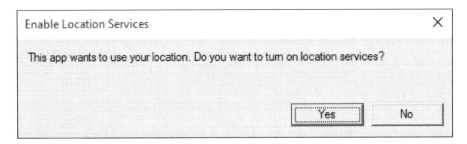

And then you will get a screen like this:

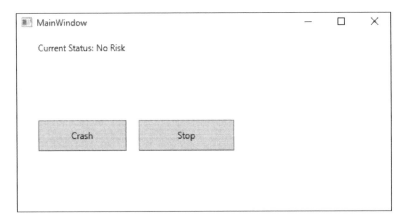

Once you completely take in the awesomeness of the user experience, stop running the application. So far, this is pretty good. If we put this application on a location-aware device (like a GPS) in the car and drive around, the status bar will warn us if we are within a quarter mile of a geolocation that might have a crash or stop risk. However, if we want to give ourselves more of a heads up, we need to add a bit more of code.

Adding distance calculations

Go back to the F# project and open up the `TrafficML.fs` file. Locate the last line of the constructor. It looks like the following code:

```
let trafficGeo' = Array.zip trafficGeo labels
                  |> Array.map(fun (tg,l) -> {Geolocation=tg.
                  Geolocation;CrashCount=tg.CrashCount;
                  StopCount=tg.StopCount;Cluster=l} )
```

Below this line, enter the following:

```
let toRadian x = (Math.PI/180.0) * x

let haversine x y =
    let dlon = toRadian (x.Longitude - y.Longitude)
    let dLat = toRadian (x.Latitude - y.Latitude)
    let a0 = pown (Math.Sin(dLat/2.0)) 2
    let a1 = Math.Cos(toRadian(x.Latitude)) *
                        Math.Cos(toRadian(y.Latitude))
    let a2 = pown (Math.Sin(dlon/2.0)) 2
    let a = a0 + a1 * a2
    let c = 2.0 * Math.Atan2(sqrt(a),sqrt(1.0-a))
    let R = 3956.0
    R * c
```

These two functions allow us to calculate the distance between geolocations. Since the earth is curved, we can't simply subtract the latitudes and longitudes between the two geolocations. The Haversine formula is the most common way to do this calculation.

Go to the end of the file and add the following:

```
member this.GetCluster(latitude: float, longitude: float,
    distance: float) =
    let geolocation = {Latitude=latitude; Longitude=longitude}
    let found = trafficGeo' |> Array.map(fun gt -> gt,
        (haversine gt.Geolocation geolocation))
                                |> Array.filter(fun (gt,d) ->
                                                d < distance)
                                |> Array.sortByDescending(fun (gt,d)
                                        -> gt.Cluster)
    match found.Length with
    | 0 -> -1
    | _ -> let first = found |> Array.head
            let gt = fst first
            gt.Cluster
```

What we are doing is overloading the GetCluster function with an additional parameter called distance. Using this input distance, we can calculate how far it is between the geolocation parameter and every geolocation in our trafficGeo array. If there are any matches, we sort by the highest number of cluster (sortByDescending) and return it.

Go back to our UI project and open the `MainWindow.xaml.cs` file and locate the `Watcher_PositionChanged` method. Find the following line of code:

```
var cluster = _trafficML.GetCluster(latitude, longitude);
```

Replace it with the following line of code:

```
var cluster = _trafficML.GetCluster(latitude, longitude, 2.0);
```

We now have a two mile heads-up to any problem area on the roads.

Augmenting with human observations

There is one more thing we want to do to our UI. If you look at some of the *crowd source* road applications like Waze, they provide real-time notifications. Our app bases its classification based on historical data. However, if we were driving down the street in an area that was classified as *low risk*, and we saw a traffic crash, we would want to elevate the location to a *high risk*. Ideally, all the users of our application would get this update and override the model's classification of the geolocation (at least for the time being) and then we would update our database so that, as we retrain our model, the information gets more accurate.

Go to the `notifyButton_Click` event holder and replace `//TODO` with the following:

```
var location = _watcher.Position.Location;
var latitude = Double.Parse(location.Latitude.
  ToString("00.000"));
var longitude = Double.Parse(location.Longitude.
  ToString("00.000"));
_trafficML.AddGeolocationToClusterOverride
  (latitude, longitude);
```

The compiler will complain to you because we have not implemented the `AddGeolocationToClusterOverride` yet. Go back over to the F# project and open the `TrafficML.fs` file. At the very bottom, add the following:

```
member this.AddGeolocationToClusterOverride(latitude: float,
    longitude: float)  =
    let clusterOverride = EntityConnection.ServiceTypes.dbo_
    ClusterOverride()
    clusterOverride.Latitude <- latitude
    clusterOverride.Longitude <- longitude
    clusterOverride.Cluster <- 2
    clusterOverride.OverrideDateTime <- DateTime.UtcNow
    context.dbo_ClusterOverride.AddObject(clusterOverride)
    context.DataContext.SaveChanges() |> ignore
```

We now have a way of updating the database for any override. Note that you will not be able to write to the shared database on Azure that was created for this book, but you will be able to write to your local copy. As a final step, go up to where we created the `trafficGeo` on the following line:

```
let trafficGeo' = Array.zip trafficGeo labels
                |> Array.map(fun (tg,l) -> {Geolocation=tg.
                Geolocation;CrashCount=tg.CrashCount;
                StopCount=tg.StopCount;Cluster=l} )
```

Replace that line with the following code block:

```
let overrides = context.dbo_ClusterOverride
                |> Seq.filter(fun co -> (DateTime.UtcNow -
                co.OverrideDateTime) > TimeSpan(0,5,0))
                |> Seq.toArray

    let checkForOverride (geoTraffic:GeoTraffic') =
    let found = overrides
                |> Array.tryFind(fun o -> o.Latitude =
                geoTraffic.Geolocation.Latitude &&
                o.Longitude = geoTraffic.Geolocation.Longitude)
    match found.IsSome with
    | true -> {Geolocation=geoTraffic.Geolocation;
            CrashCount=geoTraffic.CrashCount;
            StopCount=geoTraffic.StopCount;
            Cluster=found.Value.Cluster}
    | false -> geoTraffic

let trafficGeo' = Array.zip trafficGeo labels
                |> Array.map(fun (tg,l) ->
                {Geolocation=tg.Geolocation;
                 CrashCount=tg.CrashCount;
                 StopCount=tg.StopCount;
                 Cluster=l} )
                |> Array.map(fun gt -> checkForOverride(gt))
```

This block goes to the database and pulls down all overrides that occurred within the last 5 minutes and places them in the overrides array. It then creates a function called `checkForOverride` that takes in the `geoTraffic` value. If the latitude and longitude match the override table, the `geoTraffic` value is replaced with a new value that has the override value assigned by the database and not from the k-means model. If no match is found, the original value is returned. Finally, we pipe this function to the creation of `trafficGeo`. Note that if you try and execute this on our shared server, it will throw an exception because you don't have rights to write to the database. Hopefully, though, the intention is clear with this example. With that, we have a real-time system where we combine machine learning and human observations to give our end user the best possible predictions.

Summary

We covered a lot of ground in this chapter. We looked at k-means and PCA to help us find hidden relationships in our traffic datasets. We then built an application that took advantage of the insights we gleaned to make drivers more aware and, hopefully, safer. This application is unique because it blended both real-time machine learning modeling and human observations to provide the best possible outcome for the driver.

In the next chapter, we are going to look at some of the limitations of our coding so far in this book and see if we can improve on both model and feature selection.

8
Feature Selection and Optimization

In software engineering, there is an old saying: *make it work first, then make it fast*. In this book, we have adopted the strategy to *make it run, then make it better*. Many of the models that we covered in the initial chapters were correct in a very limited sense and could stand some optimization to make them more correct. This chapter is all about *making it better*.

Cleaning data

As we saw in *Chapter 5, Time Out – Obtaining Data*, obtaining and shaping the data (which is often the largest problem in many projects) is a snap using F# type providers. However, once our data is local and shaped, our work in preparing the data for machine learning is not complete. There might still be abnormalities in each frame. Things like null values, empty values, and values outside a reasonable range need to be addressed. If you come from an R background, you will be familiar with `null.omit` and `na.omit`, which remove all of the rows from a data frame. We can achieve functional equivalence in F# by applying a filter function to the data. In the filter, you can search for null if it is a reference type, or `.isNone` if the column is an option type. While this is effective, it is a bit of a blunt hammer because you are throwing out a row that might have valid values in the other fields when only one field has an inappropriate value.

Another way to handle missing data is to replace it with a value that will not skew an analysis. Like most things in data science, there are plenty of opinions on the different techniques, and I won't go into too much detail here. Rather, I want to make you aware of the issue and show you a common way to remediate it:

Go into Visual Studio and create a Visual F# Windows Library project called `FeatureCleaning`:

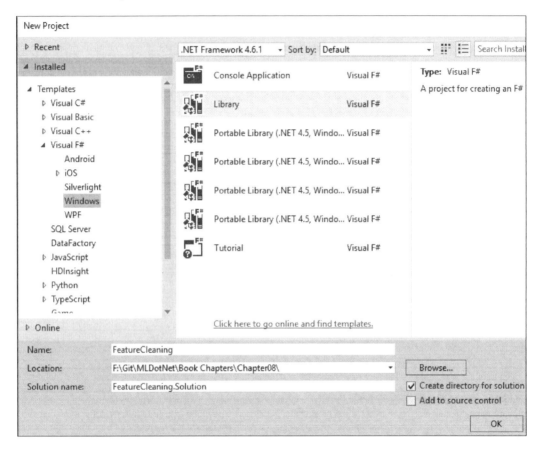

Locate `Script1.fsx` in the **Solution Explorer** and rename it `CleanData.fsx`:

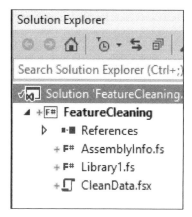

Open that script file, and replace the existing code with this:

```
type User = {Id: int; FirstName: string;
             LastName: string; Age: float}
let users = [|{Id=1; FirstName="Jim";
             LastName="Jones"; Age=25.5};
             {Id=2; FirstName="Joe";
             LastName="Smith"; Age=10.25};
             {Id=3; FirstName="Sally";
             LastName="Price"; Age=1000.0};|]
```

Sending this to the FSI gives us the following:

```
type User =
  {Id: int;
   FirstName: string;
   LastName: string;
   Age: float;}
val users : User [] = [|{Id = 1;
                       FirstName = "Jim";
                       LastName = "Jones";
                       Age = 25.5;}; {Id = 2;
                                    FirstName = "Joe";
                                    LastName = "Smith";
                                    Age = 10.25;}; {Id = 3;
                                                  FirstName = "Sally";
                                                  LastName =
     "Price";
                                                  Age =
     1000.0;}|]
```

`User` is a record type that represents the users of an application while `users` is an array of three users. It looks pretty vanilla except user 3, Sally Price, has an age of `1000.0`. What we want to do is take that age out but still keep Sally's record. To do that, let's remove 1,000 and replace it with the average of the ages of all of remaining users. Go back to the script file and enter this:

```
let validUsers = Array.filter(fun u -> u.Age < 100.0) users
let averageAge = Array.averageBy(fun u -> u.Age) validUsers

let invalidUsers =
    users
    |> Array.filter(fun u -> u.Age >= 100.0)
    |> Array.map(fun u -> {u with Age = averageAge})

let users' = Array.concat [validUsers; invalidUsers]
```

Sending this to the FSI should give you the following:

```
val averageAge : float = 17.875
val invalidUsers : User [] = [|{Id = 3;
                                FirstName = "Sally";
                                LastName = "Price";
                                Age = 17.875;}|]
val users' : User [] = [|{Id = 1;
                          FirstName = "Jim";
                          LastName = "Jones";
                          Age = 25.5;}; {Id = 2;
                                         FirstName = "Joe";
                                         LastName = "Smith";
                                         Age = 10.25;}; {Id = 3;
                                                         FirstName =
"Sally";
                                                         LastName =
"Price";
                                                         Age = 17.875;}|]
```

Notice that we create a subarray of the valid users and then get their average ages. We then create a subarray of invalid users and map in the average age. Since F# does not like mutability, we create a new record for each of the invalid users and use the `with` syntax effectively, creating a new record that has all the same values as the original record, except the age. We then wrap up by concatenating the valid users and the updated user back into a single array. Although this is a fairly rudimentary technique, it can be surprisingly effective. As you get further into machine learning, you will develop and refine your own techniques for dealing with invalid data—and you have to keep in mind that the model that you are using will dictate how you clean that data. In some models, taking the average might throw things off.

Selecting data

When we are confronted with a large number of independent variables, we often run into the problem of which values to select. In addition, the variable might be binned, combined with other variables, or altered—all of which might make or break a particular model.

Collinearity

Collinearity is when we have multiple x variables that are highly related to each other; they have a high degree of correlation. When using regressions, you always have to be on the watch for collinearity as you can't be sure which individual variable really affects the outcome variable. Here is a classic example. Suppose you wanted to measure the happiness of a college student. You have the following input variables: age, sex, money available for beer, money available for textbooks. In this case, there is a direct relationship between money available for beer and money available for textbooks. The more money spent on textbooks, the less there is available for beer. To solve for collinearity, you can do a couple of things:

- Drop one of the highly-correlated variables. In this case, perhaps drop money available for text books.

- Combine correlated variables into a single variable. In this case, perhaps just have a category of money in checking account.

A common way to test for collinearity is to run your multiple regressions several times, each time removing one x variable. If there is not a dramatic change when two different variables are removed, they are good candidates for collinearity. In addition, you can always do a visual scan of the correlation matrix of the x variables, which you can do using Accord.Net with the `Tools.Corrlelation` method. Let's take a look at this. Go back into Visual Studio and add a new script file called `Accord.fsx`. Open the NuGet Package Manager Console and add in Accord:

```
PM> install-package Accord.Statistics
Next, go into the script file and enter this:
#r "../packages/Accord.Math.3.0.2/lib/net40/Accord.Math.dll"
#r "../packages/Accord.Statistics.3.0.2/lib/net40
/Accord.Statistics.dll"

open Accord.Statistics

//Age
//Sex - 1 or 0
//money for textbooks
//money for beer

let matrix = array2D [ [ 19.0;1.0;50.0;10.0];
                       [18.0;0.0;40.0;15.0];
                       [21.0;1.0;10.0;40.0]]
let correlation = Tools.Correlation(matrix)
```

This represents three students who we interviewed. We asked each their age, their gender, how much money they had for textbooks, and how much money they had for beer. The first student is a 19-year-old, female, had $50.00 for text books, and $10.00 for beer.

When you send this to the FSI, you get the following:

```
val correlation : float [,] =
  [[1.0; 0.755928946; -0.8386278694; 0.8824975033]
   [0.755928946; 1.0; -0.2773500981; 0.3592106041]
   [-0.8386278694; -0.2773500981; 1.0; -0.9962709628]
   [0.8824975033; 0.3592106041; -0.9962709628; 1.0]]
```

It is a bit hard to read, so I reformatted it:

	Age	Gender	$ Books	$ Beer
Age	1.0	0.76	-0.84	0.88
Sex	0.76	1.0	-0.28	0.35
$ Books	-0.84	-0.28	1.0	-0.99
$ Beer	0.88	0.35	-0.99	1.0

Notice the diagonal values in matrix, 1.0, which means that age is perfectly correlated with age, sex is perfectly correlated with sex, and so on. The key thing from this example is that there is an almost perfect negative correlation between the amount of money for books and the amount of money for beer: it is -0.99. What this means is that, if you have more money for books, you have less for beer, which makes sense. By reading the correlation matrix, you can get a quick understanding of what variables are correlated and can possibly be removed.

A related topic to collinearity is to always keep your y variable as independent as possible from the x variable. For example, if you made a regression where you were trying to pick the amount of money available for beer for our student, you would not pick any independent variable that related to the amount of money the student has. Why? Because they are measuring the same thing.

Feature selection

A related topic to collinearity is feature selection. If you have a whole mess of x variables, how do you decide which ones will be the best ones for your analysis? You can start picking and choosing, but that is time-consuming and can possibly lead to errors. Instead of guessing, there are some modeling techniques that run simulations across all your data to determine the best combination of x variables to use. One of the most common techniques is called forward-selection step-wise regression. Consider a data frame that has five independent variables and one dependent variable:

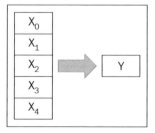

Using forward-selection step-wise regression, the technique starts out with a single variable, runs a regression, and calculates (in this case) a rmse:

Next, the technique goes back and adds in another variable and calculates the rmse:

Next, the technique goes back and further adds in another variable and calculates the rmse:

By now, you probably have the idea. Depending on the implementation, the stepwise might be re-run with different combinations of independent variables and/or different test and training sets. When the step-wise is done, you can have a good idea about what features are important and what can be discarded.

Let's take a look at a step-wise regression example in Accord. Go back to your script and enter this code (note that this is verbatim from the Accord help file on stepwise regression):

```
#r "../packages/Accord.3.0.2/lib/net40/Accord.dll"
open Accord.Statistics.Analysis

//Age/Smoking
let inputs = [|[|55.0;0.0|];[|28.0;0.0|];
               [|65.0;1.0|];[|46.0;0.0|];
               [|86.0;1.0|];[|56.0;1.0|];
               [|85.0;0.0|];[|33.0;0.0|];
               [|21.0;1.0|];[|42.0;1.0|];
```

```
              [|33.0;0.0|];[|20.0;1.0|];
              [|43.0;1.0|];[|31.0;1.0|];
              [|22.0;1.0|];[|43.0;1.0|];
              [|46.0;0.0|];[|86.0;1.0|];
              [|56.0;1.0|];[|55.0;0.0|];|]

    //Have Cancer
    let output = [|0.0;0.0;0.0;1.0;1.0;1.0;0.0;0.0;0.0;1.0;
                  0.0;1.0;1.0;1.0;1.0;1.0;0.0;1.0;1.0;0.0|]

    let regression =
        StepwiseLogisticRegressionAnalysis(inputs, output,
        [|"Age";"Smoking"|],"Cancer")
```

Send this to the FSI to get the following:

```
val inputs : float [] [] =
  [|[|55.0; 0.0|]; [|28.0; 0.0|]; [|65.0; 1.0|]; [|46.0; 0.0|]; [|86.0;
1.0|];
    [|56.0; 1.0|]; [|85.0; 0.0|]; [|33.0; 0.0|]; [|21.0; 1.0|]; [|42.0;
1.0|];
    [|33.0; 0.0|]; [|20.0; 1.0|]; [|43.0; 1.0|]; [|31.0; 1.0|]; [|22.0;
1.0|];
    [|43.0; 1.0|]; [|46.0; 0.0|]; [|86.0; 1.0|]; [|56.0; 1.0|]; [|55.0;
0.0|]|]
val output : float [] =
  [|0.0; 0.0; 0.0; 1.0; 1.0; 1.0; 0.0; 0.0; 0.0; 1.0; 0.0; 1.0; 1.0; 1.0;
1.0;
    1.0; 0.0; 1.0; 1.0; 0.0|]
val regression : StepwiseLogisticRegressionAnalysis
```

As you can tell from the comments in the code, the inputs are 20 fictional people that have been recently screened for cancer. The features are their ages and whether or not they smoke. The output is whether the person actually did have cancer.

Go back to the script and add this:

```
    let results = regression.Compute()
    let full = regression.Complete;
    let best = regression.Current;


    full.Coefficients


    best.Coefficients
```

When you send this to the FSI, you will see something very interesting. The `full.Coefficients` returns all of the variables but the `best.Coefficients` returns this:

```
val it : NestedLogisticCoefficientCollection =
  seq
    [Accord.Statistics.Analysis.NestedLogisticCoefficient
      {Confidence = 0.0175962716285245, 1.1598020423839;
       ConfidenceLower = 0.01759627163;
       ConfidenceUpper = 1.159802042;
       LikelihoodRatio = null;
       Name = "Intercept";
       OddsRatio = 0.1428572426;
       StandardError = 1.068502877;
       Value = -1.945909451;
       Wald = 0.0685832853132018;};
     Accord.Statistics.Analysis.NestedLogisticCoefficient
      {Confidence = 2.63490696729824, 464.911388747606;
       ConfidenceLower = 2.634906967;
       ConfidenceUpper = 464.9113887;
       LikelihoodRatio = null;
       Name = "Smoking";
       OddsRatio = 34.99997511;
       StandardError = 1.319709922;
       Value = 3.55534735;
       Wald = 0.00705923290736891;}]
```

You can now see that `Smoking` is the most important variable when predicting cancer. If two or more variables were considered important, Accord would have told you the number 1 variable, then the next one, and so on. Stepwise regressions are a bit on the outs these days as the community has moved to Lasso and some other techniques. However, it is still an important tool in your toolkit and is something that you should know about.

Normalization

Sometimes our models can be improved by adjusting the data. I am not talking about "adjusting numbers" in the Enron accounting or US politician sense. I am talking about adjusting the data using some standard scientific techniques that might improve the model's accuracy. The general term for this is *normalization*.

There are many different ways to normalize data. I want to show you two common ones that work well with regressions. First, if your data is clustered together, you can take the log of the values to help tease out relationships that might otherwise be hidden. For example, look at our scatterplot of product reviews from the beginning of *Chapter 2, AdventureWorks Regression*. Notice that most of the order quantity centered around 250 to 1,000.

By applying the log to the order quantity and doing the same kind of scatterplot, you can see the relationship much more clearly:

Note that taking the log typically does not change the relationship among the dependent and independent variables, so you can use it safely in replacement of the natural values in regressions.

If you go back to the solution in *Chapter 2, AdventureWorks Regression,* you can open up the regression project and add a new file called `Accord.Net4.fsx`. Copy and paste in the contents from `Accord.Net2.fsx`. Next, replace the data reader lines of code with this:

```
while reader.Read() do
    productInfos.Add({ProductID=reader.GetInt32(0);
        AvgOrders=(float)(reader.GetDecimal(1));
        AvgReviews=log((float)(reader.GetDecimal(2)));
        ListPrice=(float)(reader.GetDecimal(3));})
```

Sending this to the REPL, we get the following:

```
val regression : MultipleLinearRegression =
  y(x0, x1) = 35.4805245757214*x0 + -0.000897944878777119*x1 + -
36.7106228824185
val error : float = 687.122625
val a : float = 35.48052458
val b : float = -0.0008979448788
val c : float = -36.71062288
val mse : float = 7.083738402
val rmse : float = 2.661529335
val r2 : float = 0.3490097415
```

Notice the change. We are taking the `log()` of our x variables. Also, notice that our r2 slightly decreases. The reason for this is that although the log does not change the relationship among `AvgReviews`, it does impact how it relates to the other x variables and potentially the y variable. You can see, in this case, that it didn't do much.

Besides using log, we can trim outliers. Going back to our graph, do you notice that lonely dot at 2.2 average order quantity/3.90 average review?

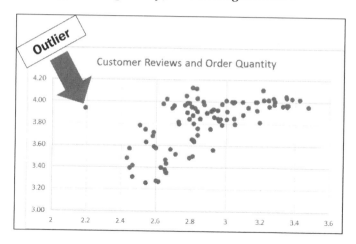

Looking at all of the other data points, we would expect that a 3.90 average review should have a 2.75 average order quantity at least. Although we might want to dive into the details to figure out what is going on, we'll save that exercise for another day. Right now, what it is really doing is messing up our model. Indeed, the biggest criticism of regressions is that they are overly sensitive to outliers. Let's look at a simple example. Go to *Chapter 2, AdventureWorks Regression*, regression project and create a new script, called Accord5.fsx. Copy the first part of the code from Accord1.fsx into it:

```
#r "../packages/Accord.3.0.2/lib/net40/Accord.dll"
#r "../packages/Accord.Statistics.3.0.2/lib/net40/Accord.Statistics.dll"
#r "../packages/Accord.Math.3.0.2/lib/net40/Accord.Math.dll"

open Accord
open Accord.Statistics.Models.Regression.Linear

let xs = [| [|15.0;130.0|];[|18.0;127.0|];[|15.0;128.0|];
[|17.0;120.0|];[|16.0;115.0|] |]
let y = [|3.6;3.5;3.8;3.4;2.6|]

let regression = MultipleLinearRegression(2,true)
let error = regression.Regress(xs,y)

let a = regression.Coefficients.[0]
let b = regression.Coefficients.[1]
```

```
let sse = regression.Regress(xs, y)
let mse = sse/float xs.Length
let rmse = sqrt(mse)
let r2 = regression.CoefficientOfDetermination(xs,y)
```

Next, let's add a child prodigy who is bored with school so he has a low GPA. Add in a student with an age of 10, an IQ of 150, and a GPA of 1.0:

```
let xs = [| [|15.0;130.0|];[|18.0;127.0|];[|15.0;128.0|]; [|17.0;120.0
|];[|16.0;115.0|];[|10.0;150.0|] |]

let y = [|3.6;3.5;3.8;3.4;2.6;1.0|]
```

Sending the entire script to the REPL gives us the following:

```
val regression : MultipleLinearRegression =
  y(x0, x1) = 0.351124295971452*x0 + 0.0120748957392838*x1 +
-3.89166344210844
val error : float = 1.882392837
val a : float = 0.351124296
val b : float = 0.01207489574
val sse : float = 1.882392837
val mse : float = 0.3137321395
val rmse : float = 0.5601179693
val r2 : float = 0.6619468116
```

Notice what happens to our model. Our r2 moves from 0.79 to 0.66 and our rmse climbs from 0.18 to 0.56! Holy cow, that's dramatic! As you can guess, how you deal with outliers will have a large impact on your model. If the intention of the model is to predict a majority of students' GPAs, we can safely remove the outlier because it's not typical. Another way of handling outliers is to use a model that does a better job of dealing with them.

With that under our belts, let's try it with real data. Add a new script file and call it AccordDotNet6.fsx. Copy and paste all of AccordDotNet2.fsx into it. Next, locate these lines:

```
while reader.Read() do
    productInfos.Add({ProductID=reader.GetInt32(0);
                        AvgOrders=(float)(reader.
                        GetDecimal(1));
                        AvgReviews=(float)(reader.
                        GetDecimal(2));
                        ListPrice=(float)(reader.
                        GetDecimal(3));})
```

```
let xs = productInfos |> Seq.map(fun pi ->
[|pi.AvgReviews; pi.ListPrice|]) |> Seq.toArray
let y = productInfos |> Seq.map(fun pi -> pi.AvgOrders)
|> Seq.toArray
```

And replace them with these:

```
while reader.Read() do
    productInfos.Add({ProductID=reader.GetInt32(0);
                        AvgOrders=(float)(reader.
                            GetDecimal(1));
                        AvgReviews=(float)(reader.
                            GetDecimal(2));
                        ListPrice=(float)(reader.
                            GetDecimal(3));})

let productInfos' = productInfos |>
Seq.filter(fun pi -> pi.ProductID <> 757)

let xs = productInfos' |> Seq.map(fun pi ->
[|pi.AvgReviews; pi.ListPrice|]) |> Seq.toArray
let y = productInfos' |> Seq.map(fun pi -> pi.AvgOrders)
|> Seq.toArray
```

Sending this to the REPL, we get the following:

```
val regression : MultipleLinearRegression =
  y(x0, x1) = 9.89805316193142*x0 + -0.000944004141999501*x1 +
-26.8922595356297

val error : float = 647.4688586

val a : float = 9.898053162

val b : float = -0.000944004142

val c : float = -26.89225954

val mse : float = 6.744467277

val rmse : float = 2.59701122

val r2 : float = 0.3743706412
```

The r2 moves up from 0.35 to 0.37 and our rmse drops from 2.65 to 2.59. Quite an improvement for removing one data point! Feel free to move this change over to the AdventureWorks project if you want. I am not going to walk you through it, but you now have the skills to do it independently. Dropping outliers is a very powerful way to make regressions more accurate, but there's a cost. Before we start dropping data elements that don't work from our model, we have to use some judgement. In fact, there are textbooks devoted to the science of what to do with outliers and missing data. We are not going to get into that in this book, other than acknowledge that the issue exists and to advise you to use some common sense when dropping elements.

Scaling

I want to acknowledge a common misperception about normalization and units of measure. You might notice that the different x variables have significantly different units of measure in *Chapter 2, AdventureWorks Regression,* and *Chapter 3, More AdventureWorks Regression.* In our examples, the Units of Customer Review is a 1-5 rating and the Price of Bikes is 0-10,000 US dollars. You might think that comparing such a large range of numbers would adversely affect the model. Without going into details, you can be rest assured that regressions are immune to different units of measure.

However, other models (especially classification and clustering models like k-NN, k-means, and PCA) are impacted. When we created these kinds of models in *Chapter 6, AdventureWorks Redux – k-NN and Naïve Bayes Classifiers,* and *Chapter 7, Traffic Stops and Crash Locations – When Two Datasets Are Better Than One,* we ran a risk that we were getting erroneous results because the data was not scaled. Fortunately, the features we selected, and the libraries we used (Numl.net and Accord), bailed us out. Numl.NET automatically scales input variables in all of the classification models. Depending on the type of model, Accord might scale for you. For example, in the PCA we wrote in *Chapter 7, Traffic Stops and Crash Locations – When Two Datasets Are Better Than One,* we passed in an input parameter called `AnalysisMethod.Center` on this line:

```
let pca = new PrincipalComponentAnalysis(pcaInput.ToArray(),
AnalysisMethod.Center)
```

This scales the input variables to the mean, which is good enough for our analysis. When we did the k-NN in *Chapter 6, AdventureWorks Redux – k-NN and Naïve Bayes Classifiers,* using Accord, we did not scale the data because our two input variables were categorical (`MartialStatus` and `Gender`) with only two possibilities (married or not, male or female) and you only need to scale continuous variables or categorical variables with more than two values. If we had used a continuous variable or a three-factor categorical variable in the k-NN, we would have had to scale it.

Let's walk through a quick example of scaling using Accord. Open up the
`FeatureCleaning` solution from this chapter and add a new script file called
`AccordKNN`:

Go into the NuGet Package Manager Console and enter this:

```
PM> install-package Accord.MachineLearning
```

Go into the `AccordKNN.fsx` file and add the code we used in *Chapter 6, AdventureWorks
Redux – k-NN and Naïve Bayes Classifiers,* for students who study and drink beer:

```
#r "../packages/Accord.3.0.2/lib/net40/Accord.dll"
#r "../packages/Accord.Math.3.0.2/lib/net40/Accord.Math.dll"
#r "../packages/Accord.Statistics.3.0.2/lib/net40/Accord.Statistics.
dll"
#r "../packages/Accord.MachineLearning.3.0.2/lib/net40/Accord.
MachineLearning.dll"

open Accord
open Accord.Math
open Accord.MachineLearning
open Accord.Statistics.Analysis

let inputs = [|[|5.0;1.0|];[|4.5;1.5|];
            [|5.1;0.75|];[|1.0;3.5|];
            [|0.5;4.0|];[|1.25;4.0|]|]
let outputs = [|1;1;1;0;0;0|]

let classes = 2
let k = 3
let knn = KNearestNeighbors(k, classes, inputs, outputs)

let input = [|5.0;0.5|]
let output = knn.Compute(input)
```

Now, let's scale the data so that studying and drinking beer are equivalent. We are going to take the simplest methodology of scaling called *mean scaling*. Go back to the script and enter this:

```
let studyingAverage = inputs |> Array.map(fun i -> i.[0])
|> Array.average
let drinkingAverage = inputs |> Array.map(fun i -> i.[1])
|> Array.average

let scaledInputs = inputs |> Array.map(fun i ->
[|i.[0]/studyingAverage; i.[1]/drinkingAverage|])
let scaledKNN = KNearestNeighbors(k, classes, scaledInputs,
outputs)
```

When you send this to the REPL, you will see the following:

val studyingAverage : float = 2.891666667

val drinkingAverage : float = 2.458333333

val scaledInputs : float [] [] =

  [|[|1.729106628; 0.406779661|]; [|1.556195965; 0.6101694915|];

   [|1.763688761; 0.3050847458|]; [|0.3458213256; 1.423728814|];

   [|0.1729106628; 1.627118644|]; [|0.4322766571; 1.627118644|]|]

val scaledKNN : KNearestNeighbors

Notice that the inputs are now relative to their means. The person who studied five hours and drank one beer now studied 73% more than the average and drank 41% less than the average. This k-NN model is now scaled and will give a better "apples to apples" comparison when used in practice.

Overfitting and cross validation

If you remember from Chapters 2, 3, and 4, one of the problems with our methodology when building models was that we were guilty of overfitting. Overfitting, the bane of predictive analytics, is what happens when we build a model that does a great job with past data but then falls apart when new data is introduced. This phenomenon is not just for data science; it happens a lot in our society: Professional athletes get lucrative contracts and then fail to live up to their prior performances; fund managers get hefty salary bumps because of last year's performance, and the list goes on.

Cross validation – train versus test

Unlike the Yankees, who never seem to learn, our profession has learned from its mistakes and has a great, if imperfect, tool to combat overfitting. We use the methodology of train/test/eval to build several models and then select the best one not based on how well it did against an existing dataset, but how it does against data it has never seen before. To accomplish that, we take our source data, import it, clean it, and split it into two subsets: training and testing. We then build our model on the training set and, if it seems viable, apply our test data to the model. If the model is still valid, we can think about pushing it to production. This is represented graphically as follows:

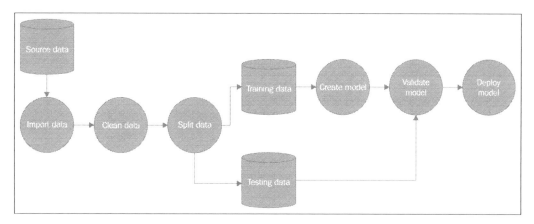

But there is one more step we can add. We can split our data several times and build new models to be validated. The actual splitting of the dataset is its own science, but typically each time the base dataset is split into **Training** and **Testing** subsets, the records are selected randomly. That means if you split your base data five times, you will have five completely different training and test subsets:

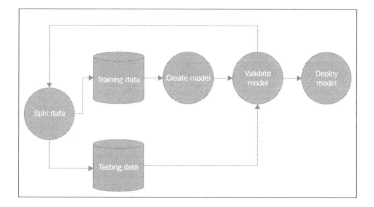

This kind of technique can be more important than the actual model selection. Both Accord and Numl do some kind of splitting under the hoods and in this book, we will trust that they are doing a good job. However, once you start working on models in the wild, you will want to dedicate a certain amount of time on every project for cross validation.

Cross validation – the random and mean test

Going back to our k-NN example of students that studied and drank beer, how do we know if we are predicting accurately? If we want to guess whether a student passed or not, we could just flip a coin: heads they pass, tails they fail. The assumption in our analysis is that the number of hours studying and the number of beers consumed have some kind of causality on the exam outcome. If our model does no better than a coin flip, then it is not a model worth using. Open up Visual Studio and go back to the `AccordKNN.fsx` file. At the bottom, enter in the following code:

```
let students = [|0..5|]
let random = System.Random()
let randomPrediction =
    students
    |> Array.map(fun s -> random.Next(0,2))
```

Sending this to the FSI, we get the following (your results will be different):

```
val students : int [] = [|0; 1; 2; 3; 4; 5|]

val random : System.Random

val randomPrediction : int [] = [|0; 1; 0; 0; 1; 1|]
```

Now, let's enter in some information about each student: the number of hours they studied and the number of beers they drank and run the unscaled k-NN on it:

```
let testInputs = [|[|5.0;1.0|];[|4.0;1.0|];
                   [|6.2;0.5|];[|0.0;2.0|];
                   [|0.5;4.0|];[|3.0;6.0|]|]

let knnPrediction =
    testInputs
    |> Array.map(fun ti -> knn.Compute(ti))
```

Sending this to the REPL gives us the following:

```
val testInputs : float [] [] =
  [|[|5.0; 1.0|]; [|4.0; 1.0|]; [|6.2; 0.5|]; [|0.0; 2.0|];
[|0.5; 4.0|];
    [|3.0; 6.0|]|]
val knnPrediction : int [] = [|1; 1; 1; 0; 0; 0|]
```

Finally, let's see how they actually did on the exam. Add this to the script:

```
let actual = [|1;1;1;0;0;0|]
```

Sending this to the FSI gives us the following:

val actual : int [] = [|1; 1; 1; 0; 0; 0|]

Combining these arrays together in a chart, will give us the following:

Student	Random	KNN	Actual
0	1	1	1
1	0	1	1
2	1	1	1
3	0	0	0
4	1	0	0
5	0	0	0

If we then scored how well the random test and k-NN did predicting the actual results, we can see that the random test correctly predicted the result 66% of the time and k-NN correctly predicted the result 100% of the time:

Student	Random Correct?	KNN Correct?
0	1	1
1	0	1
2	1	1
3	1	1
4	0	1
5	1	1
TOTAL	4	6
% Total	67%	100%

Because our k-NN did better than the random coin flip, we can consider the model useful.

This kind of yes/no random test works well when our model is a logistic regression or a classification model like k-NN, but what about when the dependent (Y) variable is a continuous value like in a linear regression? In that case, instead of using a random coin flip, we can plug in the mean of the known values. If the outcome predicts better than the mean, we probably have a good model. If it does worse than the mean, we need to rethink our model. For example, consider predicting average bike reviews from AdventureWorks:

Customer	Mean Rating	Predicted Rating	Actual
0	3.5	4.2	4.1
1	3.5	2.9	2.8
2	3.5	3.7	3.5
3	3.5	4.1	4.1
4	3.5	3.6	3.5
5	3.5	2.8	3.0

When you compare the predicted to the actual (taking the absolute value to account for being both higher and lower) and then aggregate the results, you can see that our linear regression did a better job in predicting the rating than the mean:

Customer	Abs Mean Difference	Abs Regression Difference
0	0.6	0.1
1	0.8	0.2
2	0.0	0.2
3	0.6	0.0
4	0.0	0.1
5	0.5	0.2
TOTAL	2.5	0.8
AVG	41%	13%

If you are thinking we have already done something like this in Chapters 2 and 3, you are right—this is the same concept as the RMSE.

Cross validation – the confusion matrix and AUC

Going back to our k-NN example, imagine that we ran our k-NN against many students. Sometimes the k-NN guessed correctly, sometimes the k-NN did not. There are actually four possible outcomes:

- k-NN predicted that the student would pass and they did pass
- k-NN predicted that the student would fail and they did fail
- k-NN predicted that the student would pass and they failed
- k-NN predicted that the student would fail and they passed

Each of these outcomes has a special name:

- **Predict Pass and Did Pass**: True Positive
- **Predict Fail and Did Fail**: True Negative
- **Predict Pass and Failed**: False Positive
- **Predict Fail and Passed**: False Negative

And in a chart format, it would look like this:

True Postive (Predict Pass/Actual Pass)	False Positive (Predict Pass/Actual Fail)
False Negative (Predict Fail/Actual Pass)	True Nagative (Predict Fail/Actual Fail)

Sometimes the False Positive is called a Type I error and the False Negative is called a Type II error.

If we ran the k-NN against 100 students, we could add values to that chart like this:

	Passed	Failed
	50	3
	2	40
TOTAL	52	43

Reading this chart, 52 students passed the exam. Of that, we correctly predicted 50 of them would pass, but we incorrectly predicted two of the passing students would fail. Similarly, 43 failed the exam (must have been a tough exam!), 40 of which we correctly predicted would fail, and three we incorrectly predicted would pass. This matrix is often called a *confusion matrix*.

With this confusion matrix, we can then do some basic statistics like:

Accuracy = True Positives + True Negatives / Total Population = (50 + 40) / 100 = 90%

True Positive Rate (TPR) = True Positives / Total Positives = 50 / 52 = 96%

False Negative Rate (FNR) = False Negatives / Total Positives = 2 / 52 = 4%

False Positive Rate (FPR) = False Positives / Total Negatives = 3 / 43 = 7%

True Negative Rate (TNR) = True Negatives / Total Negatives = 40 / 43 = 93%

(Note that TPR is sometimes called Sensitivity, the FNR is sometimes called Miss Rate, the False Positive Rate is sometimes called Fall-Out and the TNR is sometimes called Specificity.)

Positive Likelihood Ratio (LR+) = TPR / FPR = 96 % / 1 – 93% = 13.8

Negative Likelihood Ratio (LR-) = FNR / TNR = 4% / 93% = .04

Diagnostic Odds Ratio (DOR) = LR+ / LR- = 33.3

Since the DOR is greater than 1, we know that the model is working well.

Putting this into code, we could handwrite these formulas, but Accord.Net has already taken care of this for us. Go back into Visual Studio and open `AccordKNN.fsx`. At the bottom, enter in this code:

```
let positiveValue = 1
let negativeValue = 0

let confusionMatrix =
ConfusionMatrix(knnPrediction,actual,positiveValue,negativeValue)
```

On the next line, type `confusionMatrix` and hit dot to see all of the properties that are available to you:

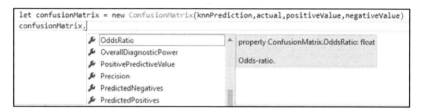

This is a very useful class indeed. Let's select the odds ratio:

```
confusionMatrix.OddsRatio
```

And then send the entire code block to the FSI:

```
val positiveValue : int = 1
val negativeValue : int = 0
val confusionMatrix : ConfusionMatrix = TP:3 FP:0, FN:0 TN:3
val it : float = infinity
```

Since our k-NN is was 100% accurate, we got an odds ratio of infinity (and beyond). In a real-world model, the odds ratio would obviously be much lower.

Cross validation – unrelated variables

There is one more technique that I want to cover to for cross-validation—adding in unrelated variables and seeing the impact on the model. If your model is truly useful, it should be able to handle extraneous "noise" variables without significantly impacting the model's result. As we saw in *Chapter 2, AdventureWorks Regression*, any additional variable will have a positive impact on most models, so this is a measure of degree. If adding an unrelated variable makes the model seem much more accurate, then the model itself is suspect. However, if the extra variable only has a marginal impact, then our model can be considered solid.

Let's see this in action. Go back into `AccordKNN.fsx` and add the following code at the bottom:

```
let inputs' = [|[|5.0;1.0;1.0|];[|4.5;1.5;11.0|];
                [|5.1;0.75;5.0|];[|1.0;3.5;8.0|];
                [|0.5;4.0;1.0|];[|1.25;4.0;11.0|]|]

let knn' = KNearestNeighbors(k, classes, inputs', outputs)

let testInputs' = [|[|5.0;1.0;5.0|];[|4.0;1.0;8.0|];
                    [|6.2;0.5;12.0|];[|0.0;2.0;2.0|];
                    [|0.5;4.0;6.0|];[|3.0;6.0;5.0|]|]

let knnPrediction' =
    testInputs'
    |> Array.map(fun ti -> knn'.Compute(ti))
```

I added a third variable that represents each student's zodiac symbol (1.0 = Aquarius, 2.0 = Pisces, and so on). When I passed in the same test input (also with random zodiac symbols), the predictions were the same as the original k-NN.

```
val knnPrediction' : int [] = [|1; 1; 1; 0; 0; 0|]
```

We can conclude that the extra variable, although it had an impact at some point in the modeling process, was not important enough to alter our original model. We can then use this model with a higher degree of confidence.

Summary

This chapter is a bit different than other machine learning books that you might have read because it did not introduce any new models, but instead concentrated on the dirty job on gathering, cleaning, and selecting your data. Although not as glamorous, it is absolutely essential that you have a firm grasp on these concepts because they will often make or break a project. In fact, many projects spend over 90% of their time acquiring data, cleaning the data, selecting the correct features, and building the appropriate cross-validation methodology. In this chapter, we looked at cleaning data and how to account for missing and incomplete data. Next, we looked at collinearity and normalization. Finally, we wrapped up with some common cross-validation techniques.

We are going to apply all of these techniques in the coming chapters. Up next, let's go back to the AdventureWorks company and see if we can help them improve their production process using a machine learning model based on how the human brain works.

9
AdventureWorks Production – Neural Networks

One day you are sitting in your office, basking in the glow of your new-found rock star status at AdventureWorks when your boss knocks on the door. She says, "Since you did such a good job with the consumer-facing portion of our existing website, we want to know if you would be interested in working on an internally-facing greenfield project." You cut her off with a resounding, "Yes!" She smiles and continues, "Okay. The problem is in our production area. Management is very interested in how we can reduce our scrap amount. Every month we get a report from Excel that looks like this:"

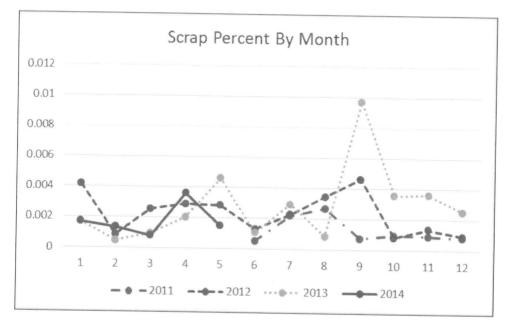

"The problem is that we don't know what to do with this data. Production is a complex workflow with many variables that can impact whether an item gets scrapped. We are looking for two things:

- A way of identifying the items that most impact whether items get scrapped
- A tool that allows our planners to alter the key variables to play *what if...* and make changes to the production process"

You tell your boss okay. Since this is a greenfield application and you have been hearing the hype around ASP.NET Core 1.0, this seems like a great place to try it. Also, you have heard about one of the hot models in data science, neural networks, and want to see whether the reality matches the hype.

Neural networks

A relative latecomer to data science, neural networks attempt to have the computer imitate how the brain operates. The gray matter between our ears is very good, up to a point, at making connections and drawing inferences. The promise of neural networks is that if we can build models that are patterned after how our brain works, we can combine the speed of computers and the pattern-matching ability of our wetware to make a learning model that can provide insights that computers or humans alone might miss.

Background

Neural networks takes their vocabulary from the actual brain; a neural network is a collection of neurons. If you remember from Biology 101 (or Crysis 2), the brain has billions of neurons that look more or less like this:

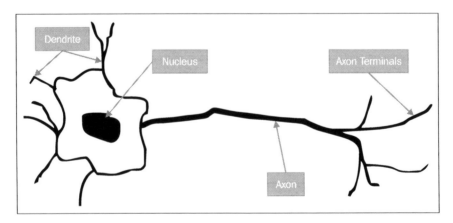

The axon terminal of one neuron connects to another neuron's dendrite. Since an individual neuron can have multiple dendrites and axon terminals, neurons can connect, and be connected to, numerous other neurons. The actual connection area between two neurons is called the synapse. Our brains use electrical signals to pass messages among neurons.

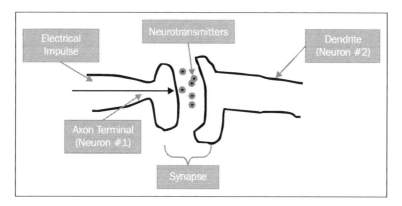

Since we are modeling the human brain for neural networks, it stands to reason that we will use the same vocabulary. In a neural network, we have a series of inputs and an output. Between the inputs and outputs, there is a hidden layer comprising neurons. Any connection from the inputs into the hidden layer, among the neurons inside the hidden layer, and from the hidden layer to the output is called a synapse.

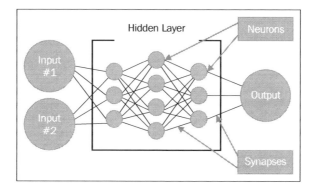

Notice that every synapse connects only to the neurons (or output) to its immediate right. Data always flows in one direction in a neural network and synapses never connect to themselves or any other preceding neuron in the network. One more thing to note is that when the hidden layer has many neurons, it is called a deep belief network (or deep learning). We will not be covering deep belief networks in this book, though it is certainly something you might want to toss around the next time you are out bowling with friends.

In a neural network, the synapse has only one job. They form a connection from one neuron to the next, applying a weight to that connection. For example, Neuron 1 activates the synapse with a weight of two, so that Neuron 2 receives an input of two:

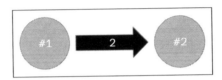

Neurons have a more complicated job. They take in the values from all of their input synapses, take input from something called a bias (I'll get to that in a second), apply an activation function to the inputs, and then either output a signal or do nothing. The activation function can treat each input separately, combine them, or do a mixture of both. There are many kinds of activation functions, ranging from simple to mind-boggling. In this example, the inputs are added together:

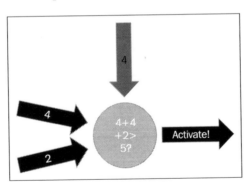

Some neural networks are smart enough to add and drop neurons as needed. For this book, we will not be doing anything like that—we will fix the number of neurons in each layer. Going back to some vocabulary that I dropped on you in the preceding paragraph, there are two kinds of inputs for any given activation function inside a neuron: the weights as transmitted by the synapses and the bias. The weights are a number that is assigned to the synapse, depending on the nature of the synapse, and does not change during the lifetime of the neural network. The bias is a global value that is assigned to all neurons (and output) which, unlike the weights, changes frequently. The machine learning component of the neural network is the many iterations that the computer does to create the best combination of weights and bias to give the optimal predictive score.

Neural network demo

With this mental model in place, let's take a look at a neural network in action. Let's look at a series of students who studied and drank beer before an exam and compare whether they passed that exam or not:

Student	Hours Studying	Beers Drank	Passed?
0	2	3	N
1	3	4	N
2	1	6	N
3	4	5	N
4	6	2	Y
5	8	3	Y
6	12	1	Y
7	3	2	Y

Since we have two input (x) variables (**Hours Studying** and **Beers Drank**), our neural network will have two inputs. We have one dependent variable (**Passed?**) so our neural network will have one output:

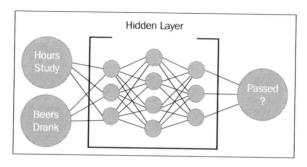

One thing to note is that the number of inputs depends on the range of values. So if we had a categorical input (such as male/female), we would have a number of inputs that correspond to the range of values in the category:

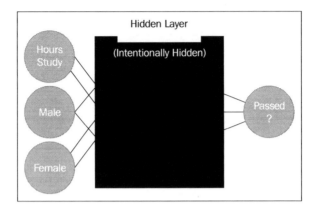

1. Go into Visual Studio and create a new C# ASP.NET web application:

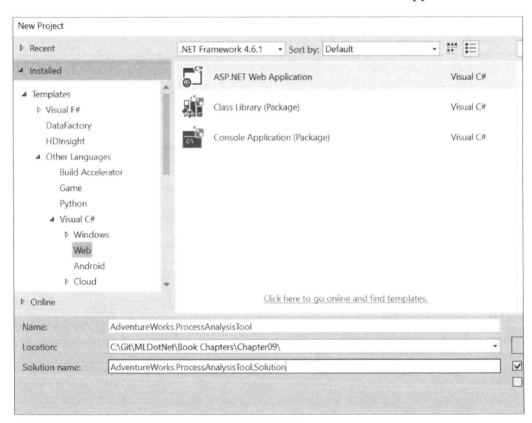

2. In the next dialog box, select **ASP.NET 5 Templates** and change the authentication type to **No Authentication**. Note that the templates will probably change from ASP.NET 5 to ASP.NET Core 1 after the writing of this book. You can consider these two terms synonymously.

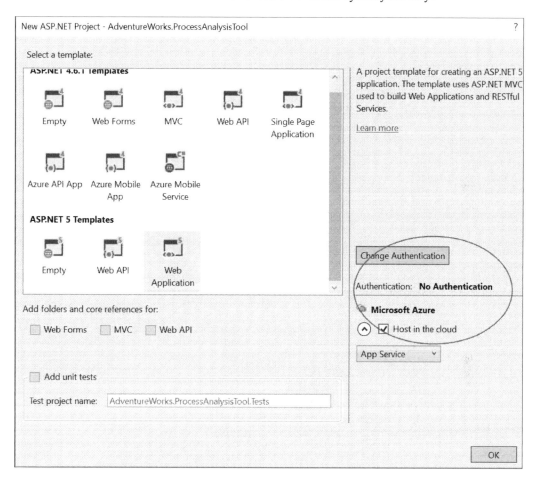

3. If everything code-gens as it should, you will get the following project:

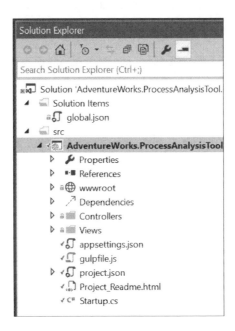

4. Next, let's add an F# Windows Library project:

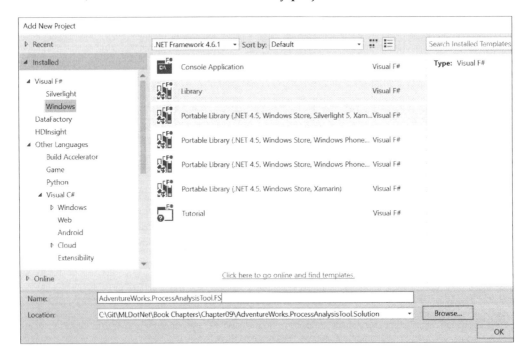

5. Once the F# project has been created, open up the NuGet Package Manager Console and install numl. Make sure that you are targeting the F# project for the NuGet installation:

```
PM> install-package numl
```

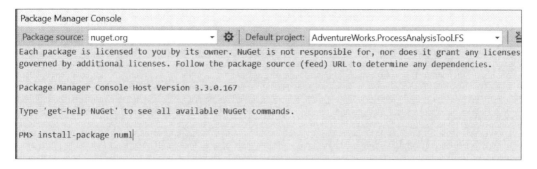

6. Rename `Scipt1.fsx` to `StudentNeuralNetwork.fsx`.

7. Go to the script and replace everything in it with this code:

```
#r "../packages/numl.0.8.26.0/lib/net40/numl.dll"

open numl
open numl.Model
open numl.Supervised.NeuralNetwork

type Student = {[<Feature>]Study: float;
                [<Feature>]Beer: float;
                [<Label>] mutable Passed: bool}

let data =
    [{Study=2.0;Beer=3.0;Passed=false};
     {Study=3.0;Beer=4.0;Passed=false};
     {Study=1.0;Beer=6.0;Passed=false};
     {Study=4.0;Beer=5.0;Passed=false};
     {Study=6.0;Beer=2.0;Passed=true};
     {Study=8.0;Beer=3.0;Passed=true};
     {Study=12.0;Beer=1.0;Passed=true};
     {Study=3.0;Beer=2.0;Passed=true};]

let data' = data |> Seq.map box
let descriptor = Descriptor.Create<Student>()
let generator = NeuralNetworkGenerator()
generator.Descriptor <- descriptor
let model = Learner.Learn(data', 0.80, 100, generator)
let accuracy = model.Accuracy
```

8. When you send this to the FSI, you will get the following:

```
val generator : NeuralNetworkGenerator
val model : LearningModel =
   Learning Model:
   Generator numl.Supervised.NeuralNetwork.NeuralNetworkGenerator
   Model:
numl.Supervised.NeuralNetwork.NeuralNetworkModel
   Accuracy: 100.00 %


val accuracy : float = 1.0
```

If you worked through the example in *Chapter 3, More AdventureWorks Regression,* this code will look familiar. The `Student` type has three properties: `Study`, `Beer`, and `Passed`. Note that `Passed` is marked as mutable because numl expects any prediction data type to be of the same type that was used when the model was created. Numl then mutates the response variable to whatever the model comes up with, so we have to use the mutable keyword. Alternative implementations would be to pass into the prediction function a type without that response variable or return a new instance so the value can be immutable. Feel free to contribute to the open source project if you feel strongly about this (I'll see you there J).

In any event, the data is an array of instances of our students. We then create a descriptor of the `Student` type and a generator of a neural network. Notice that we know the generator's `descriptor` property is mutable because we assign it using the `<-` symbol in this line:

```
generator.Descriptor <- descriptor
```

Next, we pass the generator to the learner and create the model. Under the hood, numl is scaling our data and running multiple instances of a neural network to determine the optimal solution. Once the generator has finished its work, it reports that it has an accuracy of 100%. We can then test our neural network with some new data. Go to the script and add this:

```
let testData = {Study=7.0;Beer=1.0;Passed=false}
let predict = model.Model.Predict(testData)
```

When you send this to the FSI, you will get this:

```
val testData : Student = {Study = 7.0;
                          Beer = 1.0;
                          Passed = false;}
```

```
>

val predict : obj = {Study = 7.0;
                     Beer = 1.0;
                     Passed = true;}
```

In this case, our student who studies 7 hours and has 1 beer will pass the test.

Neural network – try #1

With the theory out of the way, let's see if neural networks can help us with AdventureWorks. As in *Chapter 3, More AdventureWorks Regression*, let's see if we can use a business area expert to help us formulate some viable hypotheses. When we visit the manager of manufacturing, he says, "I think there are a couple of areas that you should look at. See if the production location has an impact. We have seven major locations":

ID	Location
10	Frame Forming
20	Frame Welding
30	Debur and Polish
40	Paint
45	Specialized Paint
50	Subassembly
60	Final Assembly

"I am curious if our **Paint** location generates more than expected defects because we have high turnover in that area."

"Also, see if there is a relationship between vendors and products with defects. In some cases, we purchase parts for a single vendor; in other cases, we have two or three vendors supplying us parts. We don't track which part came from which vendor when we build a bike, but perhaps you can find that certain vendors are associated with purchase orders that have defects."

These seem like two good places to start, so let's head over to the **Solution Explorer** and create a new script file called `AWNeuralNetwork.fsx` in the F# project:

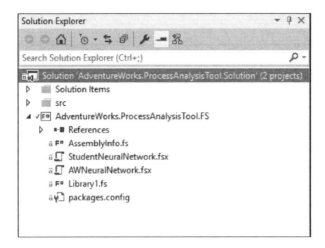

Next, open up the NuGet Package Manager and enter this:

```
PM> Install-Package SQLProvider -prerelease
```

Next, open the script file and enter this (note that the version number might be different for you):

```fsharp
#r "../packages/SQLProvider.0.0.11-alpha/lib/FSharp.Data.SQLProvider.dll"
#r "../packages/numl.0.8.26.0/lib/net40/numl.dll"
#r "../packages/FSharp.Collections.ParallelSeq.1.0.2/lib/net40/FSharp.Collections.ParallelSeq.dll"

open numl
open System
open numl.Model
open System.Linq
open FSharp.Data.Sql
open numl.Supervised.NeuralNetwork
open FSharp.Collections.ParallelSeq

[<Literal>]
let connectionString = "data
source=nc54a9m5kk.database.windows.net;initial
catalog=AdventureWorks2014;user id= PacktReader;password=
P@cktM@chine1e@rning;"
```

```
type AdventureWorks =
SqlDataProvider<ConnectionString=connectionString>
let context = AdventureWorks.GetDataContext()
```

Sending this to the REPL will give you the following:

```
val connectionString : string =
  "data source=nc54a9m5kk.database.windows.net;initial catalog=A"+[70
chars]
type AdventureWorks = SqlDataProvider<...>
val context : SqlDataProvider<...>.dataContext
```

Next, let's tackle the location hypothesis. Go to the script and enter the following:

```
type WorkOrderLocation = {[<Feature>] Location10: bool;
                          [<Feature>] Location20: bool;
                          [<Feature>] Location30: bool;
                          [<Feature>] Location40: bool;
                          [<Feature>] Location45: bool;
                          [<Feature>] Location50: bool;
                          [<Feature>] Location60: bool;
                          [<Label>] mutable Scrapped: bool}

let getWorkOrderLocation (workOrderId, scrappedQty:int16) =
    let workOrderRoutings =
    context.``[Production].[WorkOrderRouting]``.Where(fun wor ->
    wor.WorkOrderID = workOrderId) |> Seq.toArray
    match workOrderRoutings.Length with
    | 0 -> None
    | _ ->
        let location10 = workOrderRoutings |> Array.exists(fun wor
        -> wor.LocationID = int16 10)
        let location20 = workOrderRoutings |> Array.exists(fun wor
        -> wor.LocationID = int16 20)
        let location30 = workOrderRoutings |> Array.exists(fun wor
        -> wor.LocationID = int16 30)
        let location40 = workOrderRoutings |> Array.exists(fun wor
        -> wor.LocationID = int16 40)
        let location45 = workOrderRoutings |> Array.exists(fun wor
        -> wor.LocationID = int16 45)
        let location50 = workOrderRoutings |> Array.exists(fun wor
        -> wor.LocationID = int16 50)
        let location60 = workOrderRoutings |> Array.exists(fun wor
        -> wor.LocationID = int16 60)
```

```
let scrapped = scrappedQty > int16 0
Some {Location10=location10;Location20=location20;
Location30=location30;Location40=location40;
Location45=location45;Location50=location50;
Location60=location60;Scrapped=scrapped}
```

Sending this to the REPL gives you the following:

```
type WorkOrderLocation =
  {Location10: bool;
   Location20: bool;
   Location30: bool;
   Location40: bool;
   Location45: bool;
   Location50: bool;
   Location60: bool;
   mutable Scrapped: bool;}
val getWorkOrderLocation :
  workOrderId:int * scrappedQty:int16 -> WorkOrderLocation option
```

You can see we have a record type with each location as a field and an indicator if there was anything scrapped. The level of automacy for this data structure is work order. Each order might visit one or all of the locations and might have some scrap quantity. The getWorkOrderFunction takes the WorkOrderLocation table, where each location is a row in the table, and flattens into this WorkOrderLocation record type.

Next, go back to the script and enter this:

```
let locationData =
    context.``[Production].[WorkOrder]``
    |> PSeq.map(fun wo ->
    getWorkOrderLocation(wo.WorkOrderID,wo.ScrappedQty))
    |> Seq.filter(fun wol -> wol.IsSome)
    |> Seq.map(fun wol -> wol.Value)
    |> Seq.toArray
```

Sending this to the REPL gives us the following:

```
val locationData : WorkOrderLocation [] =
  [|{Location10 = true;
    Location20 = true;
    Location30 = true;
```

```
Location40 = false;
Location45 = true;
Location50 = true;
Location60 = true;
Scrapped = false;}; {Location10 = false;
                    Location20 = false;
                    Location30 = false;
                    Location40 = false;
```

This code is very much what you saw in *Chapter 5, Time Out – Obtaining Data.* We go to the database and pull in all the work orders and then map the locations into our `WorkOrderLocation` record. Notice that we are using the `PSeq` so that we can get a performance boost by making simultaneous calls to the database to get the locations for each work order.

With the data local, let's try out a neural network. Go into the script file and enter this:

```
let locationData' = locationData |> Seq.map box
let descriptor = Descriptor.Create<WorkOrderLocation>()
let generator = NeuralNetworkGenerator()
generator.Descriptor <- descriptor
let model = Learner.Learn(locationData', 0.80, 5,
generator)
let accuracy = model.Accuracy
```

Sending that to the REPL, after a long wait, will give you the following:

```
val generator : NeuralNetworkGenerator
val model : LearningModel =
  Learning Model:
  Generator numl.Supervised.NeuralNetwork.NeuralNetworkGenerator
  Model:
numl.Supervised.NeuralNetwork.NeuralNetworkModel
  Accuracy: 0.61 %


val accuracy : float = 0.006099706745
```

So, ugh, it does not look like the location can predict where defects might occur. As we saw in *Chapter 3, More AdventureWorks Regression,* sometimes you do not need a working model to make the experiment worthwhile. In this case, we can go back to the director and tell him that scraps are occurring all over his production location, not just in the painting (so much for blaming the new guy).

Neural network – try #2

Let's see if we can find anything using the director's second hypothesis that certain vendors might have higher defect rates than others. Go back to the script and enter this:

```
type  VendorProduct = {WorkOrderID: int;
                       [<Feature>]BusinessEntityID: int;
                       [<Feature>]ProductID: int;
                       [<Label>] mutable Scrapped: bool}

let workOrders = context.``[Production].[WorkOrder]`` |>
Seq.toArray
let maxWorkOrder = workOrders.Length
let workOrderIds = Array.zeroCreate<int>(1000)
let workOrderIds' = workOrderIds |> Array.mapi(fun idx i ->
workOrders.[System.Random(idx).Next(maxWorkOrder)])
                                 |> Array.map(fun wo ->
                                 wo.WorkOrderID)
```

When you send it to the FSI, you will get the following:

```
type VendorProduct =
  {WorkOrderID: int;
   BusinessEntityID: int;
   ProductID: int;
   mutable Scrapped: bool;}


     ...
   FSharp.Data.Sql.Common.SqlEntity; FSharp.Data.Sql.Common.SqlEntity;
   FSharp.Data.Sql.Common.SqlEntity; FSharp.Data.Sql.Common.SqlEntity;
...|]
val maxWorkOrder : int = 72591
val workOrderIds : int [] =
  [|0; 0; 0; 0; 0; 0; 0; 0; 0; 0; 0; 0; 0; 0; 0; 0; 0; 0; 0; 0; 0; 0;
0; 0;
    0; 0; 0; 0; 0; 0; 0; 0; 0; 0; 0; 0; 0; 0; 0; 0; 0; 0; 0; 0; 0; 0;
0; 0;
    0; 0; 0; 0; 0; 0; 0; 0; 0; 0; 0; 0; 0; 0; 0; 0; 0; 0; 0; 0; 0; 0;
0; 0;
    0; 0; 0; 0; 0; 0; 0; 0; 0; 0; 0; 0; 0; 0; 0; 0; 0; 0; 0; 0; 0; 0;
0; 0;
    ...|]
val workOrderIds' : int [] =
```

The `VendorProduct` record type should be familiar to you. The next code block creates an array of 1,000 random work order IDs. As we learned from the first experiment, neural networks take a long time to complete. We will look at some big-data solutions in the next chapter, but until then we'll do what data scientists have done for as long as they have done data science—take a sample of the larger dataset. Notice that we are using the `Array.Mapi` high-order function so that we can use the index value to locate the correct value in the work orders array. Unfortunately, we can't pass the index into the type provider and have it evaluate on the server, so the entire work order table is brought local so that we can use the index.

Next, enter this into the script:

```
let (|=|) id a = Array.contains id a

let vendorData =
    query{for p in context.``[Production].[Product]`` do
        for wo in p.FK_WorkOrder_Product_ProductID do
        for bom in
        p.FK_BillOfMaterials_Product_ProductAssemblyID do
        join pv in context.``[Purchasing].[ProductVendor]`` on
        (bom.ComponentID = pv.ProductID)
        join v in context.``[Purchasing].[Vendor]`` on
        (pv.BusinessEntityID = v.BusinessEntityID)
        select  ({WorkOrderID = wo.WorkOrderID;BusinessEntityID
        = v.BusinessEntityID; ProductID = p.ProductID; Scrapped
        = wo.ScrappedQty > int16 0})}
        |> Seq.filter(fun vp -> vp.WorkOrderID |=|
        workOrderIds')
        |> Seq.toArray
```

When you send it to the FSI, after a bit of a wait, you will get the following:

```
val ( |=| ) : id:'a -> a:'a [] -> bool when 'a : equality
val vendorData : VendorProduct [] =
  [|{WorkOrderID = 25;
    BusinessEntityID = 1576;
    ProductID = 764;
    Scrapped = false;}; {WorkOrderID = 25;
                         BusinessEntityID = 1586;
                         ProductID = 764;
                         Scrapped = false;}; {WorkOrderID = 25;
```

The first line is the `in` (`|=|`) operator that we ran across in *Chapter 5, Time Out – Obtaining Data*. The next code block hydrates the `vendorData` array with the data from the 1,000 randomly selected work orders. Notice that there is some repetition because each work order will use several parts and each part might be supplied by a variety of vendors (in this case, called business entities).

With the data local, go into the script and enter this:

```
let vendorData' = vendorData |> Seq.map box
let descriptor' = Descriptor.Create<VendorProduct>()
let generator' = NeuralNetworkGenerator()
generator'.Descriptor <- descriptor'
let model' = Learner.Learn(vendorData', 0.80, 5, generator')
let accuracy' = model'.Accuracy
```

When you send it to the FSI, you will get the following:

```
val generator' : NeuralNetworkGenerator
val model' : LearningModel =
  Learning Model:
  Generator numl.Supervised.NeuralNetwork.NeuralNetworkGenerator
  Model:
numl.Supervised.NeuralNetwork.NeuralNetworkModel
  Accuracy: 99.32 %


val accuracy' : float = 0.9931740614
```

So, this is interesting. We have a very high accuracy rate. One wonders: is this because in the case of a single vendor for a product, all of the scrapped amount will be associated with them because they are the only ones. However, since a single vendor might supply multiple input products and those products might have different scrap rates, you can use the model to predict if a given vendor and a given product will have a scrap rate. Also, notice that instead of adding an input for each vendor and product (which would have made a very sparse data frame), there is one input for vendor and one for product. Although these can be considered categorical values, we can sacrifice some precision for this exercise.

The key thing about the neural network that you will want to remember is that the neural network can't tell you how it got its answer (very much like the human brain, no?). So the neural network won't report back which combination of vendors and products will lead to defects. To do that, you would need to use a different model.

Building the application

With this neural network giving us enough of what we need, let's go ahead and build out our ASP.NET 5.0 application with the model. At the time of writing, ASP. NET 5.0 only supports C# so we will have to translate our F# into C# and port the code into the application. Once the other languages are supported by ASP.NET, we will update the sample code on the website.

If you are not familiar with C#, it is the most popular language on the .NET stack and is very similar to Java. C# is a general-purpose language that initially combined imperative and object-oriented language features. Lately, functional constructs have been bolted onto the language specifications. However, as the old carpenter axiom goes, "If it's a screw, use a screwdriver. If it's a nail, use a hammer." Since that's the case, you are much better served to do .NET functional programming with F#. I'll do my best in the next section to explain any differences in the C# implementation when we port the code over.

Setting up the models

You already have the boilerplate MVC site created. Open up NuGet Package Manager Console and install numl into it:

```
PM > install-package numl
```

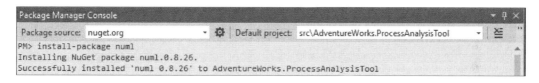

Next, create a folder called `Models` in the **Solution Explorer**:

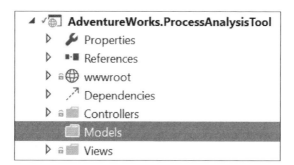

In that folder, add a new class file named `VendorProduct`:

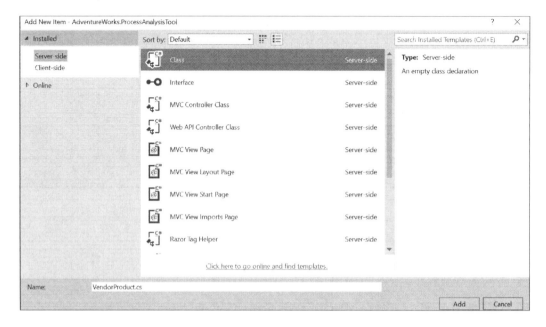

Inside that file, replace all of the code with the following:

```
using numl.Model;

namespace AdventureWorks.ProcessAnalysisTool.Models
{
    public class VendorProduct
    {
        public int WorkOrderID { get; set; }
        [Feature]
        public int BusinessEntityID { get; set; }
        [Feature]
        public int ProductID { get; set; }
        [Label]
        public bool Scrapped { get; set; }
    }
}
```

As you can guess, this is the equivalent of the record type we create in F#. The only real difference is that the properties are mutable by default (so be careful). Go to the **Solution Explorer** and find the `Project.json` file. Open it and remove this entry in the `frameworks` section:

```
:        "dnxcore50": { }
```

This section should now look like the following:

```
"frameworks": {
    "dnx451": {
        "dependencies": {
            "numl": "0.8.26"
        }
    }
},
```

Go ahead and run the website to make sure it is good:

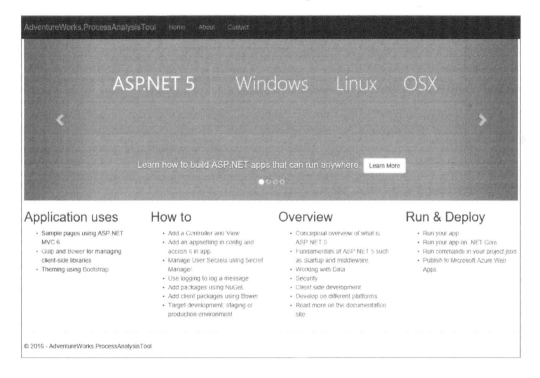

What we are doing is removing the site's dependency on .NET Core. Although numl does support .NET Core, we don't need it right now.

If the site is up and running, let's add the rest of our helper classes. Go back into the **Solution Explorer** and add a new class file named `Product.cs`. Go into that class and replace the existing code with this:

```
using System;

namespace AdventureWorks.ProcessAnalysisTool.Models
{
    public class Product
    {
        public int ProductID { get; set; }
        public string Description { get; set; }
    }
}
```

This is another record-equivalent class which will be used when the user selects the `Product` they want to model.

Go back to the **Solution Explorer** and add a new class file named `Vendor.cs`. Go into that class and replace the existing code with this:

```
using System;

namespace AdventureWorks.ProcessAnalysisTool.Models
{
    public class Vendor
    {
        public int VendorID { get; set; }
        public String Description { get; set; }


    }
}
```

Like the `Product` class, this will be used to populate the select list for the user.

Go back into the **Solution Explorer** and add a new class file named `Repository.cs`. Go into that class and replace the existing code with the following:

```
using System;
using System.Collections.Generic;
using System.Data.SqlClient;
using System.Linq;
```

```csharp
namespace AdventureWorks.ProcessAnalysisTool.Models
{
    public class Repository
    {
        public String ConnectionString { get; private set; }
        public Repository(String connectionString)
        {
            this.ConnectionString = connectionString;
        }

        public ICollection<Vendor> GetAllVendors()
        {
            var vendors = new List<Vendor>();
            using (var connection = new
            SqlConnection(this.ConnectionString))
            {
                var commandText =
                    "Select distinct V.BusinessEntityID, V.Name
                    from [Purchasing].[Vendor] as V " +
                    "Inner join[Purchasing].[ProductVendor]
                    as PV " +
                    "on V.BusinessEntityID = PV.BusinessEntityID "
                    +
                    "order by 2 asc";

                using (var command = new SqlCommand(commandText,
                connection))
                {
                    connection.Open();
                    var reader = command.ExecuteReader();
                    while (reader.Read())
                    {
                        vendors.Add(new Vendor() { VendorID =
                        (int)reader[0], Description =
                        (string)reader[1] });
                    }
                }
            }
            return vendors;
        }

        public ICollection<Product> GetAllProducts()
        {
            var products = new List<Product>();
            using (var connection = new
```

```
        SqlConnection(this.ConnectionString))
        {
            var commandText =
                "Select distinct P.ProductID, P.Name from
                [Production].[Product] as P " +
                "Inner join[Purchasing].[ProductVendor]
                as PV " +
                "on P.ProductID = PV.ProductID " +
                "order by 2 asc";

            using (var command =
            new SqlCommand(commandText, connection))
            {
                connection.Open();
                var reader = command.ExecuteReader();
                while (reader.Read())
                {
                    products.Add(new Product() { ProductID =
                    (int)reader[0], Description =
                    (string)reader[1] });
                }
            }
        }
        return products;
    }

    public ICollection<VendorProduct> GetAllVendorProducts()
    {
        var vendorProducts = new List<VendorProduct>();
        using (var connection = new
        SqlConnection(this.ConnectionString))
        {
            var commandText =
                "Select WO.WorkOrderID, PV.BusinessEntityID,
                PV.ProductID, WO.ScrappedQty " +
                "from[Production].[Product] as P " +
                "inner join[Production].[WorkOrder] as WO " +
                "on P.ProductID = WO.ProductID " +
                "inner join[Production].[BillOfMaterials]
                as BOM " +
                "on P.ProductID = BOM.ProductAssemblyID " +
                "inner join[Purchasing].[ProductVendor]
                as PV " +
                "on BOM.ComponentID = PV.ProductID ";
```

```
        using (var command =
        new SqlCommand(commandText, connection))
        {
            connection.Open();
            var reader = command.ExecuteReader();
            while (reader.Read())
            {
                vendorProducts.Add(new VendorProduct()
                {
                    WorkOrderID = (int)reader[0],
                    BusinessEntityID = (int)reader[1],
                    ProductID = (int)reader[2],
                    Scrapped = (short)reader[3] > 0
                });
            }
        }
    }

    return vendorProducts;
}

public ICollection<VendorProduct>
GetRandomVendorProducts(Int32 number)
{
    var returnValue = new List<VendorProduct>();
    var vendorProducts = this.GetAllVendorProducts();
    for (int i = 0; i < number; i++)
    {
        var random = new System.Random(i);
        var index = random.Next(vendorProducts.Count - 1);
        returnValue.Add(vendorProducts.ElementAt(index));
    }
    return returnValue;
}
    }
}
```

As you can probably guess, this is the class that calls out to the database. Since C# does not have type providers, we need to handwrite the ADO.NET code. We will need to add a reference to `System.Data` to make this code work. Go into the **References** in **Solution Explorer** and add it:

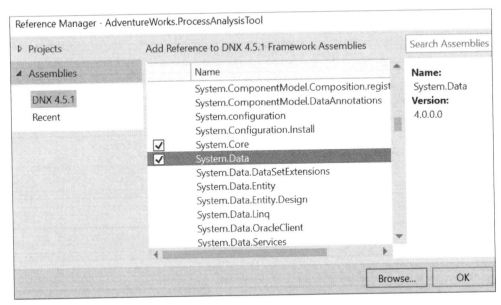

You can run the site again to make sure we are on the right track. In the **Solution Explorer**, add a class file called `NeuralNetwork.cs`. Replace all of its code with this:

```
using numl;
using numl.Model;
using numl.Supervised.NeuralNetwork;
using System;
using System.Collections.Generic;

namespace AdventureWorks.ProcessAnalysisTool.Models
{
    public class NeuralNetwork
    {
        public ICollection<VendorProduct> VendorProducts
        { get; private set; }
        public LearningModel Model { get; private set; }

        public NeuralNetwork(ICollection<VendorProduct>
        vendorProducts)
        {
            if(vendorProducts ==  null)
```

```
        {
            throw new ArgumentNullException("vendorProducts");
        }
        this.VendorProducts = vendorProducts;
        this.Train();
    }

    internal void Train()
    {
        var vendorData = VendorProducts;
        var descriptor = Descriptor.Create<VendorProduct>();
        var generator = new NeuralNetworkGenerator();
        generator.Descriptor = descriptor;
        var model = Learner.Learn(vendorData, 0.80, 5,
        generator);
        if (model.Accuracy > .75)
        {
            this.Model = model;
        }
    }

    public bool GetScrappedInd(int vendorId, int productId)
    {
        if(this.Model == null)
        {
            return true;
        }
        else
        {
            var vendorProduct = new VendorProduct()
            {
                BusinessEntityID = vendorId,
                ProductID = productId,
                Scrapped = false
            };
            return
            (bool)this.Model.Model.Predict((object)vendorProduct);
        }
    }
  }
}
```

This class does the heavy lifting of the neural network calculations for us. Notice that the class is data–agnostic, so it can be ported over to .NET Core easily. All we need is a collection of VendorProducts to be passed into the constructor for the neural network to calculate.

With all of these classes created, your solution explorer should look like this:

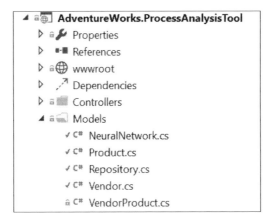

You should be able to compile and run the website. Let's now implement a user interface for the neural network.

Building the UX

The following steps will guide you to build the UX:

Go into the **Solution Explorer** and select **AdventureWorks.ProcessAnalysisTool**. Navigate to **Add | New Item**:

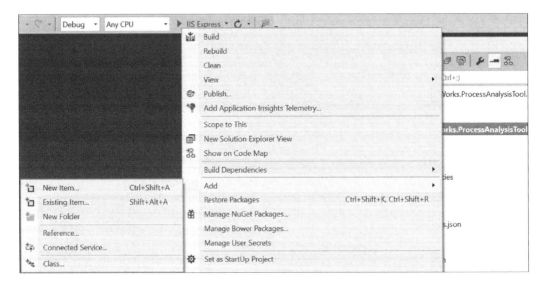

In the next dialog, select **Class** and name it `Global.cs`:

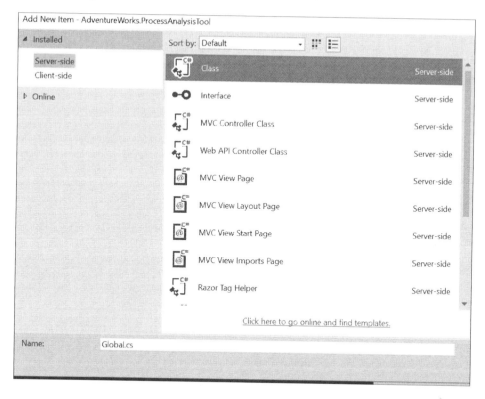

Go to the `Global` class and replace all of the contents with the following:

```
using AdventureWorks.ProcessAnalysisTool.Models;

namespace AdventureWorks.ProcessAnalysisTool
{
    public static class Global
    {
        static NeuralNetwork _neuralNetwork = null;

        public static void InitNeuralNetwork()
        {
            var connectionString =
            "data source=nc54a9m5kk.database.windows.net;
            initial catalog=AdventureWorks2014;
            user id= PacktReader;
            password= P@cktM@chine1e@rning;";
            var repository = new
            Repository(connectionString);
            var vendorProducts =
            repository.GetRandomVendorProducts(1000);
```

```
        _neuralNetwork = new
        NeuralNetwork(vendorProducts);
    }

    public static NeuralNetwork NeuralNetwork
    { get
        {
            return _neuralNetwork;
        }
    }
  }
}
```

This class creates a new neural network for us. We can access the neural network's functions via the read-only property called `Neural Network`. Because it is marked static, the class will stay in memory as long as the application is running.

Next, locate the `Startup.cs` file in the main site:

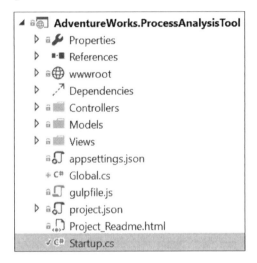

Open the file and replace the constructor (called `Startup`) with this code:

```
public Startup(IHostingEnvironment env)
{
    // Set up configuration sources.
    var builder = new ConfigurationBuilder()
        .AddJsonFile("appsettings.json")
        .AddEnvironmentVariables();
        Configuration = builder.Build();

    Global.InitNeuralNetwork();
}
```

When the website starts up, it will create a global neural network that all requests can use.

Next, locate the `HomeController` in the `Controllers` directory.

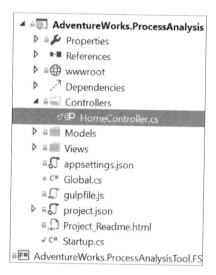

Open that file and add this method to populate some drop lists of vendors and products:

```
[HttpGet]
public IActionResult PredictScrap()
{
    var connectionString =
    "data source=nc54a9m5kk.database.windows.net;
    initial catalog=AdventureWorks2014;
    user id= PacktReader;password= P@cktM@chine1e@rning;";
    var repository = new Repository(connectionString);
    var vendors = repository.GetAllVendors();
    var products = repository.GetAllProducts();

    ViewBag.Vendors = new SelectList(vendors, "VendorID",
    "Description");
    ViewBag.Products = new SelectList(products,
    "ProductID", "Description");

    return View();
}
```

Next, add this method to run `Calculate` on the global neural network when the vendor and product are posted back to the server:

```
[HttpPost]
public IActionResult PredictScrap(Int32 vendorId,
Int32 productId)
{
    ViewBag.ScappedInd = Global.NeuralNetwork
    .GetScrappedInd(vendorId, productId);

    var connectionString =
    "data source=nc54a9m5kk.database.windows.net;
    initial catalog=AdventureWorks2014;
    user id= PacktReader;password= P@cktM@chine1e@rning;";
    var repository = new Repository(connectionString);
    var vendors = repository.GetAllVendors();
    var products = repository.GetAllProducts();

    ViewBag.Vendors = new SelectList(vendors,
    "VendorID", "Description", vendorId);
    ViewBag.Products = new SelectList(products,
    "ProductID", "Description", productId);

    return View();
}
```

If you collapse to definitions, the `HomeController` will look like this:

```
namespace AdventureWorks.ProcessAnalysisTool.Controllers
{
    0 references | Jamie Dixon, 7 days ago | 1 author, 1 change
    public class HomeController : Controller
    {
        0 references | Jamie Dixon, 7 days ago | 1 author, 1 change
        public IActionResult Index()...

        0 references | Jamie Dixon, 7 days ago | 1 author, 1 change
        public IActionResult About()...

        0 references | Jamie Dixon, 7 days ago | 1 author, 1 change
        public IActionResult Contact()...

        0 references | Jamie Dixon, 7 days ago | 1 author, 1 change
        public IActionResult Error()...

        [HttpGet]
        0 references | 0 changes | 0 authors, 0 changes
        public IActionResult PredictScrap()...

        [HttpPost]
        0 references | 0 changes | 0 authors, 0 changes
        public IActionResult PredictScrap(Int32 vendorId, Int32 productId)...

    }
```

Next, go into **Solution Explorer** and navigate to **AdventureWorks. ProcessAnalysisTool | Views | Home**. Right-click on the folder and navigate to **Add | New Item**:

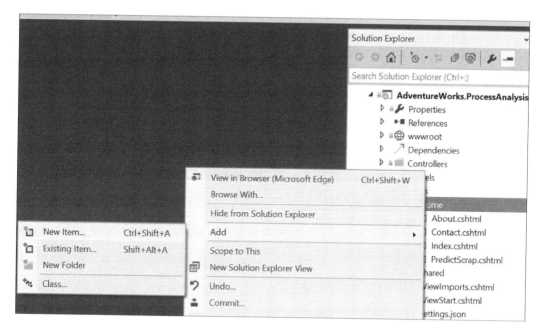

In the next dialog box, select **MVC View Page** and name it `PredictScrap.cshtml`:

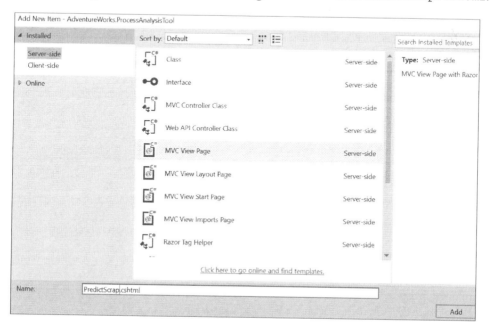

Open this page and replace all of the contents with the following:

```
<h2>Determine Scrap Rate</h2>

@using (Html.BeginForm())
{
    <div class="form-horizontal">
        <h4>Select Inputs</h4>
        <hr />

        <div class="form-group">
            <div class="col-md-10">
                @Html.DropDownList("VendorID",
                (SelectList)ViewBag.Vendors,
                htmlAttributes: new { @class = "form-control" })
                @Html.DropDownList("ProductID",
                (SelectList)ViewBag.Products,
                htmlAttributes: new { @class = "form-control" })
            </div>
        </div>
        <div class="form-group">
            <div class="col-md-offset-2 col-md-10">
                <input type="submit" value="Predict!"
                class="btn btn-default" />
            </div>
        </div>
        <h4>Will Have Scrap?</h4>
        <div class="form-group">
            <div class="col-md-offset-2 col-md-10">
                @ViewBag.ScappedInd
            </div>
        </div>
    </div>
}
```

This is the input form that will allow users to select vendors and products and see what the neural network will predict—whether this combination will have scrap. When you run the site and navigate to `localhost:port/home/PredictScrap` for the first time, you will see the droplists ready for you:

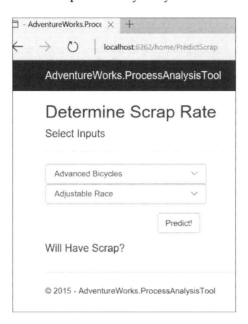

Select a vendor and a product and click on **Predict!**:

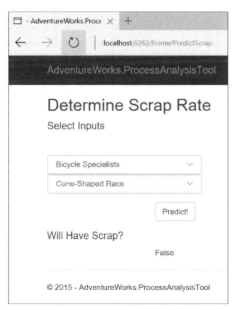

We now have a fully functioning ASP .NET Core 1.0 website that uses a neural network to predict AdventureWorks scrap percentages. With this skeleton, we can hand the site off to a UX expert to make the site have a better look and feel—with the core functionality in place.

Summary

This chapter broke some new ground. We dove into ASP.NET 5.0 for our website design. We used numl to create two neural networks: one that showed that there is no relationship between the area of the company and the scrap rate, and another that can be used to predict if there will be scrap based on the vendor and product. We then implemented the second model in our website.

10
Big Data and IoT

Up to this point, this book has followed a pattern of extracting data, cleaning and shaping the data, and then building machine learning models. A common element in all of the examples is that when we've extracted data, we have brought it from the server (or other external sources) locally to our machine. This means our analysis is confined to whatever data fits in the memory on our local machines. While this is good for small- and medium-sized datasets, there are plenty of datasets and questions that do not fit in RAM. The last couple of years have seen the rise of big data, where we can ask questions of datasets that are too large, unstructured, or fast-moving to be analyzed using our conventional machine learning techniques. One domain that fits well with big data is the proliferation of small, inexpensive devices that can send a vast quantity of data to a server for analysis. These **Internet of Things** (**IoT**) devices have the potential to reshape the world around us in ways that typical computers and smartphones cannot. In this chapter, let's run though a potential big data and the Internet of Things scenario at AdventureWorks.

AdventureWorks and the Internet of Bikes

One day you are sitting in your office, your boss comes in and says, "Since you did such a great job on helping reduce our scrap rate, we would like you to work on a proof of concept with our research and development department. Last month, the management team went to a conference about the Internet of Things and we think we have an interesting use case: the **Internet of Bikes** (**IoB**). We are going to put sensors on a bike model that can read certain diagnostic information about the bike and its riding patterns. We think that a certain segment of our customers would love to have a "smart bike".

You head over to the research and development area, where they have tricked out a bike like this:

- Tire pressure sensors
- Speedometer sensor
- Gear sensor
- A Raspberry Pi 2 mounted under the seat
- A wireless Ethernet shield attached to the PI
- A GPS shield attached to the PI

The head of the R&D department tells you, "We are trying to find cost-effective wireless sensors. Until then, we are stringing wires through the frame's tube to the PI. We initially thought of using the bike rider's phone as the CPU, but we went with the PI because it is less bulky and weighs much less than a phone—bike riders are very concerned about weight. The PI gets its power from a rechargeable battery and when the bike gets docked at home to recharge, all of its on-board data is uploaded to our servers at that time. We want to transmit data from the PI to our servers only at the bike's home for security reasons and so the riders are not hit with data plan limitations by using cell networks."

The head of R&D continues, "We envision a dashboard for people to keep track of their cycling route, their biking habits, and whatnot. Where you come in is on the machine learning piece. We need a way of analyzing these huge amounts of data we are going to collect to provide an enhanced customer experience when they are riding this bike."

Data considerations

You look at the data (called telemetry) coming from the bike as two different problems. Problem one is getting the data to the server from individual bikes and problem two is having the data in a format that allows for machine learning on a large scale. You decide to solve both those problems by using the Microsoft Azure IoT suite to stream the data from the bikes into the current Northwind SQL Azure database. You add a table called `telemetry` and add a foreign key to `PurchaseOrderHeader`.

You then populate the table with some data from riders in the AdventureWorks Early Adopter program. Although there is not much data in the table to start, it is expected to grow rapidly. The level of atomacy of the table is a single reading that occurs about every second. That means for a 30-minute bike ride, we capture 1,800 rows of data. Since we have about 200 bike riders in our early adopter program, we will generate about 360,000 rows of data every time they take a ride. This one ride generates about as much data as the current AdventureWorks database maintains for the entire company. After one month of data where these bikers go out about every other day, we will have 5.4 million rows of data.

One of the data elements that we are capturing is latitude and longitude. Fortunately, all of our bike riders live in Enderlin, North Dakota, and all travel on the straightest road in the United States, Highway 46 (`https://en.wikipedia.org/wiki/North_Dakota_Highway_46 (54st SE)`). This means our longitude does not change. Also, we are capturing feet per second as a speed gauge so we can easily compare how riders perform against each other.

With the data in place, let's take a look at how to analyze data at scale.

MapReduce

Open Visual Studio and create a new Visual F# Windows Library called
`AdventureWorks.IOB`:

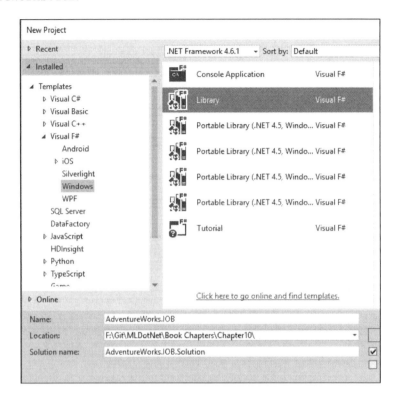

Go into the NuGet Package Manager Console and enter this:

PM> install-package Accord.MachineLearning

Next, rename `script1.fsx` to `MapReduce.fsx`. Now, enter in the same code from
Chapter 5, Time Out – Obtaining Data, that created a k-NN:

```
#r"../packages/Accord.3.0.2/lib/net40/Accord.dll"
#r"../packages/Accord.Math.3.0.2/lib/net40/Accord.Math.dll"
#r"../packages/Accord.Statistics.3.0.2/lib/net40/Accord.Statistics.
dll"
#r"../packages/Accord.MachineLearning.3.0.2/lib/net40/Accord.
MachineLearning.dll"

open Accord
open System
open Accord.Math
```

```
open Accord.MachineLearning

let inputs = [|[|5.0;1.0|];[|4.5;1.5|];[|5.1;0.75|];[|1.0;3.5|];[|0.5;
4.0|];[|1.25;4.0|]|]
let outputs = [|1;1;1;0;0;0|]

let classes = 2
let k = 3
let knn = new KNearestNeighbors(k, classes, inputs, outputs)

let input = [|5.0;0.5|]
let output = knn.Compute(input)
```

Sending this to the FSI gives us the following:

```
val inputs : float [] [] =
  [|[|5.0; 1.0|]; [|4.5; 1.5|]; [|5.1; 0.75|]; [|1.0; 3.5|]; [|0.5;
4.0|];
    [|1.25; 4.0|]|]
val outputs : int [] = [|1; 1; 1; 0; 0; 0|]
val classes : int = 2
val k : int = 3
val knn : Accord.MachineLearning.KNearestNeighbors
val input : float [] = [|5.0; 0.5|]
val output : int = 1
```

Notice this line:

```
let output = knn.Compute(input)
```

We called `knn.Compute` to do a calculation on a single input after the k-NN model was created.

This works well enough or a single calculation, but what if we want to do thousands of calculations? For example, let's call `knn.Compute()` on 250,000 random samples. After we finish all 250,000 calculations, let's add up the results and then divide that total by the number of observations and see if the dataset is biased towards a particular category.

First, let's create a function that will create a random input:

```
let createInput i =
    let random = Random(i)
    [|float(random.Next(0,6)) + Math.Round(random.NextDouble(),2);
      float(random.Next(0,6)) + Math.Round(random.NextDouble(),2);|]
```

Sending this to the FSI gives us the following:

```
val createInput : i:int -> float []
```

Next, let's create an array of 250,000 items and populate it with the random values:

```
let observations = Array.zeroCreate<int> 250000
let inputs' =
    observations
    |>Array.mapi (fun idx _ -> createInput idx)
```

Sending this to the REPL gives us the following:

```
val observations : int [] =
  [|0; 0; 0; 0; 0; 0; 0; 0; 0; 0; 0; 0; 0; 0; 0; 0; 0; 0; 0; 0; 0;
0; 0;

    0; 0; 0; 0; 0; 0; 0; 0; 0; 0; 0; 0; 0; 0; 0; 0; 0; 0; 0; 0; 0;
0; 0;

    0; 0; 0; 0; 0; 0; 0; 0; 0; 0; 0; 0; 0; 0; 0; 0; 0; 0; 0; 0; 0;
0; 0;

    0; 0; 0; 0; 0; 0; 0; 0; 0; 0; 0; 0; 0; 0; 0; 0; 0; 0; 0; 0; 0;
0; 0;

    ...|]
val inputs' : float [] [] =
  [|[|4.82; 4.56|]; [|1.11; 2.77|];
```

With our data ready, let's do our calculation. I added a timer to give us an idea of the performance hit for running 250,000 records:

```
let stopwatch = System.Diagnostics.Stopwatch()
stopwatch.Start()
let predictionTotal =
    inputs'
    |>Seq.map(fun i -> knn.Compute i)
    |>Seq.reduce(fun acc i -> acc + i)

let predictionBias = float predictionTotal/float 250000
stopwatch.Stop()
stopwatch.Elapsed.TotalSeconds
```

Sending this to the FSI will give us the following:

```
val stopwatch : Diagnostics.Stopwatch
val predictionTotal : int = 109826
val predictionBias : float = 0.439304
val it : float = 0.1787221
```

The interesting piece of code is this:

```
let predictionTotal =
    inputs'
    |>Seq.map(fun i -> knn.Compute i)
    |>Seq.reduce(fun acc i -> acc + i)
```

Notice that we are mapping and reducing. Mapping is old hat to you by now, but you might not be familiar with reducing. Reduce is a high-ordered function that takes in two parameters: an accumulator and a value. Both parameters are of the same type (in this case, `int`). What reduce is doing is going through each of the items of the array and applying a function. It then takes the results of that calculation and adds it to the accumulator. In this case, the accumulator `acc` is added to the value from the `array (i)`.

Visually, this looks like the following:

	i	acc	acc + i
Element 0	0	0	0
Element 1	2	0	2
Element 2	1	2	3
Element 3	2	3	5

You might have heard the expression map/reduce used in the context of big data. That's because some of the pioneers in big data analytics such as Google and Yahoo created Hadoop based on the concept of map/reduce. Hadoop is a platform for big data, including a filesystem (HDFS), query languages (Hive and PIG), and machine learning (Mahdut). Typically, when you hear people talking about Hadoop and map/reduce, they are talking about a specialized implementation using key/value pairs. Also, usually the *map* part of map/reduce is distributed across thousands of commodity machines. The *reduce* can be distributed depending on the nature of the function that is passed to reduce. If the function does a `groupBy` or some other calculation on a section of the entire dataset, it can be distributed. In this chapter, we are going to distribute map and are not going to distribute reduce.

To illustrate why map/reduce is popular for big data, let's distribute the mapping across all of the cores on my machine. This can simulate the way Hadoop distributes processing across thousands of networked computers. Go into Visual Studio and open the NuGet Package Manager and enter this:

```
PM> Install-Package FSharp.Collections.ParallelSeq
```

Next, go into `MapReduce.fsx` and enter this at the bottom:

```
#r"../packages/FSharp.Collections.ParallelSeq.1.0.2/lib/net40/FSharp.
Collections.ParallelSeq.dll"
open FSharp.Collections.ParallelSeq

let stopwatch' = new System.Diagnostics.Stopwatch()
stopwatch'.Start()
let predictionTotal' =
    inputs'
    |>PSeq.map(fun i -> knn.Compute i)
    |>Seq.reduce(fun acc i -> acc + i)
let predictionBias' = float predictionTotal'/float 250000
stopwatch'.Stop()
stopwatch'.Elapsed.TotalSeconds
```

Sending this to the FSI gives us the following:

```
val stopwatch' : Diagnostics.Stopwatch

val predictionTotal' : int = 109826

val predictionBias' : float = 0.439304

val it : float = 0.0700362
```

Notice that the code is identical to the preceding code except that we are now implementing `PSeq` for the mapping function, so we are distributing it across all of my cores. You can see that the time dropped significantly by implementing parallelism to the mapping function.

If you are thinking we have an answer for our big data scenario, you are incorrect. Look what happens when we try and do 5.4 million records:

```
System.OutOfMemoryException: Exception of type 'System.
OutOfMemoryException' was thrown.

>    at Microsoft.FSharp.Collections.ArrayModule.ZeroCreate[T](Int32
count)
```

We can't analyze the data only with my machine. To do map/reduce and distribute the mapping across many machines, we could implement Hadoop or its faster cousin, Spark, but then we would have to leave Visual Studio and .NET, and journey into the JVM. Also, we would have to learn Java/Python/Scala and be unable to easily integrate with our existing .NET applications. As an alternative, we could use the Azure implementation called HDInsight, but then we are locked-in to a specific cloud vendor. Instead, let's use `MBrace` to handle our distributed computations.

MBrace

MBrace is an open source project for scalable data scripting using F# or C#. You can find the website at http://mbrace.io/. MBrace supports a local simulation of distributed computing and actual implementation on Azure and, coming soon, AWS. For this chapter, we are going to stick with the local simulation so you don't have to get an Azure or AWS subscription to work through the samples.

Go back to Visual Studio, open the NuGet Package Manager, and enter this:

```
PM> Install-Package MBrace.Thespian -pre
```

Once all of the packages install, go into MapReduce.fsx and add this at the bottom (note that the version number might be different for you):

```
#load"../packages/MBrace.Thespian.1.0.19/MBrace.Thespian.fsx"


open MBrace.Core.Builders
open MBrace.Thespian
open MBrace.Core
open MBrace.Library.Cloud

//Spin up your clusters
let cluster = ThespianCluster.InitOnCurrentMachine(4)

//Basic Example
let number = cloud { return 5 + 10 } |> cluster.Run
```

Sending this to the REPL gives us the following:

```
namespace FSI_0007.MBrace

>

val cluster : ThespianCluster

>

val number : int = 15
```

But also notice what is happening outside of Visual Studio on your machine. You probably got this dialog:

If so, click on **Allow access**.

Next, four dialog boxes popped up, representing the four machines that you initialized on this line:

```
let cluster = ThespianCluster.InitOnCurrentMachine(4)
```

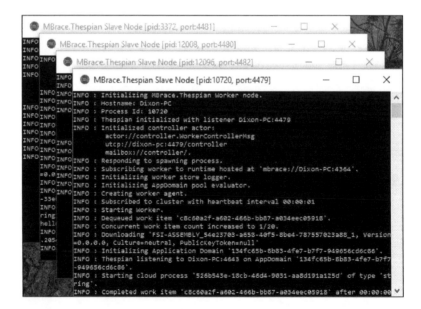

If you cycle through the dialog boxes, you will notice that one of them looks like this:

```
INFO : Starting Worker.
INFO : Dequeued work item '1fced20f-87b2-4e58-bf47-b59b796bb313'.
INFO : Concurrent work item count increased to 1/20.
INFO : Downloading 'FSI-ASSEMBLY_f898db71-941d-4273-b891-9671e15672b8_2, Version
=0.0.0.0, Culture=neutral, PublicKeyToken=null'
INFO : Initializing Application Domain '49111d5f-4324-4bf0-bc74-6ca73e2e872a'.
INFO : Thespian listening to Dixon-PC:8951 on AppDomain '49111d5f-4324-4bf0-bc74
-6ca73e2e872a'.
INFO : Starting cloud process 'b18053d9-c6ba-4ea6-a362-062f5e8a48e2' of type 'in
t'.
INFO : Completed work item '1fced20f-87b2-4e58-bf47-b59b796bb313' after 00:00:00
.2309159
INFO : Concurrent work item count decreased to 0/20.
```

Consider executing the following line:

```
let number = cloud { return 5 + 10 } |> cluster.Run
```

MBrace sends the job to one of the four consoles. When working with MBrace, everything inside of the curly braces { } is executed. In this case, it is 5 + 10, but soon enough it will contain much more complicated calculations.

Go back into `MapReduce.fsx` and add this script at the bottom:

```
let mBraceTotal =
    inputs'
    |>Seq.map(fun i ->cloud { return knn.Compute i })
    |> Cloud.Parallel
    |> cluster.Run
    |>Seq.reduce(fun acc i -> acc + i)

let mBracePrediction = float mBraceTotal/float 250000
```

When you send this to the REPL, nothing much will happen for quite a while. If you look at the four console windows, you will see that they are working hard calculating `knn.map` on each of those 250,000 values:

Since this is on our local machine and there is overhead passing data to the different processes, it is much slower than running the in-memory map/reduce that we have seen earlier in the chapter. However, out in the real world when we have more data than any one machine can handle and we can spin up several machines on Azure or AWS, MBrace really shines. You will also notice that we did nothing to install Accord.NET on those four other machines. Vagabond, part of the MBrace NuGet package, handles installing missing assemblies for us. This is a brand of awesome that should never be on sale. Instead of worrying about standing up and configuring machines, we can let MBrace handle all of that for us.

There is one last bit of syntax we want to use. Go back into `MapReduce.fsx` and add this at the bottom:

```
let mBraceTotal' =
    inputs' |>Balanced.map(fun i -> knn.Compute i) |> cluster.Run
           |>Seq.reduce(fun acc i -> acc + i)

let mBracePrediction' = float mBraceTotal/float 250000
```

Sending it to the REPL has the same effect as the first MBrace example. Consider the following line:

```
|>Balanced.map(fun i -> knn.Compute i) |> cluster.Run
```

This line replaces these lines from the first MBrace example:

```
|>Seq.map(fun i ->cloud { return knn.Compute i })
|> Cloud.Parallel
|> cluster.Run
```

This is the syntax we will be using for the AdventureWorks implementation. If you want to dig into MBrace further, download the starter pack found on GitHub at https://github.com/mbraceproject/MBrace.StarterKit/blo. With our intro to MapReduce and MBrace out of the way, let's see what we can do with AdventureWorks data.

Distributed logistic regression

In the Visual Studio **Solution Explorer**, add a new F# script file called AdventureWorksLR. Go back into Visual Studio, open up the NuGet Package Manager, and enter this:

```
PM> Install-Package SQLProvider -prerelease
```

In that script, add the following code (your version number might be different):

```
#r "../packages/SQLProvider.0.0.11-
alpha/lib/net40/FSharp.Data.SQLProvider.dll"

open System
open System.Linq
open FSharp.Data.Sql

[<Literal>]
let connectionString = "data
source=nc54a9m5kk.database.windows.net;initial
catalog=AdventureWorks2014;user id=PacktReader;password=
P@cktM@chine1e@rning;"

type AdventureWorks = SqlDataProvider<ConnectionString=
connectionString>
let context = AdventureWorks.GetDataContext()

type Telemetry = {ID:int; BusinessEntityID: int;
                  TimeStamp: System.DateTime;
```

```
                    Longitude: float; Latitude: float;
                    FrontTirePressure: float;
                    BackTirePressure: float;
                    GearId: int; TireSpeed: float; RiderLevel: int}

    let telemetry = query {for t in context.''[Person].[Telemetry]''
    do
       join rl in context.''[Person].[RiderLevel]'' on
       (t.BusinessEntityID = rl.BusinessEntityID)
       select {ID=t.ID; BusinessEntityID=t.BusinessEntityID;
               TimeStamp=t.TimeStamp;
               Longitude=t.Longitude; Latitude=t.Latitude;
               FrontTirePressure=t.FrontTirePressure;
               BackTirePressure=t.BackTirePressure;
               GearId=t.GearID;TireSpeed=t.TireSpeed;
               RiderLevel=rl.RiderLevel}}
       |>Seq.toArray
```

Sending this to the FSI gives us the following:

```
    val connectionString : string =
       "data source=nc54a9m5kk.database.windows.net;initial
       catalog=A"+[72 chars]
    type AdventureWorks = FSharp.Data.Sql.SqlDataProvider<...>
    val context : FSharp.Data.Sql.SqlDataProvider<...>.dataContext
    type Telemetry =
       {ID: int;
        BusinessEntityID: int;
        TimeStamp: System.DateTime;
        Longitude: float;
        Latitude: float;
        FrontTirePressure: float;
        BackTirePressure: float;
        GearId: int;
        TireSpeed: float;
        RiderLevel: int;}
    val telemetry : Telemetry [] =
       [|{ID = 1;
          BusinessEntityID = 295;
          TimeStamp = 12/30/2015 3:19:02 PM;
          Longitude = 46.6297;
          Latitude = -97.6087;
          FrontTirePressure = 100.0;
          BackTirePressure = 100.0;
          GearId = 2;
```

```
        TireSpeed = 20.04;
        RiderLevel = 0;}; {ID = 2;
                        BusinessEntityID = 775;
```

There is no new code here. We are creating a `telemetry` type that contains all of the useful data that we are capturing from the IoT bikes. We then create an array of telemetries from all of the data in the database. If you were wondering, there are 360,000 records in the `telemetry` table.

Go back to the script and enter this:

```
#r"../packages/Accord.3.0.2/lib/net40/Accord.dll"
#r"../packages/Accord.Math.3.0.2/lib/net40/Accord.Math.dll"
#r"../packages/Accord.Statistics.3.0.2/lib/net40/
  Accord.Statistics.dll"
#r"../packages/Accord.MachineLearning.3.0.2/lib/net40/Accord.
MachineLearning.dll"

open System
open Accord
open Accord.Math
open Accord.Statistics
open Accord.MachineLearning
open Accord.Statistics.Models.Regression.Linear

Tools.Shuffle(telemetry)
let attachmentPoint = float telemetry.Length * 0.7 |> int
let train = telemetry.[..attachmentPoint]
let test = telemetry.[attachmentPoint+1..]

let trainInputs = train |> Array.map(fun t -> [|float t.GearId;
float t.RiderLevel|])
let trainOutputs = train |> Array.map(fun t -> t.TireSpeed)
let target = new MultipleLinearRegression(2, false)
target.Regress(trainInputs, trainOutputs)
```

Sending this to the FSI gives us the following:

```
                    RiderLevel = 1;}; ...|]
val trainInputs : float [] [] =
  [|[|1.0; 1.0|]; [|2.0; 2.0|]; [|2.0; 1.0|]; [|3.0; 1.0|];
[|1.0; 0.0|];
    [|3.0; 1.0|]; [|4.0; 2.0|]; [|2.0; 0.0|]; [|3.0; 1.0|];
[|1.0; 0.0|];
  ...|]
```

```
val trainOutputs : float [] =
  [|23.3934008; 30.5693388; 18.2111048; 19.3842; 14.007411; 21.861742;
    36.6713256; 14.5381236; 16.2; 25.451495; 25.4571174; 14.5671708;
    20.1900384; 19.3655286; 27.8646144; 21.6268866; 19.3454316; ...|]
val target : MultipleLinearRegression =
  y(x0, x1) = 5.72463678857853*x0 + 6.83607853679457*x1
val it : float = 18472679.55
```

This chunk of code creates a multiple linear regression to predict bike speeds based on the level of the rider and the gear they are using. Instead of looking at the r2, let's do a sniff test. Go back to the script and add this:

```
let possible =
    [|0..4|]
    |> Array.collect(fun i -> [|0..2|]
                              |> Array.map(fun j ->
                              [|float i; float j|]))
let predict =
    possible
    |> Array.map(fun i -> i, target.Compute(i))
```

Sending this to the REPL, gives us the following:

```
val possible : float [] [] =
  [|[|0.0; 0.0|]; [|0.0; 1.0|]; [|0.0; 2.0|]; [|1.0; 0.0|]; [|1.0; 1.0|];
    [|1.0; 2.0|]; [|2.0; 0.0|]; [|2.0; 1.0|]; [|2.0; 2.0|]; [|3.0; 0.0|];
    [|3.0; 1.0|]; [|3.0; 2.0|]; [|4.0; 0.0|]; [|4.0; 1.0|]; [|4.0;
2.0|]|]
val predict : (float [] * float) [] =
  [|([|0.0; 0.0|], 0.0); ([|0.0; 1.0|], 6.836078537);
    ([|0.0; 2.0|], 13.67215707); ([|1.0; 0.0|], 5.724636789);
    ([|1.0; 1.0|], 12.56071533); ([|1.0; 2.0|], 19.39679386);
    ([|2.0; 0.0|], 11.44927358); ([|2.0; 1.0|], 18.28535211);
    ([|2.0; 2.0|], 25.12143065); ([|3.0; 0.0|], 17.17391037);
    ([|3.0; 1.0|], 24.0099889); ([|3.0; 2.0|], 30.84606744);
    ([|4.0; 0.0|], 22.89854715); ([|4.0; 1.0|], 29.73462569);
    ([|4.0; 2.0|], 36.57070423)|]
```

In this script, `possible` is a jagged array of all the possible combination of gears (values 0 to 4) and biker level (values 0 to 2). We then populate this matrix with the results of the `Compute()` method. When you take this data and put it in a more user-friendly way, you can see that there is a relationship—the elite cyclists go faster in all gears than the beginners and it looks like the beginners don't use the lowest gear at all:

			Biker Level		
			0	1	2
			Beginner	Average	Elite
Gear	0	Low	0.00	6.84	13.67
	1	Med Low	5.72	12.56	19.40
	2	Medium	11.45	18.29	25.12
	3	Med High	17.17	17.17	24.00
	4	High	22.90	29.73	36.57

With this model created, we can then run classifiers on the data and get expected speeds for a given gear and biker level. Go into the script file and enter this:

```
#load"../packages/MBrace.Thespian.1.0.19/MBrace.Thespian.fsx"

open MBrace.Core.Builders
open MBrace.Thespian
open MBrace.Core
open MBrace.Library.Cloud

let cluster = ThespianCluster.InitOnCurrentMachine(4)

let testInputs = test |> Array.map(fun t -> [|float t.GearId; float
t.RiderLevel|])

let mBraceTotal =
    testInputs
    |> Balanced.map(fun i ->
                    target.Compute(i)) |> cluster.Run
```

When you send this to the REPL, you will see that the console windows pop up and start doing work. After a couple of minutes, you will get this:

```
val mBraceTotal : float [] =
  [|36.57070423; 25.12143065; 36.57070423; 18.28535211; 5.724636789;
    24.0099889; 5.724636789; 25.12143065; 24.0099889; 18.28535211;
24.0099889;
```

```
5.724636789; 36.57070423; 12.56071533; 24.0099889; 11.44927358; 0.0;
11.44927358; 25.12143065; 12.56071533; 30.84606744; 12.56071533;
11.44927358; 18.28535211;
```

You might be wondering if there is a way to distribute the creation of the model (the `target.Regress(trainInputs, trainOutputs)` line). The short answer is no, you cannot be using the frameworks that we are using to do that. However, some models might lend themselves to distribution and then re-aggregation, but you would have to extend what is offered in numl and Accord.

The IoT

But before we leave machine learning and IoT, let's get crazy. The PI is not just an input device—heck, it is more powerful than the laptop you bought five years ago. Let's make our Raspberry PI-enabled bike the ultimate power in the tri-state area.

PCL linear regression

Go into Visual Studio and add a new Visual F# Windows Portable Library (.NET 4.5) called `AdventureWorks.IOB.PCL`:

Once the project is created, go into the NuGet Package Manager Console and enter this:

```
PM> Install-Package portable.accord.statistics
PM> Install-Package portable.accord.MachineLearning
```

Make sure that the default project is pointed to `AdventureWorks.IOB.PCL`:

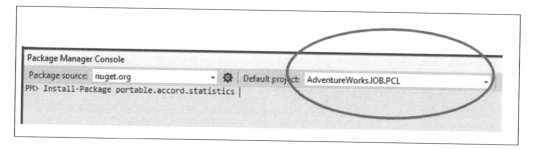

One of the issues when dealing with PCLs is that since they are a slimmed-down version of the .NET Framework, they have no data access support. This means we can't use our friendly neighborhood type provider to get the telemetry data to train our models. Instead, we will need to get our data from a different project and push that data into the PCL for it to train the model. Another "gotcha" is that the script file created in the PCL project is evaluated inside the FSI, which is a full-on .NET Framework. This means you can't assume that all of the code you write inside the .fsx file can be copied and pasted into the .fs file. Since we are building on code we already wrote, we won't be using the script file for this section. I know...take a deep breath...functional programming without an REPL.

Go into the PCL project and delete the `Script.fsx` file and rename `PortableLibrary1.fs` to `SpeedModel.fs`.

Inside the `SpeedModel.fs` file, replace all of the existing code with this:

```
namespace AdventureWorks.IOB.PCL

open System
open Accord
open Accord.Math
open Accord.Statistics
open Accord.MachineLearning
open Accord.Statistics.Models.Regression.Linear

typeTelemetry = {ID:int; BusinessEntityID: int;
                 TimeStamp: System.DateTime;
                 Longitude: float; Latitude: float;
```

```
                    FrontTirePressure: float;
                    BackTirePressure: float;
                    GearId: int; TireSpeed: float; RiderLevel: int}
typeSpeedModel() =
letmutable model = newMultipleLinearRegression(2, false)

member this.CurrentModel
with get() = model
and set (value) = model <- value

member this.Train(telemetries:Telemetry array) =
        Tools.Shuffle(telemetries)
let inputs = telemetries |>Array.map(fun t -> [|float t.GearId;
        float t.RiderLevel|])
let outputs = telemetries |>Array.map(fun t -> t.TireSpeed)
        model.Regress(inputs, outputs)

member this.Classify telemetry =
let input = [|float telemetry.GearId; float telemetry.RiderLevel|]
        model.Compute(input)
```

This code creates two .NET classes. The `Telemetry` class is equivalent to a read-only DTO/POCO that you would see in C# or VB.NET. The `SpeedModel` class is a bit more involved. The class has one property and two methods:

- `CurrentModel` is a property that allows the linear regression model to be set. Note that the model is an internal variable that is mutable.

- `Train` is a method where an array of telemetries is passed and the linear regression model will be updated. The implementation of `Train()` can be copied and pasted from the script file that you worked on previously.

- `Classify` is a method where a single telemetry is passed and the linear regression computes the score. The implementation of `Classify()` can be copied and pasted from the script file that you worked on previously.

You can check to see if everything is OK by compiling the project.

Service layer

With our PCL ready, let's build a service layer to deploy the model to devices in the field:

1. Go into Visual Studio and add a new Visual C# Web **ASP.NET Web Application**:

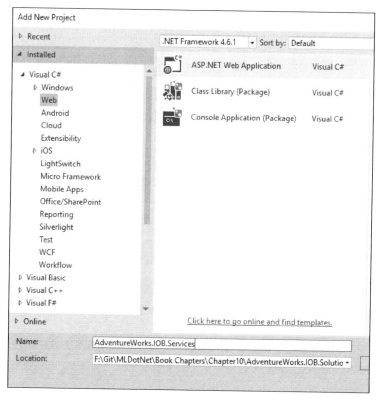

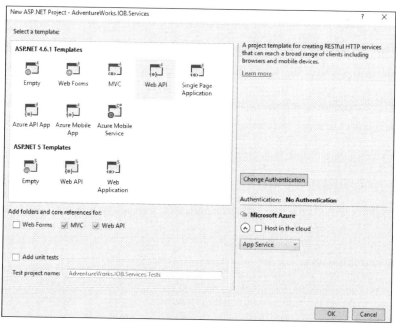

2. Add a reference:

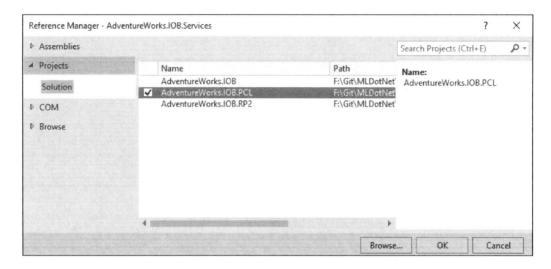

3. Next, go into the NuGet Package Manager Console and add a reference to `Accord.Statistics`. Make sure the **Default project** is pointing to `AdventureWorks.IOB.Services`:

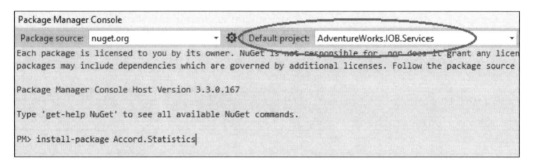

4. Next, go into the `Web.Config` file and add a connection string entry:

```
<configuration>
<connectionStrings>
<addname="Northwind"connectionString="data source=nc54a9m5kk.
database.windows.net;initial catalog=AdventureWorks2014;user
id=PacktReader;password= P@cktM@chine1e@rning;" />
</connectionStrings>
<appSettings>
<addkey="webpages:Version"value="3.0.0.0" />
```

5. Head over to the `Global.asax.cs` file and replace the entire contents with the following:

```
using System;
using System.Collections.Generic;
using System.Web.Http;
using System.Web.Mvc;
using System.Web.Optimization;
using System.Web.Routing;
using AdventureWorks.IOB.PCL;
using System.Threading;
using System.Configuration;
using System.Data.SqlClient;

namespace AdventureWorks.IOB.Services
{
publicclassWebApiApplication : System.Web.HttpApplication
    {
staticObject _lock = newObject();
Timer _timer = null;
staticSpeedModel _speedModel = null;

protectedvoid Application_Start()
        {
AreaRegistration.RegisterAllAreas();
GlobalConfiguration.Configure(WebApiConfig.Register);
FilterConfig.RegisterGlobalFilters(GlobalFilters.Filters);
RouteConfig.RegisterRoutes(RouteTable.Routes);
BundleConfig.RegisterBundles(BundleTable.Bundles);

            _speedModel = newSpeedModel();
            _timer = newTimer(TrainModel, null, 0,
            TimeSpan.FromMinutes(5).Milliseconds);

        }


protectedTelemetry[] CreateTelemetries(String
connectionString)
        {
var telemetries = newList<Telemetry>();

using (var connection = newSqlConnection(connectionString))
            {
var commandText = "Select T.*,RL.RiderLevel from
[Person].[Telemetry] as T " +
```

```
"inner join[Person].[RiderLevel] as RL " +
"on T.BusinessEntityID = rl.BusinessEntityID";
using (var command = newSqlCommand(commandText,
connection))
                {
                        connection.Open();
var reader = command.ExecuteReader();
while(reader.Read())
                        {
                                telemetries.Add(newTelemetry
                                ((int)reader[0], (int)reader[1],
                                (DateTime)reader[2],
                                (double)reader[3],
                                (double)reader[4],
                                (double)reader[5],
                                (double)reader[6], (int)reader[7],
                                (double)reader[8],
                                (int)reader[9]));
                        }
                }
        }

return telemetries.ToArray();
        }

        private void TrainModel(object state)
        {
            var connectionString =
            ConfigurationManager.ConnectionStrings
            ["Northwind"].ConnectionString;
            var telemetries =
            CreateTelemetries(connectionString);
            lock (_lock)
            {
                SpeedModel.Train(telemetries);
            }
        }

publicstaticSpeedModel SpeedModel
        {
get
                {
lock (_lock)
                        {
return _speedModel;
```

```
                                }
                            }
            set
                            {
            lock (_lock)
                            {
                                _speedModel = value;
                            }
                        }
                    }
                }
            }
```

You can compile the project now. This code is much like *Chapter 3, More AdventureWorks Regression,* in that we create a timer that fires every 5 minutes. Also, we use a lock to prevent the model being read in an illegal state. When the timer fires, the model is recreated, based on the data from the database. Notice that this is where the C# application is responsible for getting the data that is passed into the `SpeedModel` class.

Head over to the `Controllers` and rename `ValuesController` to `SpeedModelController`. Go into the file and replace all of the code with this:

```
using System.Web.Http;
using System.Net.Http;
using System.IO;
using System.Xml.Serialization;
using System.Net;

namespace AdventureWorks.IOB.Services.Controllers
{
  publicclassSpeedModelController : ApiController
    {
    // GET api/SpeedModel
      publicHttpResponseMessage Get()
        {
          HttpResponseMessage result = null;

          if (WebApiApplication.SpeedModel != null)
            {
              using (MemoryStream stream = newMemoryStream())
                {
                  var formatter = newXmlSerializer(
                  typeof(double[]));
```

```
            formatter.Serialize(stream, WebApiApplication.
            SpeedModel.CurrentModel.Coefficients);
            var content = stream.ToArray();

            result = Request.CreateResponse(
            HttpStatusCode.OK);
            result.Content = newByteArrayContent(content);
            return result;
        }
    }
      else
    {
      return Request.CreateResponse(HttpStatusCode.Gone);
    }
    }
    }


    }
    }
```

If you compile the project and run the website, when you navigate to the controller, you will get this:

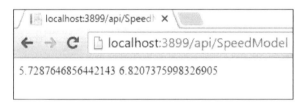

We now have a way of creating a model based on all the data in the database that we can share to individual clients.

Universal Windows app and Raspberry Pi 2

This universal app has a couple of moving parts:

- When the app is connected to its home network, it will:
    - Upload all of the telemetry that is collected to Azure's IoT Suite
    - Download the most recent global model that was created based on all the riders in the AdventureWorks database from our service layer

- When the app is running, it will collect telemetry data from the sensors hooked up to the bike. After a certain point, it will start generating its own local model and compare it to the global AdventureWorks model. If the local model begins diverging from the expected speed of the global model, it will instruct the biker to shift. The app will keep the telemetry data on local storage until it is connected to the network, then it will upload the data.

Let's code this up:

1. Go into the **Solution Explorer** and add a new Visual C# Windows Universal Blank App named `AdventureWorks.IOB.RP2`:

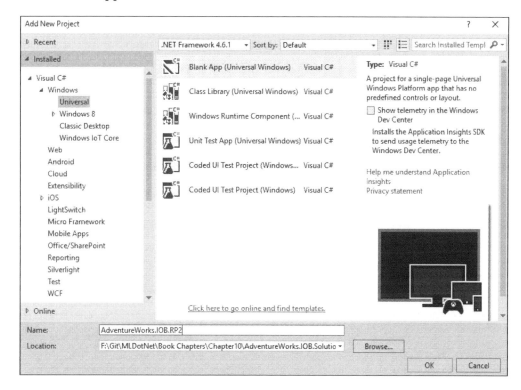

2. Once the project is created, go to its **References** section and select
   Add Reference:

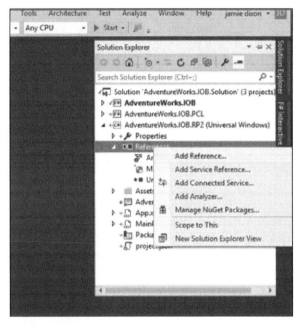

The Add Reference... option

3. Then navigate to **Projects | Solution** and select the location of your
   PCL project:

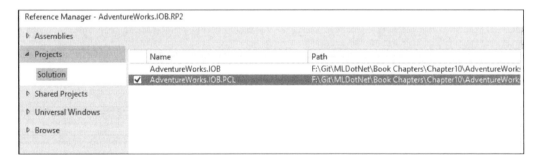

4. Now navigate to **Universal Windows | Extensions | Windows IoT Extensions for the UWP**:

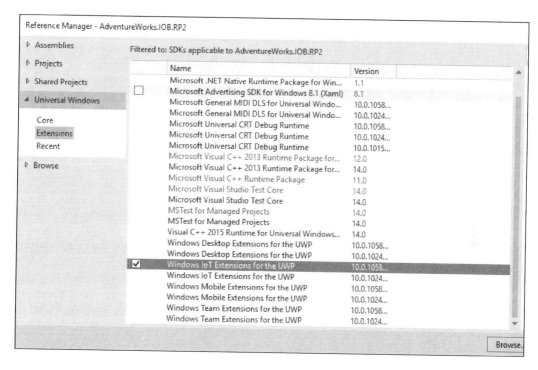

5. Next, go into the NuGet Package Manager Console and enter this:

```
PM> Install-Package portable.accord.statistics
```

6. Make sure that the **Default project** is pointing to AdventureWorks.IOB.RP2:

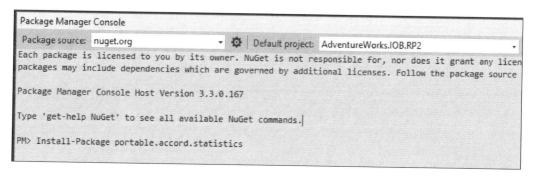

Build the project to make sure all is well.

7. Next, go to the **Solution Explorer** and add a new folder called `Sensors`:

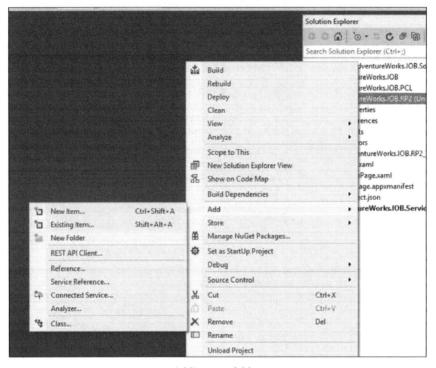

Adding new folder

8. Navigate to the `Sensors` folder:

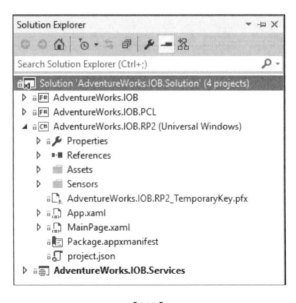

9. Add a new class called `TelemetryEventArgs.cs`:

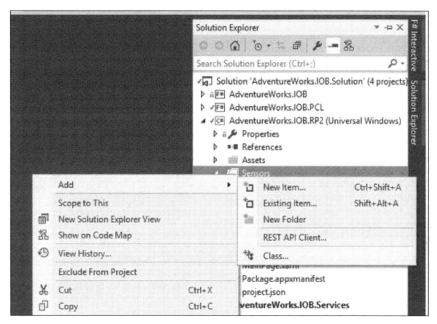

Adding a new class

10. In `TelemetryEventArgs.cs`, replace the existing code with the following:

```
using AdventureWorks.IOB.PCL;
using System;

namespace AdventureWorks.IOB.RP2.Sensors
{
    Public class TelemetryEventArgs : EventArgs
        {
            Public Telemetry Telemetry { get; set; }
        }
}
```

11. In the sensors folder, add a new interface called `IBikeController`. After it is created, replace all of the code with the following:

```
using System;

namespace AdventureWorks.IOB.RP2.Sensors
{
Public interface IBikeController
    {
```

```
        Event EventHandler
        <TelemetryEventArgs> TelemetryCreated;
        void SwitchGear(int targetGear);
    }
}
```

This interface will be used by the main app to, well, interface with the
Raspberry Pi. The Pi communicates back to the main app via an event
called TelemetryCreated. The reason that we used an interface (versus
talking directly to the PI) is that we want to borrow a bit from the SOLID
principles and have several implementations for our app: an in-memory bike
controller that we can use to make sure everything is hooked up correctly
and a Raspberry Pi bike controller that actually talks to the hardware that
we currently have available. Also, there are so many sensors available on
the market, we need a way of adding in new sensors without changing the
existing code.

12. Go into the Sensors folder and add a new class called
    InMemoryBikeController. Replace the existing code with this:

```
using AdventureWorks.IOB.PCL;
using System;
using System.Threading;

namespace AdventureWorks.IOB.RP2.Sensors
{

    public class InMemoryBikeController : IBikeController
    {
        Timer _timer = null;

        public InMemoryBikeController()
        {
            _timer = new Timer(GenerateTelemetry, null, 0,
            TimeSpan.FromSeconds(1).Milliseconds);
        }

        public event EventHandler<TelemetryEventArgs>
        TelemetryCreated;

        private void GenerateTelemetry(object state)
        {
            var telemetry = new Telemetry
            (0, 0, DateTime.UtcNow, 46.6297, -97.6087,
            100.0, 100.0, 2, 10.0, 1);
            var args = new TelemetryEventArgs() {
              Telemetry = telemetry };
```

```
        if (TelemetryCreated != null)
        {
            TelemetryCreated(this, args);
        }
    }

    public void SwitchGear(int targetGear)
    {

    }
  }
}
```

This code simulates an actual Raspberry Pi. Every second, it fires an event with some hardcoded telemetry data. It also has a method stub for the SwitchGears that does nothing.

13. Make sure everything compiles and jumps over to the MainPage.xaml file and replace all of the contents with this:

```
<Page
  x:Class="AdventureWorks.IOB.RP2.MainPage"
  xmlns="http://schemas.microsoft.com/winfx/2006/xaml/
  presentation"
  xmlns:x="http://schemas.microsoft.com/winfx/2006/xaml"
  xmlns:local="using:AdventureWorks.IOB.RP2"
  xmlns:d="http://schemas.microsoft.com/expression/
  blend/2008"
  xmlns:mc="http://schemas.openxmlformats.org/
  markup-compatibility/2006"
  mc:Ignorable="d">

  <Grid Background="{ThemeResource
    ApplicationPageBackgroundThemeBrush}">
  <StackPanel HorizontalAlignment="Center"
    VerticalAlignment="Center">
  <TextBox x:Name="StatusMessage" Text="IOB Ready!"
    Margin="10" IsReadOnly="True"/>
  </StackPanel>
  </Grid>
</Page>
```

This creates a status box that you can use for debugging. When you deploy this app to the Raspberry Pi, this is unnecessary because there is no graphical user interface.

14. Next, go into the `MainPage.xaml.cs` file and replace everything with this:

```
using System;
using System.IO;
using System.Linq;
using Windows.UI.Xaml;
using Windows.Web.Http;
using AdventureWorks.IOB.PCL;
using Windows.UI.Xaml.Controls;
using System.Xml.Serialization;
using System.Collections.Generic;
using AdventureWorks.IOB.RP2.Sensors;
using Windows.Networking.Connectivity;
using Accord.Statistics.Models.Regression.Linear;

namespace AdventureWorks.IOB.RP2
{
    publicsealedpartialclassMainPage : Page
    {
        String _networkName = String.Empty;
        SpeedModel _globalSpeedModel = null;
        SpeedModel _localSpeedModel = null;
        List<Telemetry> _telemetries = null;
        IBikeController _bikeController = null;
        DispatcherTimer _timer = null;

        public MainPage()
        {
            this.InitializeComponent();
            _networkName = "MySafeNetwork";
            _globalSpeedModel = newSpeedModel();
            _localSpeedModel = newSpeedModel();
            _telemetries = newList<Telemetry>();
            _bikeController = newInMemoryBikeController();
            _timer = newDispatcherTimer();

            _timer.Interval = newTimeSpan(0, 0, 1);

            NetworkInformation.NetworkStatusChanged +=
            NetworkInformation_NetworkStatusChanged;
            _bikeController.TelemetryCreated +=
            _bikeController_TelemetryCreated;
```

```csharp
    _timer.Tick += _timer_Tick;


}

privatevoid _timer_Tick(object sender, object e)
{
  if(_telemetries.Count > 300)
    {
      _localSpeedModel.Train
      (_telemetries.ToArray());

      var targetGlobalGear = _globalSpeedModel
      .Classify(_telemetries.Last());
      var targetLocalGear = _localSpeedModel
      .Classify(_telemetries.Last());
      if (targetGlobalGear < targetLocalGear)
        {
          _bikeController.SwitchGear
          ((int)targetGlobalGear);
        }
    }
}

privatevoid _bikeController_TelemetryCreated(
object sender, TelemetryEventArgs e)
{
    _telemetries.Add(e.Telemetry);
}

privatevoid NetworkInformation_NetworkStatusChanged
(object sender)
{
  var connectionProfile = NetworkInformation
  .GetInternetConnectionProfile();
  if (connectionProfile.ProfileName ==
  _networkName)
    {
      GetGlobalModel();
      UploadLocalTelemetryData();
    }
}

privateasyncvoid GetGlobalModel()
```

```
{
  var client = newHttpClient();
  var uri = newUri("http://localhost:3899/api
  /SpeedModel");
  try
    {
      var response = await client.GetAsync(uri);
      if (response.IsSuccessStatusCode)
        {
          var content = await response.Content
          .ReadAsInputStreamAsync();
          using (var stream =
          content.AsStreamForRead())
            {
              var formatter = newXmlSerializer(
              typeof(double[]));
              var coefficients = (
              double[])formatter.Deserialize(
              stream);
              var regression =
              newMultipleLinearRegression(2);
              Array.Copy(coefficients,
              regression.Coefficients,
              coefficients.Length);
              _globalSpeedModel.CurrentModel =
              regression;
            }
        }
    }
  catch (Exception e)
  {
      this.StatusMessage.Text = e.ToString();
  }

}

  privateasyncvoid UploadLocalTelemetryData()
  {
//TODO: Send _telemetries to Azure IoT Suite
  }

    }
}
```

This is where the heavy lifting occurs. When the app starts, it begins a timer that fires every second (`_timer_Tick`). If there are over 5 minutes' worth of data in the local collection, it generates a `SpeedModel`. It then compares this speed model to the global one and if the global output is less than the local one, it signals the biker via the `.SwitchGear()`. The actual implementation is up to the controller. As you will see in a minute, the Raspberry Pi controller turns on an LED that the biker can see. In other examples, we could hook the Pi up to the bike's shifting assembly and shift the gears for the biker — an automatic transmission for the bike, as it were.

15. Next, go into the **Solution Explorer** and right-click on **Properties** and change the startup project to **Multiple startup projects** with the `Services` and `RP2` projects changed to **Start**. The `Services` project has to be listed before the `RP2` one:

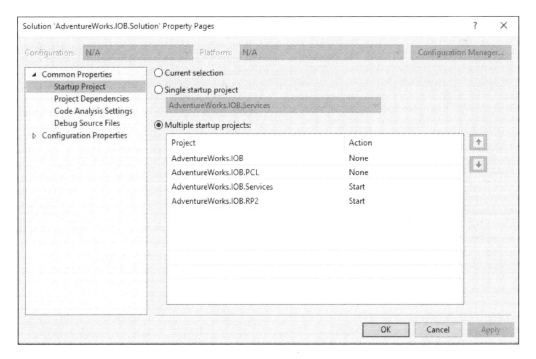

16. One last thing you need to do before we run this is to deploy the Universal Windows application. If you ask me why you need to deploy it first, I will tell you, "Because Microsoft said so." Go into the **Solution Explorer** and right-click on the Rp2 project and select **Deploy**:

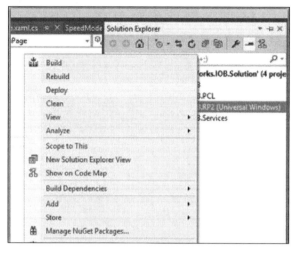

The Deploy option

17. Now you can run the app and both, the browser will pop up for the service layer and the universal Windows app will start:

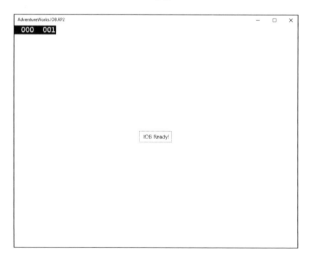

Notice nothing much is happening—at least on the screen. That is pretty typical of IoT projects; the action is on the device and connected peripherals. If the device fired the `NetworkStatus_Changed` event, the device would get the most recent global model and upload the global model. You can simulate this by placing `GetGlobalModelinMainPage()` and then write it to the status box if you are the type of person who wants to see something on the screen.

Let's build out the Raspberry Pi implementation of the `BikeController`. Since this is a book on machine learning and not on IoT, I will not be covering the details of setting up a Raspberry Pi and doing all of the wiring and coding. As a frame of reference, I used the example found at http://ms-iot.github.io/content/en-US/win10/samples/Potentiometer.htm. Basically, each of the sensors would be considered an analog input device (such as a potentiometer) that converts its signal to a digital signal. For each of the inputs, a `SpiConnection` was created like this:

```
privateasyncTask<SpiDevice> InitSPI(int pin)
    {
        var settings = newSpiConnectionSettings(pin);
        settings.ClockFrequency = 500000;
        settings.Mode = SpiMode.Mode0;

        string spiAqs = SpiDevice.GetDeviceSelector("SPI0");
        var deviceInfo =
        awaitDeviceInformation.FindAllAsync(spiAqs);
        returnawaitSpiDevice.FromIdAsync(deviceInfo[0].Id,
        settings);
    }
```

And every second, each device's buffer was read:

```
privatevoid SensorTimer_Tick(ThreadPoolTimer timer)
        {
byte[] readBuffer = newbyte[3];
byte[] writeBuffer = newbyte[3] { 0x00, 0x00, 0x00 };
        writeBuffer[0] = 0x06;

//Gear
        _gear.TransferFullDuplex(writeBuffer, readBuffer);
var gear = convertToInt(readBuffer);
```

The readings were aggregated into telemetry data and the event was raised:

```
var telemetry = newTelemetry(0, _businessEntityID,
            DateTime.UtcNow,
            latitude, longitude, frontTire, backTire, gear,
            tireSpeed, _riderLevel);
var args = newTelemetryEventArgs() { Telemetry = telemetry };

if (TelemetryCreated != null)
        {
            TelemetryCreated(this, args);
        }
```

Meanwhile, a different timer was running and shutting off the LED every two seconds. The LED was set when the `SwitchGear` method was called:

```
public void SwitchGear(int targetGear)
        {
            _led.Write(GpioPinValue.Low);
        }
```

So the controller app can turn the LED on, and then the Pi turns it off after two seconds. You can see the final result in the code sample that accompanies the book.

Next steps

I glossed over some important IoT issues that would need to be addressed to make this bike app fully functional:

- There are hundreds of input devices that I could have used. You will have to write a specific implementation for the devices that you are interested in. Thank goodness we have an interface!

- How to deploy this app to a Raspberry Pi is beyond the scope of this book. You can learn more about this at https://dev.windows.com/en-US/iot.

- Telemetry to local storage is beyond the scope of this book. This is a universal Windows app issue that can be researched at https://msdn.microsoft.com/en-us/library/windows/apps/dn894631.aspx.

- Uploading the data to the Azure IoT suite is beyond the scope of this book. You can find more information on that at https://www.microsoft.com/en-us/server-cloud/internet-of-things/azure-iot-suite.aspx.

Summary

This was a fairly ambitious chapter. We looked at some of the challenges of big data and how to use MBrace to help us with distributed machine learning. We then created a sample IoT project to show an example of how big data is generated and how we can deploy ML models to devices. The IoT app used two ML models to give optimal results. We then looked (briefly) at how we can use the power of .NET to build multiple input devices so that we can extend across the variety of hardware that is, and will be, available for IoT.

Index

Symbol

.NET
about 2, 3
advantages 2, 3
URL 4
version 3, 4

A

Accord 110-117
Accord.NET
about 20, 37
regression 37, 38
regression, against actual data 41-45
regression evaluation, RMSE used 38-40
regression, using with real world 40, 41
URL 20
AdventureWorks
about 135, 168
and Internet of Bikes (IoB) 289
and k-NN 179
and Naïve Bayes 180, 181
data, making available 168-178
URL 41
AdventureWorks app
about 45
environment, setting up 46, 47
existing web project, updating 47-49
regression, implementing 50-52
AdventureWorks data
and k-NN 179
database 130
logistic regression, applying 73-77
multiple linear regression, applying 59-61

application
building 271
logistic regression, adding 81-89
models, setting up 271-280
UX, building 280-288
attachment point, logistic regressions 79
Azure IoT suite
URL 328

B

Bing Map API
URL 148

C

classification models discoveries
data, making available 181-183
features, expanding 183, 184
using 181
clean data block 92
Code-4-Good application
about 209
distance calculations, adding 220-222
human observations, augmenting
      with 222-224
machine learning assembly 209-212
UI 213-220
collinearity 229, 230
cross validation
about 242
AUC 247-249
confusion matrix 247-249
mean test 244-246
random test 244-246

28070575R00197

Printed in Great Britain
by Amazon